8988

An

INTRODUCTION TO MUSIC

BY MARTIN BERNSTEIN

ASSISTANT PROFESSOR OF MUSIC, NEW YORK UNIVERSITY

New York : 1937

PRENTICE-HALL · INC ·

7/8 2

PREFACE

IN THE preparation of this volume the author has had but one objective in mind: the presentation of such information as will make
for intelligent listening to the music that is heard today in the concert
hall, in the opera house, and through modern instruments of transmis-
sion and reproduction. This book is consequently neither a history
of music nor a technical manual. In order to concentrate on this objective, the author found certain compromises necessary. There is no
discussion of many significant composers and their works, and detailed study begins at so recent a stage in the evolution of the art of
music as that represented by the compositions of Johann Sebastian
Bach.

It is a familiar axiom that an appreciation of music cannot be
acquired by the reading of books. Much space, therefore, has been
devoted to discussions of representative works with the hope that they
will be read in conjunction with actual hearing of the music. Thematic quotations from an unfamiliar composition have little value;
it is only when the reader has had the experience of listening to the
work from which they have been extracted that they can be of aid
in the recognition of formal outlines.

The writer of a work of this type is often compelled to resort to
summary pronouncements and facile generalizations. Lists of suggested readings have therefore been included to enable the reader
to find in the books mentioned the necessary expansions and qualifica-
tions of the statements made in the text.

For valuable suggestions and friendly interest the author is indebted
to his colleagues at New York University, Professor Philip James and
Mr. Gustave Reese, and to Doctor Howard Hanson of the Eastman
School of Music; and for painstaking assistance in the reading of
proofs, to Miss Mary S. Schieffelin. The author wishes especially to

v

express his gratitude to Professor Casper J. Kraemer, Jr. of New York University for the interest he has shown in this volume since its inception, and for his many constructive criticisms of the manuscript.

M. B.

Acknowledgments

Excerpts from Debussy's *L'Après midi d'un faune* and *Nuages* are reprinted with kind permission of Jean Jobert, of Paris, and Elkan-Vogel Co., Inc., copyright owners in the U. S. A., and excerpts from Debussy's *La Cathédrale engloutie, Jumbo's Lullaby, Voiles, Pelléas et Mélisande,* and Dukas' *L'Apprenti sorcier* with kind permission of Durand & Cie. of Paris, and Elkan-Vogel Co., Inc., copyright owners in the U. S. A.

Excerpts from Holst's *The Planets* and Vaughan Williams' *Pastoral Symphony* are reprinted by kind permission of J. Curwen & Sons, Ltd., of London.

Excerpts from Schoenberg's *Drei Klavierstücke,* Sibelius' Symphony No. 2, and Strauss' *Ein Heldenleben* are used by kind permission of the copyright owners, Associated Music Publishers, Inc., New York.

The excerpt from Stravinsky's *L'Histoire du soldat* is reprinted by kind permission of the publishers, J. & W. Chester, Ltd., of London.

The excerpt from Strauss' *Burleska* is reprinted by special permission of the Society of European Stage Authors and Composers, Inc., of New York, and Steingraeber Verlag, Leipzig.

TABLE OF CONTENTS

CHAPTER   PAGE

I   THE CHARACTERISTICS OF A MUSICAL TONE 1

II   MUSICAL INSTRUMENTS 5

III   FUNDAMENTAL MUSICAL CONCEPTS: RHYTHM AND MELODY . 28

IV   FUNDAMENTAL MUSICAL CONCEPTS: POLYPHONY AND HAR-
MONY 39

V   FUNDAMENTAL MUSICAL CONCEPTS: FORM 49

VI   JOHANN SEBASTIAN BACH 57

VII   GEORGE FRIDERIC HANDEL 96

VIII   CHRISTOPH WILLIBALD GLUCK 109

IX   THE VIENNESE SCHOOL: JOSEPH HAYDN 114

X   THE VIENNESE SCHOOL: WOLFGANG AMADEUS MOZART . . . 134

XI   THE VIENNESE SCHOOL: LUDWIG VAN BEETHOVEN 155

XII   ROMANTICISM IN MUSIC 185

XIII   FRANZ SCHUBERT 189

XIV   CARL MARIA VON WEBER 201

XV   FELIX MENDELSSOHN 211

XVI   ROBERT SCHUMANN 219

XVII   FRÉDÉRIC CHOPIN 231

XVIII   HECTOR BERLIOZ 239

XIX   FRANZ LISZT 248

XX   ITALIAN OPERA OF THE EARLY NINETEENTH CENTURY . . . 263

XXI   RICHARD WAGNER 270

XXII   ITALIAN OPERA OF THE LATE NINETEENTH CENTURY . . . 291

XXIII   JOHANNES BRAHMS 297

XXIV   NATIONALISM IN MUSIC 314

XXV   RUSSIAN NATIONALISM 319

XXVI   FRENCH NATIONALISM 337

CHAPTER   PAGE

XXVII   POST-WAGNERIAN MUSIC IN GERMANY AND AUSTRIA   . . 348

XXVIII JEAN SIBELIUS 361

XXIX   CLAUDE DEBUSSY 370

XXX   SOME RECENT TRENDS 380

INDEX OF MUSICAL EXAMPLES 387

GENERAL INDEX 392

LIST OF ILLUSTRATIONS

	PAGE
Orchestral Wood-Wind Instruments	9
Orchestral Brass Instruments	15
Johann Sebastian Bach	59
George Frideric Handel	97
Joseph Haydn	115
Wolfgang Amadeus Mozart	135
Ludwig van Beethoven	157
Franz Schubert	191
Carl Maria von Weber	203
Felix Mendelssohn	213
Robert Schumann	221
Frédéric Chopin	233
Hector Berlioz	241
Franz Liszt	249
Gioacchino Rossini	265
Richard Wagner	271
Giuseppe Verdi	293
Johannes Brahms	299
Nicholas Rimsky-Korsakoff	323
Peter Ilitch Tchaikovsky	331
Richard Strauss	349
Jean Sibelius	363
Claude Debussy	371

Chapter I

THE CHARACTERISTICS OF A MUSICAL TONE

THREE men, one in the concert hall listening to a symphony of Beethoven, another in the opera house listening to a presentation of one of Wagner's music-dramas, a third in his own home listening to a sentimental tune sung by a radio performer, are all doing the same thing, or rather, are having the same thing done to them: the atmosphere about them is supplying them with oxygen and transmitting to them waves of compressions and rarefactions set up by certain vibrating bodies. The waves so produced fall on the men's ears, and each of them would describe his own particular sensation as "music." It is obvious that the works which these persons are hearing have certain things in common. No matter what the artistic value of the works performed may be, their renditions consist of successions and combinations of atmospheric disturbances which we designate as *musical tones*. Each and every musical tone has four characteristics: *duration, pitch, intensity,* and *quality.*

The *duration* of a musical tone may be defined purely in terms of the time elapsing between its commencement and its cessation. In actual practice the ear never measures the absolute time interval. It is, however, continually making comparisons between the relative time values of different tones, and between the time values of groups of tones.

The term *pitch* refers to the relative highness or lowness of a tone. The tone of a toy whistle is of high pitch, that of the human voice as used in ordinary speech, of medium pitch, and that of a large church bell, of low pitch. There is, however, an accurate and precise way of describing pitch. The pitch of a musical tone may be shown to depend wholly on the number of vibrations per second set up by the sounding body. This number of vibrations per second is known as the *frequency* of vibration. The art of music employs frequencies ranging from 16 to 4,224 vibrations per second; but the ear can respond to frequencies in the neighborhood of 20,000. The modern piano has a range which extends from 27 to 4,224 vibrations per second. Precisely as in the case of *duration*, our ears seldom measure the absolute number of vibrations, but rather are continually comparing the relative value of the vibrations of tones sounded either simultaneously or successively. The most elementary relationship is the *octave*—a ratio of 1:2.

Ex. 1

 512 vibrations per second

256 vibrations per second

Intensity is the measure of the loudness of a tone. As in the case of the two previously mentioned characteristics, our measurement of intensity is purely relative; acoustical engineers have, however, devised a unit of intensity, the *decibel*. The loudness of a tone for any given pitch depends on the amplitude of the vibrations: i.e., the extent to which the sounding body moves from its normal position of rest as it vibrates to and fro. The easiest way to demonstrate this is to strike a key on the piano. The loudness of the tone will depend entirely on how forcefully the key is depressed, that is, on how far the string is displaced from its position of rest by the blow of the hammer. The intensity of a tone also depends on its pitch.[1]

The *quality* of a musical tone enables us to distinguish between notes which, although they may possess the same pitch and intensity, are produced by different instruments. One can very easily distinguish between a bugle-call played on a bugle and the identical notes played on a violin; nor does it take a sensitive ear to recognize a difference in the quality of the tones of two similar instruments, such as two pianos or two violins. We speak of the *tone-quality,* or the *tone-color*, or the *timbre* of a sound. The quality of a musical tone is one of its most interesting and at the same time one of its most

---

[1] Stated more precisely, the amplitude remaining constant, the intensity of a tone varies as the square of its frequency. The frequency remaining constant, the intensity varies as the square of the amplitude.

elusive aspects. There is an infinite variety of tonal qualities. Each and every instrument has its own unique timbre which depends not only on the instrument itself, but also on the skill of the performer. There is no better proof of this than to listen to the same piece of music played in turn on the same instrument by several competent performers.

On what then does the quality of a musical tone depend? Before this question can be answered it will be necessary to investigate in some detail the behavior of a sounding body. Let us take a taut wire as our example. If the wire is plucked, a characteristic sound will be heard. By means of specially devised instruments known as resonators, a physicist could easily demonstrate that this wire was producing not one but many simultaneous sounds; or he could show with equal ease, that the wire was vibrating not only as a whole, but also in fractions of itself. The vibrations of the wire as a whole are the strongest vibrations and they produce a tone called the *fundamental*. When we refer to the pitch of a tone we are really referring to the pitch of the fundamental, the loudest of the several tones that we are hearing. The tones produced by the fractional vibrations of the wire are known as *overtones*. These vary in number and intensity, depending on many factors—the composition of the wire, the way in which it is held taut, the manner in which it is sounded, and so forth. The quality of a musical tone depends entirely on the number and the relative intensities of these overtones.

In reality, therefore, when we strike a note on the piano we are not hearing one tone, but several tones. We can readily distinguish the loudest, the fundamental; but many other tones of lesser intensity are also heard, and while we may seem unable to distinguish them from the fundamental, they do nevertheless actuate our ear drums sufficiently for us to be conscious of them. A pure tone, a tone without overtones, can be produced only by a tuning fork. All other sounds which we hear are a combination of a fundamental and numerous overtones. Overtones whose frequencies are exact multiples of the frequency of the fundamental are known as *harmonics*. The harmonics of a violin string may be heard by lightly touching the finger to a point half the string-length from the bridge, a third of the string-length, etc., and by applying the bow. Such tones are frequently used in writing for the violin. An instrument like the flute gives forth a prominent fundamental with but few overtones, most of which are faint. The violin also has a prominent fundamental, and a few strong overtones. The orchestral horn, on the other hand, gives out a prominent fundamental together with more than twenty overtones. The following illustration will show the series of harmonics which may sound with a given fundamental. These tones are known as the *harmonic series*:

Ex. 2

We have now discussed each individual characteristic of a musical tone. It must be borne in mind, however, that these various aspects cannot be divorced from one another; no one is more important than any other, and with the exception of duration, each is continually influencing the others. A sensitive musical performance consists of a most meticulous regard for these four values. (In the case of instruments like the organ and the piano, however, the performer need not concern himself with the correctness of pitch. This has been attended to in advance by the tuner.) The art of interpretation is largely the performance of each and every individual tone of a composition with what the player or singer deems to be its correct duration, pitch, intensity, and quality.

SUGGESTED READINGS

Any standard text book of physics contains a discussion of elementary acoustical phenomena. Dayton C. Miller's treatise *The Science of Musical Sounds* (Macmillan), while out-dated in many respects, is a readable and valuable discussion. More recent investigations of a popular nature are John Mill's *A Fugue in Cycles and Bels* (van Nostrand), and Otto Ortmann's article, What Is Tone-Quality?, in the October 1935 issue of *The Musical Quarterly*.

Chapter II

MUSICAL INSTRUMENTS

MANY of the musical instruments of the Occident are found in a large and diversified aggregation called a "symphony orchestra." [1] The orchestra as we know it today is a comparatively new arrival on the musical scene; for the constitution of the orchestra did not take on any semblance of regularity until the close of the eighteenth century, and many of the instruments in it were not perfected until the nineteenth century.

The instruments of the orchestra may be divided into four large groups—the strings, the wood-winds, the brasses, and the percussion. Of these the string group is the most important. A full-sized symphony orchestra includes about one hundred players, more than half of whom are performers on string instruments.

THE STRING INSTRUMENTS

The string section owes its importance to the fact that it is far superior to any other group in purity of intonation, range of dynamic value, and variety of tone-color. It must not be forgotten that a string instrument is in truth several instruments in one. Each of the strings of the violin, for example, has a different tone-color. The violin may be described, therefore, as four instruments with a common resonator. So versatile is the string group that many works have been written for strings alone.

The best-known instrument of this group is the *violin,* too familiar to warrant description here. There are usually thirty-six violins in

---

[1] The term *symphony orchestra* is somewhat of a misnomer. It indicates, of course, an orchestra capable of playing music of symphonic dimensions. There is, however, no difference between an opera orchestra and a symphony orchestra.

the orchestra, divided into two sections—the first and the second violins. These designations are merely arbitrary and by no means do they indicate the relative importance of the two groups. Modern composers have not hesitated to carry the process of division further and have divided the violins into as many as eight groups. The orchestral range of the instrument is:

Ex. 1

The *viola* is held like the violin, and from a distance it looks exactly like one. On comparing the instruments, however, one discovers that the viola is about 1 1/7 times as large. It is pitched four tones lower than its smaller colleague and has a sombre and elegiac tone-quality. It is an instrument of great inherent dignity and nobility, not at all deserving of the title which has sometimes been bestowed upon it—"a violin in mourning." There are usually ten violas in the orchestra. The orchestral range of the instrument is:

Ex. 2

There are prominent passages for the viola in the following works:

    Bach—Brandenburg Concerto No. VI
    Strauss—*Don Quixote*
    Ippolitoff-Ivanoff—*In the Village* from *Caucasian Sketches*

The *'cello* (the common abbreviation of *violoncello*) may be readily identified as the only string instrument held between the player's knees, the weight of the instrument being borne by a pin which rests on the floor. It is a vigorous masculine instrument possessing a very expressive, occasionally penetrating tone-quality. The 'cello is nominally a bass instrument; but so great is its range that it may be considered a tenor and an alto instrument as well. Modern composers have made excellent use of the versatility of the 'cellos, and there is hardly a work by composers such as Brahms, Wagner, or Strauss without a characteristic passage for them. There are usually ten 'cellos in the orchestra. The orchestral range of the instrument is:

Ex. 3

Characteristic passages will be found in the following works:

Rossini—Overture to *William Tell*
Brahms—Symphony No. 3—Third Movement
Wagner—Prelude to *Tristan und Isolde*
Strauss—*Don Quixote*

The *double bass* (known also as bass viol, contrabass, string bass, or bass) is a huge instrument which needs no description inasmuch as the semi-circle of double bass players at the rear of the orchestra is a familiar sight. The instrument has been so named because for many years it was entrusted with the humble task of doubling the bass of the orchestral harmonies as played by the 'cellos. The double basses are seldom used independently except for some special effect, but in consort with instruments like the 'cellos they furnish the orchestra with a rich and firm foundation. Because of its size and the thickness of its strings, the double bass does not lend itself to solo performances. These obstacles, however, have not prevented certain intrepid individuals from becoming virtuoso players on the instrument. There are usually ten double basses in the orchestra. The range of the instrument is:

Ex. 4

There are prominent passages for the double bass in the following works:

Beethoven—Symphony No. 5—Third Movement
Beethoven—Symphony No. 9—Fourth Movement
Saint-Saëns—*L'Eléphant* from *Le Carnaval des animaux*

The Wood-Wind Instruments

The name given to this group describes it with some degree of accuracy. All of the instruments in it except the flute have air columns which are set in motion by a reed, and each has associated with it one or two related instruments mechanically so similar to it that players can change from one to the other without difficulty. The timbres of the wood-wind instruments are much more striking than those of the strings; but by the same token, the ear tires of them more quickly. They are unique tone-colors which must be handled with circumspection. Like the human voice, the wind instruments have a somewhat different color for each of their several divisions or "registers."

The *flute* may be very readily identified: it and its related instruments are the only wind instruments that are held parallel to the plane of the floor. It also is the only instrument in this group which is seldom made of wood, silver having been found to be preferable. The flute is made to sound by blowing across a hole, the *embouchure,* at the end of the instrument. The air-column strikes the sharp edge of the hole and sets up vibrations in the flute. The frequency of vibration may be altered by opening or closing the holes drilled in the side of the instrument and by increasing the force of the air-stream blown against the embouchure (overblowing). The flute is an instrument of almost unbelievable agility. No passages are too fast or too complicated for it. Its tone-color is uniformly bright, except in the lowest register where it tends to become somewhat cool and velvety. Because of its lightness and daintiness, the flute is always associated with the elves and fairies of orchestral music, as in the Scherzo from Mendelssohn's *Midsummer Night's Dream.* The flute is also used in conjunction with other wood-wind instruments and with the violins to add brilliancy. There are usually three flutists in the orchestra, one of whom will play the related instrument—the *piccolo.* This instrument is half the size of the flute. Its name is an abbreviation of the Italian designation, *flauto piccolo* (little flute). Its tone is extremely penetrating; one piccolo playing loudly can easily make itself heard above the rest of the orchestra. Possessing an ultra-vivid color,

FLUTE

PICCOLO

OBOE

CLARINET

ENGLISH
HORN

BASS CLARINET

BASSOON

Orchestral Wood-Wind Instruments

Scale:—One inch equals 8¾ inches

Courtesy of H. & A. Selmer, Inc.

the piccolo is usually held in reserve to be unleashed at the crucial moment. The range of the flute is:

Ex. 5

and of the piccolo:

Ex. 6

There are typical passages for the flute in the following works:

> Mozart—Concerto for Flute in D major (K. V. 314)
> Rossini—Overture to *William Tell*
> Debussy—*L'Après-midi d'un faune* (see page 378, Example 5)

and for the piccolo in the following works:

> Berlioz—*Minuet of the Will-o'-the-Wisps* from *The Damnation of Faust*
> Tchaikovsky—*Chinese Dance* from *The Nutcracker Suite*
> Sousa—*The Stars and Stripes Forever*
> Pierné—*Entry of the Little Fauns* from *Cydalise*

The *oboe* is an instrument of conical bore whose air-column is actuated by a comparatively small double reed held tightly in the mouth of the player. It is one of the oldest, one of the most difficult and one of the most expressive instruments in the orchestra. The difficulty in playing the instrument arises from the nature and dimensions of the double reed. This reed, composed of two fine and unusually thin pieces of cane bound together, is so small that very little breath is required to make the oboe sound. The oboe player's problem, therefore, is the converse of that of the player of any other wind instrument. He must have a rest not to fill his lungs, but rather to rid them of the air which he has been unable to release. The most obvious characteristic of the instrument is its intensity. No better example could be quoted than the celebrated passage from the first movement of the Fifth Symphony of Beethoven. The entire orchestra is silent as the oboe sings:

Ex. 7

The tone of the instrument is pungent, nasal, occasionally acrid and above all "reedy." This reedy quality will serve to differentiate the oboe from any other wind instrument There are usually three oboists in the orchestra and of these three players, one will play the related instrument—the *English horn.*

The origin of the name of this instrument is disputed, though one explanation seems logical—that the name is a translation of the French *cor anglais* which in turn is a corruption of *cor anglé* (bent horn). (The earlier instruments were bent.) No matter what the explanation for it may be, the name is a complete misnomer. The instrument is neither "English" nor a "horn." It is simply an oboe of lower pitch, an alto oboe. To be more precise, it bears exactly the same relationship to the oboe as the viola does to the violin. It is much longer than the oboe and terminates in a pear-shaped "bell." The double reed is larger than that of the oboe, and the oboe's problems of breath control are not duplicated in the case of its relative. The instrument is one of the most serious and most profound in the entire orchestra. It has about it a reserve, a nostalgia, a gravity, which render it admirably suitable for music of sorrow, of regret, of solitude. There is no better example of the English horn's ability to evoke an atmosphere of forlornness than the melancholy shepherd's tune which is played off-stage after the curtain is raised for the third act of Wagner's *Tristan und Isolde*:

Ex. 8

The range of the oboe is:

Ex. 9
(a)

of the English horn:

(b)

Characteristic oboe passages are to be found in the following works:

> Schubert—Symphony No. 7—Second Movement
> Tchaikovsky—Symphony No. 4—Second Movement (see page 335, Example 18)
> Brahms—Concerto for Violin—Second Movement (see page 312, Example 20)

Characteristic English horn passages are to be found in the following works:

> Wagner—*Tristan und Isolde,* Act III (Shepherd's Tune)
> Franck—Symphony in D minor—Second Movement (see page 345, Example 16)
> D'vorák—Symphony in E minor (*From the New World*)—Second Movement
> Sibelius—*The Swan of Tuonela*

The *clarinet* is a cylindrical instrument about two feet long, with a large single reed, held with comfort by the player. From a distance it may seem to resemble the oboe; but comparison of the dimensions of the reeds will dispel all doubts. The clarinet is an instrument of considerable agility, of great range, and possessed of a pleasant and, at the same time, variable tone-color. It is so versatile that in arrangements of orchestral music for concert band, it plays all the passages previously executed by violins. The tone of the instrument is smooth and clear, often resembling that of the human voice and possessing a certain feminine quality which has caused it to be called the prima donna of the orchestra. The player has complete control over the dynamic value of the tone. It can be produced at the level of a whisper, which is more than can be said for any of the other wood-wind instruments. There are usually three clarinetists in the orchestra. The related instrument is the *bass clarinet*.

This instrument, which might be mistaken for a saxophone if it were not for its wooden pipe, is, as its name indicates, a larger clarinet of lower pitch. Its tone is serious and grave. Another instrument related to the clarinet appears but rarely. Known as the *E-flat clarinet*, it is a much smaller instrument with a penetrating incisive tone not far removed from a squeal. Richard Strauss uses the instrument in *Till Eulenspiegel's Merry Pranks* to depict the hanging of Till.[1] The range of the clarinet is:

Ex. 10
(a)

of the bass clarinet:

(b)

There are prominent passages for the clarinet in the following works:

> Mozart—Symphony in E-flat major (K. V. 543)—Trio of the Minuet
> Brahms—Symphony No. 1—Third Movement
> Brahms—Clarinet Quintet in B minor, Opus 115
> Tchaikovsky—Symphony No. 5—First Movement

and for the bass clarinet in the following works:

> Wagner—*Tristan und Isolde,* Act II (King Mark Scene)
> Wagner—*Tristan und Isolde,* Act III (Commencement of the *Liebestod*)

The *bassoon,* with a double reed, is the bass of the wood-wind family. In appearance it is very much like two long poles bound together; in fact the Italian name for the instrument is *fagotto,* from its resemblance to a bundle of fagots. The bassoon has a hollow, dry tone, of

---

[1] See page 355.

some seriousness, and possesses quite a degree of flexibility which, coupled with the inherent solemnity of the instrument, enables it to execute complicated passages with cold unconcern. There is no better example of this unique faculty of the bassoon than the commencement of the *vif* section of Dukas' *L'Apprenti sorcier* (The Sorcerer's Apprentice):

Ex. 11

But it must not be thought that the bassoon is limited to macabre music. In its upper register it can well suggest the sound of the human voice, while in its lower register it can be used for clownish effects. It can also intone solemn passages with commensurate gravity. There are usually three bassoonists in the orchestra, one of whom will play the related instrument, the *double bassoon*. This instrument is rarely heard independently. The range of the bassoon is:

Ex. 12

There are prominent passages for the bassoon in the following works:

Rimsky-Korsakoff—*Scheherazade*—Second Movement
Dukas—*L'Apprenti sorcier*
Tchaikovsky—Symphony No. 6 (*Pathétique*)—First Movement

THE BRASS INSTRUMENTS

The principles underlying the construction and manipulation of brass instruments have been known since ancient times. The walls of Jericho are said to have been blown down by trumpets. Many brass instruments were used by the Romans for military signals. No matter what the shape or dimensions of these instruments have been through the ages, they are all based on three acoustical facts: (1) that the human lips can be made to act as reeds and that their tension may be varied by means of the facial muscles; (2) that if the taut lips are ap-

TRUMPET

FRENCH HORN

TROMBONE

TUBA

Orchestral Brass Instruments

Scale:—One inch equals 8¾ inches

Courtesy of H. & A. Selmer, Inc.

plied to a tube and air is blown through them, the air-column in the tube commences to vibrate; and (3) that by altering the tension of the lips the frequency of vibration can be changed (within certain limitations, that is, only certain notes can be produced). It will be found that the notes produced from any tube so blown have the same pitch relationship to each other as the notes of the harmonic series given on page 4. Experience has shown that brass is the best material to use; that because of the length of tubing required, the instruments may be rendered more manageable by suitable coiling of the tube; and that control of the air-column, and manipulation of the lips are facilitated by the use of a mouthpiece. The design of the mouthpiece has a great effect on the production of overtones.

This limitation of available notes to the harmonic series is by no means an insuperable one. On examination of the series it becomes apparent that from the third overtone on, it is quite possible to construct simple melodies. The common bugle is nothing more than a coiled brass tube about four feet long. Merely by changing the tension of the lips, melodies like the following can be played:

Ex. 13

Composers found these limitations of the brass instruments irksome, but it was not until the 1830's that the problem was finally solved. The problem was this: to supply the brass instruments with a mechanical device which would (1) enable the player to alter instantaneously the length of the tube, thereby shifting the harmonic series, and (2) allow the player to effect so many alterations with their resultant changes of harmonic series that all of the notes of the scale could be produced. The solution of this problem was rendered quite difficult because of certain acoustical laws. It was finally effected in this manner—lengths of tubing were added to the instrument and, by means of mechanical devices known as "valves," these additional lengths of tubing could be added to or removed from the main tube at will. It was found that three different lengths of tubing, each with its valve to cut it in or out of the main tube, would, when used in combination, suffice to give every note of the chromatic scale (a scale of half-tones.

See page 38). We are now prepared to discuss the individual members of the brass group.

The *horn* [1] is the most expressive and poetic instrument of this group, and the most difficult to play. The flaring bell and the complicated coils of tubing enable one to identify it easily. Long before the horn was introduced into the orchestra, it was widely used for calls of the hunt. The old French name, *cor-de-chasse* (horn of the chase), and the old German names *Waldhorn* (forest horn) and *Jagdhorn* (hunting horn), tell us much about the use of the instrument, and to this very day the horn retains these associations. Up to the time of Beethoven composers had to content themselves with horns without valves—the so-called *natural* horns. The limitations of the harmonic series were partially overcome by the great range of the horn. Furthermore it was discovered that the length of the tubing might be altered, though somewhat inconveniently, by changing certain sections of pipe, probably the first use of interchangeable parts. These interchangeable sections of pipe were known as *crooks*. During the performance of a long work such as an opera by Mozart, the horn players would continually be changing crooks between the various numbers. The following passages will show the style of writing for two natural horns as well as the melodic possibilities of the harmonic series:

Ex. 14. Hunting call.

Ex. 15. Mozart—Symphony in G minor (K. V. 550)—Third Movement.

Ex. 16. Beethoven—Symphony No. 8 in F major—Third Movement.

[1] Occasionally called the French horn because of its extensive use at the French courts.

With the addition of valves, the horn was emancipated and to its capacity for producing a full and warm tone there was added the ability to play a complete scale, and this over a wide range, the widest of any of the brass instruments. So warm and round, that is, so rich in overtones is the horn tone that the instrument is used very frequently with the string instruments and with the wood-winds. Seldom are the horns silent for any length of time. They are in truth instruments of heroic qualities, and many heroes have had their musical portraits drawn by them. There are usually four horns in the orchestra, though as many as eight are called for in the works of Wagner. Haydn, Mozart and Beethoven (in his earlier symphonies) called for only two. Four horns have become standard equipment, however, since the second decade of the nineteenth century. The range of the instrument is:

Ex. 17

There are prominent horn passages in the following works:

Beethoven—Symphony No. 3 (*Eroica*)—Trio of the Third Movement
Wagner—*Götterdämmerung*—*Siegfried's Rhine Journey*
Tchaikovsky—Symphony No. 5—Second Movement
Wagner—*Die Meistersinger*—Prelude to Act III

The instrument which Haydn, Mozart and Beethoven used and which they called a *trumpet* would look exactly like a bugle to us. It was an instrument without valves, a *natural* trumpet. Of much smaller range than the horn, the natural trumpet was used but sparingly by these composers, and found its application principally in military calls like the famous ones in Beethoven's *Leonore No. 3* overture. It was not until valves were added that the trumpet could be used with any freedom. A brilliant instrument possessed of great flexibility, it has numerous usages today. It can play broad melodies, complicated and involved passages; it can be serious and dignified one instant, flippant the next. It can intone majestic themes with truly stentorian quality. Then, too, its tone can be completely changed by the insertion of a *mute,* a pear-shaped device made of cardboard. This gives the instrument a pleasantly nasal tone wholly unlike that of the unmuted trumpet. The muted trumpet is familiar through its extensive application in dance music. (Trumpeters in dance orchestras use several different kinds of mutes, each with its characteristic tone.) There are usually three trumpets in the orchestra. The range of the instrument is:

Ex. 18

There are prominent passages for the trumpet in the following works:

Beethoven—*Leonore No. 3* overture
Strauss—*Ein Heldenleben*
Wagner—Prelude to *Parsifal*
Debussy—*Fêtes*

The *trombone* is the simplest of all the brass instruments. In place of a complicated valve mechanism, the trombone has a pair of concentric tubes which slide one over the other. It is a simple matter, therefore, for the player to change the length of tubing. Since the tube is comparatively free from bends and constrictions, the trombone is blown freely and easily, but, unfortunately, with rapid consumption of the player's air-supply. The trombone is inherently stately and dignified. Its tone can be almost overpowering; but never does the instrument belie its native majesty except for purposes of deliberate burlesque. The best example of the use of the trombone occurs in the well-known overture to Wagner's *Tannhäuser*. Here, to the energetic accompaniment of the rest of the orchestra, three trombones peal forth the melody sung in the opera by the chorus of pilgrims. The broad melody comes through above all the excitement of the accompaniment in a manner that seems almost effortless. There are three trombones in the orchestra. The usual range of the instrument is:

Ex. 19

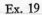

There are prominent passages for the trombone in the following works:

Wagner—Overture to *Tannhäuser*
Rimsky-Korsakoff—Overture *The Russian Easter*

The *tuba*, a huge coil of brass ending in an enormous bell, is the double bass of the brass group. Like its relative, it is seldom used independently but serves rather to strengthen the foundations of the orchestral harmonies. As a solo instrument it seems to have definite zoölogical propensities; Wagner uses it to depict the dragon *Fafner* in the *Ring* operas, and Stravinsky uses it to depict the bear in Scene IV of his ballet *Petrouchka*. There is one tuba in the orchestra. The range of the instrument is:

Ex. 20

There are prominent passages for the tuba in the following works:

Wagner—Prelude to *Siegfried*
Stravinsky—Suite from *Petrouchka*

THE PERCUSSION INSTRUMENTS

The percussion group is frequently called "the battery," which is slightly maligning as far as the many players in this group are concerned. The section embraces a host of instruments of diverse shapes and uses, all, however, having one thing in common—they are sounded by being struck.

The *timpani*, or *kettledrums*, are the oldest and most important members of the percussion group. The kettledrums differ from all other drums in that they can be rapidly tuned to definite pitches. Heads of sheep- or calfskin are stretched across large copper "kettles," and are made to sound by striking them with hammers with large felt ends. The pitches of the drums may be changed by altering the tension of the heads by means of large screws on the circumferences; though kettledrums will occasionally be seen which have a foot lever and an internal mechanism to permit faster tuning. The performer on the kettledrums must be a very gifted musician. He must, in the

first place, possess what is known as absolute pitch, that is, he must
know the pitch of any note in the scale. Secondly, he must be able
to tune his drums quietly to the required pitch no matter what the rest
of the orchestra may be playing. Thirdly, he must count his "rests"
while doing all this, so that he may strike his correctly tuned drum at
the right moment. The kettledrums can be used for producing loud
thunderous peals, for rhythmic accentuation, and, if enough drums be
available, for melodic purposes. Beethoven was one of the first composers to realize the musical potentialities of the kettledrums. They
play an important part in the second movement of his Ninth Symphony:

Ex. 21

Richard Strauss, in his *Burleska* for piano and orchestra, allows the
principal theme of the work to be announced by four kettledrums:

Ex. 22

There is usually one player assigned to the kettledrums, and he will
have from two to four drums under his care. The range of the kettledrums is:

Ex. 23

There are prominent passages for the kettledrums in the following
works:

Beethoven—Symphony No. 9—Second Movement
Wagner—*Siegfried's Funeral March* from *Götterdämmerung*
Strauss—*Burleska* for piano and orchestra

The rest of the percussion section comprises a great many miscellaneous instruments, too numerous to be described in detail. They are

used chiefly to achieve unique sound effects. Mere mention and brief description will suffice:

Snare Drum: A small untuned drum played with wooden sticks. It has metallic "snares" which strike against the lower head. A brilliant drum.

Bass Drum: A large untuned drum.

Cymbals: Large, slightly tapered disks of brass which are struck together.

Glockenspiel: A series of small tuned metal bars, struck with small hard hammers.

Xylophone: A series of small tuned wooden bars, struck with small hard hammers.

Bells: Large tubes sounding like church bells, struck with a mallet.

Gong: A huge disk of brass giving forth an ominous sound when struck with a large felt-headed stick.

Triangle: A metal bar bent into the shape of a triangle and struck with a small metal rod. It gives forth a pleasant tinkle.

Some other percussion instruments are the *castanets,* the *rattle,* the *woodblock,* the *tambourine,* and the *field-drum.*

OTHER INSTRUMENTS OF THE ORCHESTRA

Instruments Whose Strings Are Plucked

The *harp,* one of the most ancient of instruments, is the only member of this group that has won for itself a permanent place in the orchestra. Like the brass instruments, the harp was not made available for orchestral purposes until early in the nineteenth century when the French instrument maker, Sébastien Erard, perfected what is known as the "double-action" mechanism. By means of seven pedals located in the base of the instrument, the pitches of the forty-seven strings of the harp may be raised or lowered a half-tone or a whole-tone, thus enabling the instrument to be played in any key. The characteristic musical figure associated with the harp is the wide-spread chord of many notes played not simultaneously, but in quick succession. The name for this figure is *arpeggio* (from the Italian *arpa*). Another idiomatic harp figure is the *glissando*—a quick sweep over the strings. The harp can be used for simple accompaniment, accentuation, and for coloristic purposes. Wagner uses six harps in *Das Rheingold* to depict the glittering rainbow on which the gods march into *Walhall.* Some of the most effective harp parts are to be found in the orchestral works of the French composer, Claude Debussy. The range of the harp is:

Ex. 24

There are prominent passages for the harp in the following works:

Ravel—*Introduction and Allegro* for harp, string quartet and wood-winds.
Debussy—*L'Après-midi d'un faune*
Strauss—*Tod und Verklärung*

Other instruments in the plucked-string group that are employed in the orchestra only on very rare occasions are the *guitar* and *mandolin*.

Keyboard Instruments

The *celesta* looks like a small portable organ. Its sounding mechanism consists of a series of small metal bars placed over suitable resonators and struck by hammers controlled by a keyboard exactly like that of a piano, but with only about four-sevenths of its range. Its tones, pure and crystalline, resemble those of soft chimes, but lack their dissonant overtones. The only prominent passage for celesta is in the *Dance of the Sugarplum Fairy* from Tchaikovsky's *Nutcracker Suite*.

The *piano* (the common abbreviation for *pianoforte*) is a string instrument whose strings are struck by hammers. These hammers are actuated by the keys on the keyboard, a series of levers faced with ivory or ebony and arranged in two tiers so as to bring a greater number of notes under the hand. The piano has not yet become a regular member of the orchestral forces, though modern composers employ it occasionally.

The piano is one of the most satisfying musical instruments. It possesses a great range, enables the performer to play many notes simultaneously, and at the same time makes but slight physical demands. The piano can adequately reproduce many of the sounds of an orchestra and offers more varied possibilities of musical expression than any other single musical instrument.

The *organ* is an instrument composed of literally thousands of pipes of different timbres and pitches, into which air is admitted by valves.

These are controlled, usually electrically, by a player performing at the *console,* which is a group of keyboards for both hands and feet. The keyboards actuated by the hands are called manuals; the keyboard actuated by the feet is known as the pedal-board, or simply, the pedals. The organ may be likened to an orchestra composed of many different wind instruments which may be made to sound by mechanical devices and which by means of various ingenious mechanisms can be brought under the control of one player. Some large modern organs have as many as one hundred and eighty different kinds of pipes. A set of pipes of one timbre is known as a stop; the art of choosing and varying the stops is called registration. While the organ offers a greater variety of color and a greater range of gross dynamic value than any other instrument, it suffers from a vital defect which proves the designation "King of Instruments" to be a hyperbole. The serious drawback of the organ is the gap which exists between the player and the sounding medium. Because of the mechanical perfection of the instrument, it is impossible to vary the intensity of individual tones; the dynamic level can be changed only gradually by opening or closing shutters in front of the pipes or by adding or removing stops. Accent of the necessary degree of refinement is, therefore, impossible to attain. When one remembers that the organist's hands and feet are well occupied with the manuals and pedals, and that changes in registration and dynamics have to be sandwiched in, in some miraculous manner, one is inclined to be sympathetic towards the individual who has ventured to perform upon this unwieldy mechanism. Withal, no amount of admiration that we may feel for the ingeniousness of the mechanism and the virtuosity of the performer compensates for the devastating impersonality of this instrument. An occasional virtuoso can, however, when playing some of the great works of Bach, effectively conceal the limitations of the organ. Seldom used in orchestral music, its widest application is in church services where its excellent ability to sustain a tone renders it a valuable adjunct in the performance of choral music.

The Orchestra as a Whole

We have now examined the individual components of the orchestral body. The tones of these individual instruments may be likened to primary colors capable of being combined in an infinite number of ways; and these tone-colors must be chosen by the composer with due regard for the limitations of the instruments which produce them. Musical instruments have their unique idioms which, like the idioms of languages, are usually untranslatable. A melody played by a trombone is not the same music as the identical melody played by a bassoon. There is also the question of blending. The composer must continually ask himself if the colors that he proposes to use will mix. Will the ear hear them as a homogeneous whole or as dissociated sounds? The problem of balance must be considered, since certain instruments are inclined to be penetrating or overpowering. These are merely a few of the problems involved in *orchestration*, the art of setting music for orchestra, as distinguished from the actual composition of the music.

The appreciation of tone-color is one of the easiest musical habits to acquire. An individual eager to acquire this faculty should, when attending symphony concerts, occupy a seat which will allow him to see the entire orchestra. Before the concert commences he can become acquainted with the appearance of the various instruments. When the music starts, aural identification of the source of the sound may then be confirmed by the eye. A work which may be recommended purely as an elementary study of orchestration is the *Boléro* of Maurice Ravel. With the exception of a change of key near the end, this composition consists merely of the reiteration, in different orchestral colors, of two themes. Orchestration is the easiest of all the various techniques that enter into the composition of music; and brilliant orchestration may frequently conceal poverty of musical inspiration.

Coördination of the Orchestral Instruments— The Conductor

To many persons the dominating feature of the orchestra is the conductor. Concert-goers often overestimate the significance of the conductor, and for many individuals he is apparently more important than the composer who has created the music for him to conduct. The prospectus of a symphony orchestra inviting subscriptions for a coming season always gives the names of the conductors; but it seldom, if ever, mentions the compositions that will be performed.

The conductor does three things: he chooses the program, he rehearses the players, and he conducts the concert. The conductor selects the program that he proposes to give, although if a soloist is to be included on the program, the soloist himself decides what he will play. Program-making is like arranging a meal; the various courses must be well planned and cannot follow one another haphazardly. More than one new work has been unfavorably received because of its poor position on a program.

After the program has been chosen, the conductor must rehearse the orchestra. Rehearsal is, in fact, instruction; the conductor instructs the orchestra in the performance of the work, explains various passages, clarifies difficulties, makes sure that every individual is playing precisely what the composer has written for his instrument, and adjusts the balance between the various orchestral groups. The greater part of the conductor's task is thus accomplished at the rehearsal.

The concert is largely the product of the rehearsal, for at the concert the conductor cannot speak with his players. Only two media of communication are available: gesture, and facial expression. Gesture is made more visible by use of a baton. The conductor apparently "beats time" with the baton. It would, however, be more accurate to say that with the baton he dictates the speed, that is, the *tempo* [1] of the work being performed. Besides, this tempo is being constantly varied. Given a fine orchestra, the problem of the conductor is largely a choice of the right tempo and of the necessary alterations within that tempo.

Much of the explanation of the art of the conductor, however, rests on a much more intangible basis—personality. The conductor must convey to the players a zeal and enthusiasm for the work in hand; he must make each and every one of the one hundred performers under his control play as if the conductor's eyes were focussed on him and him alone; he must make every instrumentalist outdo himself. The orchestra is really an instrument on which the conductor plays. Concert audiences are prone to judge a conductor by his appearance on the podium, or by whether he conducts with or without a score, and so forth, but the only criterion is the quality of the orchestral performance as determined by our ears.

[1] See page 31.

SUGGESTED READINGS

The standard treatise on the instruments of the orchestra is Cecil Forsyth's *Orchestration* (Macmillan). The development of the art of orchestration is treated by Adam Carse in *A History of Orchestration* (Dutton). The following works will be of assistance in the study of orchestral scores: Hans Gal—*Directions for Score Reading* (Philharmonia); Martin Bernstein—*Score Reading* (Witmark).

Chapter III

FUNDAMENTAL MUSICAL
CONCEPTS: RHYTHM AND MELODY

THE CHARACTERISTICS of a single tone and the customary instruments for the creation of tones have been discussed, but as yet we have not dealt with music itself. Tones in themselves are merely raw material; it is not until they are arranged in some systematic manner that they produce what we call music. Various arrangements of tones produce the three great elements of the language of Occidental music—rhythm, melody, and harmony. Opinions differ as to the relative importance of these elements, and a history of music might be written in terms of changing conceptions of them through the centuries. A close study of these three elements as found in well-known music will serve as a point of orientation in the survey which will be made later in this volume. The primary purpose of this investigation will be clarification, but it should not be forgotten that in the process of analysis each element will be lifted out of its context, while in practice, all three are coexistent and are continually interacting on each other.

Rhythm

If successive sounds appear in some systematic order, the ear will at once be conscious of the existence of the system and, in so doing, arrange these sounds in groups. The best proof of this is the manner in which our ears group such regularly occurring sounds as those created by the wheels of a rapidly moving railway car as they strike the rail joints. Although the sounds so created may be of equal intensity, the ear in so arranging them either perceives, or imagines that it perceives, an accent on the first sound of the group. Another excellent demonstration is to listen to the absolutely equal beats of a metronome. It will be found impossible not to group the notes and to assign an accent to the first member of each fancied group. The perception of rhythm in music thus arises in a comparison of the duration of tones, or groups of tones; but inasmuch as these groups of tones are marked by stresses or accents, rhythm is concerned at the same time with accentuation.

Careful listening to music will show that of the various successive tones used some are relatively stronger, and that these relatively stronger (accented) tones appear in a regular pattern. The simplest pattern is one in which a strong pulse, or beat, alternates with a weak one. The most familiar example of this is the rhythm used for marching, in which the step of the left foot invariably is executed on the strong beat. This rhythm, produced by a group of two pulses, is called duple rhythm. Groups of three pulses produce triple rhythm and those of four pulses, quadruple rhythm. Our perception of rhythm is heightened when the number of tones appearing between pulses is varied, as is shown by the following example from the *Allegretto* of the Seventh Symphony of Beethoven:

Ex. 1

Instances of tones of equal value recurring for any length of time are rare; the effect would be monotonous. The following examples will illustrate the more fundamental rhythms:

Ex. 2. Duple rhythm. *Le Pont d'Avignon* (Anonymous).

Ex. 3. Triple rhythm. *Come, Thou Almighty King* (Giardini).

Ex. 4. Quadruple rhythm. *Adeste Fideles* (Anonymous).

A rhythm based on groups containing five pulses, that is, quintuple rhythm, while common enough in folk music and contemporary music, is seldom found in the works of the earlier masters. The most familiar instance of the use of quintuple rhythm is the second movement of Tchaikovsky's Sixth Symphony (*Pathétique*).

Ex. 5

If groups of pulses are heard rapidly, our ears will tend to simplify matters and arrange these groups into larger, more inclusive patterns. The second movement of Beethoven's Ninth Symphony is in triple rhythm; but inasmuch as the groups appear in rapid succession, the ear, by a process which might be called "aural accommodation," hears larger groups in a quadruple rhythm:

Ex. 6

In the course of the movement Beethoven changes the rhythmic system so that the groups arrange themselves in triple rhythm:

Ex. 7

Many other examples could be cited of this tendency of the ear to arrange rhythmic groups into larger patterns.

It must not be inferred, however, that the accents of music appear with mechanical regularity. While the first pulse (beat) of a group (measure) may bear a strong accent, many other secondary accents may be found. The effect of music played with regular emphasis on the first pulse is similar to that of reading verse in a sing-song manner which brings out the rhythmic scheme and yet destroys the poetry. Modern composers are continually striving to expand our concepts of rhythm. An extreme example is the brutal *Danse sacrale* which closes Igor Stravinsky's *Le Sacre du printemps* (The Rites of Spring).

Syncopation, the stressing of one or more normally unaccented beats, is one of the oldest methods of producing rhythmic interest. A few examples will demonstrate the simpler types of syncopation.

Ex. 8. Beethoven—*Leonore No. 3* Overture.

Ex. 9. Franck—Symphony in D minor—First Movement.

Ex. 10. Brahms—Symphony No. 2—Fourth Movement.

Tempo

The rate at which groups of pulses progress is described by the term *tempo*. Tempo and rhythm should not be confused. Rhythm refers to a system of stresses, tempo to the pace at which these stress groups progress. In an artistic rendition of any musical work, one of the chief concerns of the executant is the choice of a proper tempo. Within the confines of this underlying tempo all manner of deviations—slight accelerations at one point, slight retardations at another—are made by an understanding performer.

It is customary on concert programs to describe the several movements of larger works, such as symphonies and sonatas, by giving the indications of pace and general mood supplied by the composer. The long ascendancy of Italian music and musicians accounts for the predominance of Italian terms. Some of the most frequently employed designations are:

Adagio—Very slow   *Largo*—Broad, stately
Allegro—Fast, lively   *Presto*—Quick
Andante—Somewhat slow   *Vivace*—Lively, animated

MELODY

Melody may be defined as a meaningful succession of single tones. The relationships between these tones are those of duration and accent, that is, rhythmic relationship, and those of pitch. The term *melody* suffers from vagueness of usage and is frequently confused with *tune* or *air,* designations which should be restricted to melodies of a simpler type. The perception of melody in music demands an ability to sense the relationship between successive tones. Much music that is heard with pleasure today was at first condemned as lacking in melody by auditors unaccustomed to the new relationships involved.

The listener desires melody more than anything else in music. Confusion has arisen, however, from failure to differentiate between the two large types of melodies, *vocal* and *instrumental,* though the characteristics of these types are not so well marked that a hard and fast differentiation may be made. There are, to be sure, hundreds of instrumental melodies that may be sung effectively. Melodies like the following, however, are intrinsically instrumental:

Ex. 11.   Bach—Concerto for Two Violins.

Ex. 12.   Beethoven—Symphony No. 9—First Movement.

Ex. 13. Strauss—*Ein Heldenleben.*

Not all melodic relationships make themselves manifest on a first hearing, though some of the world's greatest melodies have been essentially simple. Listeners are prone to call more readily appreciated melodies "tuneful," indicating their quick grasp of the relationships between individual tones; but the effort necessary to perceive more subtle relationships, particularly as found in modern music, should not predispose one to hasty evaluation.

The number of tones available to the composer depends on the vocal or instrumental medium he has chosen. The violin, for example, affords about forty-eight tones, the piano eighty-eight, the average human voice about twenty-four, and the flute thirty-seven.

Scales

Music has much in common with another medium of communication, namely speech. Musical tones may be likened to the letters employed in speech. Precisely as letters are arranged in an alphabet, the tones used for the construction of melodies are arranged into chains of successive notes which are called *scales* [1] or *modes*. The relationship which is felt to exist in most melodies derives in large measure from the scale relationships of the tones employed. Examination of a few melodies will demonstrate at once the scales on which they are based. The tones used in *Come, Thou Almighty King* (p. 29) may be systematically arranged as:

Ex. 14

[1] The name is derived from the Latin *scala*, because of an analogy between the steps of a scale and the steps of a ladder. Cf. the German *Tonleiter*.

The essential tones employed for this motive from Wagner's *Parsifal*:

Ex. 15
(a)

as:

(b)

The tones employed for Schumann's *The Merry Farmer*:

Ex. 16
(a)

as:

(b)

It will be observed that the tones are arranged within the limits of an octave. Conversely a scale may be defined as the division of the octave for musical purposes, but this definition holds true only for Western music.

It will be noticed in the case of the three examples given above that although their scales commenced on different pitches, they were identical in pattern: each scale consisted of eight tones arranged in wholesteps or half-steps in the following manner:

1–2—whole-step	5–6—whole-step
2–3—whole-step	6–7—whole-step
3–4—half-step	7–8—half-step
4–5—whole-step	

Any scale may therefore be defined in terms of the tone on which it is based and on the arrangement of tones within it. The arrangement which we have just encountered when constructed on any tone produces a *major* scale. The scale on which Schumann's *The Merry Farmer* is based is therefore called the scale of F major.

Another type of scale is called the *minor* scale. The formation of this scale may be shown by the following model, constructed on the tone A:

Ex. 17

There are half-steps between the second and third, fifth and sixth, seventh and eighth tones. For melodic purposes the minor scale is frequently altered and there are as many as three forms. Western music during the seventeenth, eighteenth, and nineteenth centuries has used the major and minor scales almost exclusively. Prior to this period other scale types were extensively employed. Six of these "modes" in their simplest form were:

Ex. 18. The Dorian Mode.

Ex. 19. The Phrygian Mode.

Ex. 20. The Lydian Mode.

Ex. 21. The Mixolydian Mode.

Ex. 22. The Aeolian Mode.

Ex. 23. The Ionian Mode.

The names given to these modes derive from a curious twisting of the terms used by the ancient Greeks. It is evident that the Ionian mode is identical with our major scale, that the Aeolian mode is one of the forms of our minor scale. These older scales have come to be called *modal* scales, and music based on them is known as modal music. Many folk songs are modal in character. Composers of the late nineteenth and early twentieth centuries have manifested considerable interest in the possibilities of modal music, for example:

Ex. 24. Debussy—*Jumbo's Lullaby.*

(Aeolian mode)

Ex. 25. R. Vaughan Williams—*Pastoral Symphony*—Third Movement.

(Mixolydian mode)

On playing a scale it will be noticed that certain tones seem to be more important than others and that they possess a marked relationship or affinity to other notes of the scale. The tones of the scale which are most outstanding are the first, the *tonic*; the fifth, the *dom-*

inant; and the seventh, the *leading tone*. The complete list of the names employed for the tones of the scale is: [1]

First tone, *Tonic*
Second tone, *Supertonic*
Third tone, *Mediant*
Fourth tone, *Subdominant*

Fifth tone, *Dominant*
Sixth tone, *Submediant*
Seventh tone, *Leading tone*
Eighth tone, *Octave*

The *interval,* that is, the difference in pitch between any two tones, is reckoned in terms of the relationship they would possess if arranged in a scale. Intervals are calculated inclusively from the lower note. The actual difference in pitch between C and E, for example, is two whole tones; but, in reckoning the interval, C itself is included so that the interval C-E is called a third. A table of intervals from C is:

Ex. 26

The interval between any two tones is, from the standpoint of acoustics, the ratio existing between their rates of vibration, that is to say, between their frequencies. The interval of an octave exists between two tones whose frequencies are to each other as 1:2, the interval of a fifth between two tones whose frequencies are to each other as 2:3, and so on.

The major and minor scales mentioned above are known as *diatonic*

---

[1] It is by no means necessary for the non-professional reader to memorize these names. They are found in program notes, for instance, with a fair degree of regularity and one should at least possess a general, though not necessarily active, knowledge of them.

scales. In addition to these scales other divisions of the octave are possible. The *chromatic* scale is a division of the octave into twelve half-tones:

Ex. 27

The *whole-tone* scale is a division of the octave into six whole tones:

Ex. 28

The examples here given, however, by no means exhaust the possibilities of scale formation.

Tonality

The relationships existing between the tones of a melody as summarized in its scale give rise to our feeling for tonality. On playing over the hymn *Come, Thou Almighty King* quoted on page 29, it will be observed that the melody not only employs the scale based on G, but that the tone G serves as a basic note around which the melody gravitates and to which it returns at the conclusion, or more accurately stated, the return to which induces a feeling of rest and termination. The tonality of a composition may therefore be defined in terms of this focal tone, the *tonic,* and the type of scale constructed on it.

Our feeling for tonality is deeply rooted. Although most people cannot describe the tonality of a work in the technical terms employed by musicians, they are keenly aware of its existence and recognize departures from it and the return to it. Our feeling for tonality is an important factor in the formal design of music, as will be shown later. Change of tonality in the course of composition is known as *modulation.* For most purposes, the terms *tonality* and *key* are interchangeable.

Chapter IV

FUNDAMENTAL MUSICAL CONCEPTS: POLYPHONY AND HARMONY

Polyphony

THE EARLIEST technical account of music consisting of more than one melodic line dates from about 900 A.D. Many theories have been advanced to explain one of these first forms of melodic combination, a system in which one melody was paralleled by another melody removed from it by intervals, which were most frequently, but not exclusively, fourths and fifths.[1] This procedure was in marked contrast to classical and modern music, which considers thirds and sixths to be consonances. Melodic combination based on fourths and fifths was called *organum,* a simple form of which is shown in the following example:

Ex. 1

Tu pa - tris sem - pi - ter - nus es fi - li - us.

It is obvious, however, that the degree of parallelism between the voices of the above-quoted example is too inflexible to permit the added voice to have any individuality. Over two hundred years elapsed before this parallelism yielded to a style which exhibited a marked preference for melodies moving in opposite directions, with the result that they were endowed with a degree of independence and also produced other intervals than the fourth and the fifth. A science of writing combined melodies known as *counterpoint* (point against point, that is, note against note) developed; and in order to furnish

[1] See page 37.

some regulating device with which to synchronize the movement of several melodies, a rhythmic system was evolved. The first great school of polyphonic (many-voiced) writing based on the intervals of fourths and fifths arose in the thirteenth century, with Paris as its principal center of activity. A second great school whose standards of consonance were built around the third and the sixth reached its height at the close of the sixteenth century in the works of Lassus (1532–1549), Palestrina (1525[?]–1594), Victoria (ca. 1540–1611), and the great English school of madrigalists.

The sixteenth-century composers of polyphonic music strove to impart melodic and rhythmic independence to each component part of their compositions. Parts might be individualized by having them imitate each other at their successive entries, or through contrasts in rhythm, or through differences in direction of melodic flow. The excerpt on page 41 from the *Exaltabo Te, Domine* of Palestrina illustrates the state of perfection which polyphonic writing achieved during the sixteenth century. It is of the utmost importance that the five parts of this excerpt be played or sung individually in order to demonstrate that each is a complete, self-contained melody.

Consonance and Dissonance

For melodies to allow of combination, it is necessary that those pitches which are to sound simultaneously possess certain relationships. These may be classified as consonances or dissonances. Consonances are satisfying, restful combinations which produce an effect of completeness and do not demand that they be followed by some other combination. The following combinations of two notes are consonances.

Ex. 2

Consonantal combinations are not limited to two notes, but can be further enlarged by adding certain other pitches. Dissonances are not necessarily unpleasant, but they produce a tension which demands that they be followed by an eventual consonance, this process being call

Ex. 3

resolution. A few dissonances and the consonances into which they resolve are shown here:

Ex. 4

Dissonances need not necessarily be resolved at once, but may proceed into other dissonances before arriving at the final tension-relieving consonance.

The problem of the composer of polyphonic music is, therefore, a twofold one. The tones which comprise his work must arrange themselves as meaningful successions (melodies) and as logical combinations (consonances and correctly resolved dissonances). The combination of melodies produces *polyphony*; the combination of tones produces *harmony*. Up to the year 1600, composers were interested primarily in the flow of melodies, in the motion of individual parts rather than in the effects of simultaneously sounding pitches, though to be sure, these effects had to be taken into consideration.

The Canon

A polyphonic device which has found frequent application is the *canon,* a method of polyphonic writing in which there is a literal imitation of one voice by a succeeding voice or voices. An excellent example of the canon is the two-part Invention in F major of Bach:

Ex. 5

The Minuet of the String Quartet in D minor, Opus 76, No. 2 of Haydn commences with a spirited canon:

Ex. 6

A canon, it will be observed, may be regarded as a polyphonic composition in which a melody is combined with succeeding parts of itself. The imitating voices may repeat the melody of the antecedent voice at the unison, the octave, the fifth, or at any other interval; but the first two kinds of imitation are employed most frequently. A *round,* such as the familiar *Three Blind Mice,* is a canon at the unison or octave, in which the performers enter at regular intervals and make the circuit from the beginning to the end and back again without ceasing.

Short passages in a canonic style are frequently found in symphonic music. Beethoven concludes his Fifth Symphony with a triumphant canonic statement of the first theme of the last movement;[1] Franck writes in a similar manner in the first and last movements of his Symphony in D minor. An example of modern canonic writing will be found on page 383 in the excerpt from Holst's *The Planets.*

HARMONY

Polyphony and harmony arose side by side; but since the seventeenth century polyphony has relinquished its former position of priority and harmonic considerations have become important factors in the construction of musical works. The origin of harmony in polyphony

[1] Quoted on page 176.

may be shown by an examination of the following excerpt from Palestrina's *Stabat Mater,* written in a block-like style in which all the voices commence and progress together.

Ex. 7

Despite the fact that these blocks represent cross-sectional cuts made through layers of melody, they possess certain features which have enabled musicians to regard them as separate entities to which the name *chords* has been given. The polyphonic composers were not concerned with chords *per se* although they were well acquainted with the power of certain ones to establish tonality.

Homophony

The rapid rise of the opera, dating from about 1600, was responsible for an acceleration in the development of a musical idiom in which emphasis was placed on a single voice accompanied by chords. The polyphonic style, consisting of the interweaving of several independent and equally important melodies, thus gave way to a new method in which one melody predominated while the rest of the musical texture, grouped into chords, fulfilled an auxiliary function. The style is therefore called homophonic because of this emphasis on one voice.

Since the beginning of the seventeenth century, music has been predominantly harmonic in character, but the basic principles of melody formation still govern the progression of chords. The deciding factor between the rival claims on the listener's ear of the harmonic and the polyphonic aspects of any composition is the degree of musical interest, that is, the melodiousness, of its component parts. In the following excerpt from Johann Strauss' *The Beautiful Blue Danube,* the chordal accompaniment which serves as a simple underpinning for the melody possesses largely rhythmic interest.

Ex. 8

But in this excerpt from the chorale which concludes Bach's cantata *Alles nur nach Gottes Willen* (B.G.No.72), the three accompanying voices not only form chords, but also possess strong melodic individuality.[1]

Ex. 9

Wer Gott ver-traut,fest auf ihn baut, den will er nicht ver - las - - sen.

Chords

A chord may be defined as a combination of several tones sounded simultaneously. A combination of three tones capable of arrangement as a fundamental note and two superimposed thirds is called a *triad*. A triad composed of a major third and a perfect fifth is called a major triad. The major triad erected on C is:

Ex. 10

A minor triad is composed of a minor third and a perfect fifth. Either of these triads is known as a common chord.

Ex. 11

The chord of four tones, resulting from the addition of another third to a triad, is called a seventh chord, since it consists of a fundamental, third, fifth, and seventh. The most important of the numerous types of seventh chords is that formed on the dominant (the fifth scale degree) and consequently called the dominant seventh chord. The dominant seventh chord is a dissonant chord of great importance in the definition of tonality. The following illustration shows a seventh chord and a conventional resolution:

Ex. 12

Additional chords may be created by adding more thirds, raising or lowering the component intervals, or by changing the position of the fundamental tone. The number of possible chords is vast indeed, and new chord-structures and new chord-progressions are continually being evolved.

Chords may be classified as consonant or dissonant, depending on the intervals composing them and the context in which they are found. One dissonant chord is often followed by another, constituting either a new dissonance or a partial resolution, but a state of rest is not reached until a consonant chord is achieved. The art of harmonization consists of the judicious employment of both consonance and dissonance. Too much consonance is stultifying; too much dissonance is either vitiating or confusing.

It is not necessary that tones be sounded simultaneously to give the effect of a chord. The ear possesses the faculty of realizing the harmonic implications of successive tones when they are arranged in groups such as:

Ex. 13

This excerpt, the first four measures of the Prelude in C major, Part I, No. I, of Bach's *The Well-Tempered Clavichord*, consists of the adornment of the following chords by breaking them up into graceful arpeggios.

Ex. 14

Melodies themselves often have chordal implications. The following themes from *Das Rheingold* of Wagner, for example, are based on the notes of the common chord.

Ex. 15
(a)

(b)

A sustained bass note over which a series of chords progresses is called a *pedal*. Other names are pedal-point and organ-point. The pedal is an ancient harmonic device tracing its origins to the primitive *drone,* still a distinctive feature of the Scotch bagpipe. The modern name is derived from the custom of sustaining such bass notes by means of the organ pedal.

The tonic or the dominant, the first and fifth scale degrees, are usually employed as pedals. A tonic pedal is found at the conclusion of the Fugue in C minor, Part I, No. 2, of *The Well-Tempered Clavichord* of Bach:

Ex. 16

A pedal may also appear in an upper voice, in which case it is called an inverted pedal. The following example from the overture to Wagner's opera *Der Fliegende Holländer* (The Flying Dutchman) shows an inverted pedal, the effectiveness of which is enhanced by momentary deviation from the pedal tone.

Ex. 17

etc.

Chapter V

FUNDAMENTAL MUSICAL CONCEPTS: FORM

INDIVIDUAL tones have been likened to the letters of the alphabet. We have also observed how these tones may be grouped in some orderly manner to produce melodies. In examining the structure of melody further analogies with the structure of language may be observed. It will be recalled that letters are grouped into words, words into phrases, phrases into clauses or sentences, and the latter into paragraphs. Paragraphs may be grouped into chapters and a series of chapters into a complete book. Analogous procedures may be observed in the composition of musical works.

The Motive, the Phrase, and the Sentence

The smallest meaningful unit of musical thought is the *motive* [1]—a compact group of notes having a pattern or design sufficiently unique to differentiate it from other groups. A few well-known motives will illustrate the meaning of the term:

Ex. 1. Beethoven—Symphony No. 5—
First Movement.

Ex. 2. Beethoven—Symphony No. 9—
Second Movement.

Ex. 3. Wagner—*Die Walküre*.

---

[1] The "leading-motive," a special type of motive, is discussed on page 282.

Ex. 4.   Wagner—*Siegfried*.

Ex. 5.   Franck—Symphony in D minor—
First Movement.

Motives may be likened to words. The *phrase,* the next larger unit, consists of either several repetitions of the same motive, or of several motives. It is analogous to the phrase in language, which is composed of several words comprising a unit of thought. Musical phrases, like written or spoken ones, have a measure of self-subsistence, but they lack complete sense until they are arranged in a *sentence* or *clause.* The more conventional musical phrase is four measures long, and the more conventional musical sentence consists of two or more musical phrases.

The following excerpts will serve to illustrate the construction of the musical sentence:

Ex. 6.   Smith—*The Star-Spangled Banner*.

Ex. 7.   Foster—*The Old Folks at Home*.

Ex. 8.   Beethoven—Sonata, Opus 13 (*Pathétique*)—Second Movement.

Ex. 9.   Beethoven—Symphony No. 9—Fourth Movement.

Cadences

Each phrase in the above sentences concludes with a *cadence*. The cadences of a musical composition may be likened to the pauses, to the rising and falling of the voice in spoken language. They indicate the completion of some unit of the structure and are powerful factors in the establishment of tonality. Cadences vary in conclusiveness. The more common cadences are called the perfect cadence, the plagal cadence, the half-cadence and the deceptive cadence.

The perfect cadence is analogous to the fall of the voice at a period. A typical example is:

Ex. 10

Almost every musical composition ends with a perfect cadence, additional examples of which will be found at the conclusion of the sentences quoted in Examples 6–9. The perfect cadence is produced by following the chord based on the fifth degree of the scale, the dominant, with one based on the first degree, the tonic.

The plagal cadence is produced by following the chord based on the fourth degree of the scale, the subdominant, with the chord based on the tonic:

Ex. 11

This cadence, while equally as conclusive as the perfect cadence, has an atmosphere of dignity and impressiveness. It is invariably used for the *Amen* in church music. An excellent instance of the use of the plagal cadence is found at the close of Wagner's Prelude to *Lohengrin*:

Ex. 12

The half-cadence is analogous to the fall of the voice at a semicolon. It may be produced by following any chord with one based on the dominant:

Ex. 13
(a)

or

(b)

The deceptive cadence, also called the interrupted cadence, is produced when the chord based on the dominant is followed not by the awaited chord based on the tonic, but rather by a wholly unexpected chord; in fact, the deceptive cadence is not a cadence at all in that it wholly negates any feeling of conclusiveness. The effect of the deceptive cadence is always one of surprise, for the expected conclusion fails to materialize. The Prelude in E-flat minor from Part One of *The Well-Tempered Clavichord* of Bach possesses two dramatic deceptive cadences:

Ex. 14
(a)

instead of:

(b)

and

Ex. 15
(a)

instead of:

(b)

The more conventional cadences mentioned here by no means exhaust the list of possible sentence endings. Cadences of much originality are to be found in more recent music.

The sentences quoted in Examples 6–9 are all eight measures long, divided into two phrases of four measures each. The structure of musical works would be uninteresting, however, if all sentences were so constructed. Many other arrangements are not only feasible but extraordinarily common. Phrases may be shortened, extended, or overlapped without doing violence to our feeling for balance and symmetry.

Musical Forms

The term *form* permits of two broad interpretations, the first of which is essentially subjective in nature. We say that an art work possesses form when the relationships and arrangement of its component parts give rise to a feeling of unity and proportion. A musical composition thus possesses form when the ear perceives it as a unified and well-proportioned structure in sound. The first interpretation of form is therefore the concern of aesthetics. The second interpretation of form is essentially objective. Many composers have chosen to present their musical thoughts in patterns which possess a certain degree of similarity. It is in this sense that we may refer to the *sonata,* the *overture,* the *fugue,* and so on. But the forms employed by composers should not be regarded as molds for the facilitation of mass production of musical works. No great composer has meekly accepted the forms of his time as invariable codes of procedure to which he must conform.

Recognition of the form of a composition demands perception of the identities and diversities of its constituent parts, for musical form is the product of repetition and contrast. Every element of music mentioned in Chapters III and IV—melody, rhythm, and harmony—may be involved in the creation of these identities or diversities. The ear also demands that the various constituent parts of a composition possess some temporal symmetry, that is to say, durational balance.

The Two-Part Form

The simplest musical form consists of two complete sentences, a structure which divides naturally into two parts and is consequently called a *binary form,* or a *two-part form.* This form is to be found in many folk songs, hymns, and shorter piano pieces. A beautiful example is the folk-like song of Brahms—*Wiegenlied* (Lullaby):

Ex. 16

This melody consists of two sentences, each eight measures in length. Employing letters to designate the two sentences, its form may be schematically represented as A B.

Both halves of a two-part form may be considerably extended; that is, they may consist of several sentences. The perfect balance exhibited by the example quoted will not be retained invariably, nor will the second part always remain in the same key. But no matter how extended or complex the two sections may become, the structure consists of two distinct parts. Many examples of extended pieces in two-part form are to be found in the clavier suites of J. S. Bach.

The Three-Part Form

From the theoretical standpoint the number of musical forms is an infinite one. It can be shown, however, that one principle of construction has been employed more frequently than any other. This principle may be set forth as: *Statement—Digression—Restatement.* The form itself is called either the *three-part form,* the *ternary form,* or the *three-part song-form.*

The nature of this fundamental form may well be demonstrated by the familiar *Drink To Me Only With Thine Eyes:*

The song consists of only two phrases; the first is heard three times, the second once. Using letters to represent these phrases the form of this song may be given as A A B A, or in musical notation, A:‖B A, signifying Statement (repeated)—Digression—Restatement. *Drink To Me Only With Thine Eyes* is, of course, a very elementary example of three-part form. In more extended works, the B section presents a more vivid contrast than that found in the simple example quoted above. Such contrast may be obtained by change of key, rhythm or tempo, or by employment of new thematic material. Nor is the first part always repeated literally.

Further instances of the three-part form are legion in number. Detailed descriptions of other works employing the form will be discussed as they appear in the historical development of music. One of the surest routes to a rich appreciation of music is through a study of form. No opportunity for analysis of any work should be overlooked, but such analysis should at first be conducted along broad lines. Intelligent listening to folk-songs, hymns and short piano pieces will create an excellent background for the perception of the more subtle, identities and diversities to be found in the larger forms. Much modern dance music is quite regular in design, and the average fox-trot makes an easy study of the first principles of musical form.

Chapter VI

JOHANN SEBASTIAN BACH

JOHANN Sebastian Bach, the greatest of a line of over fifty Thuringian musicians to bear this family name, was born in Eisenach on the 21st of March, 1685. Left an orphan at the age of ten, he was taken into the family of an older brother who served not only as a foster parent, but also as his instructor in music. Like most of the musicians of this period, Bach became an expert performer not only on the organ and the clavier (a generic name which includes the various keyboard instruments of the period), but also on the violin. Bach's academic education consisted of ten years of *Gymnasium,* upon the completion of which, at the age of eighteen, he held posts as organist in two small German towns, Arnstadt and Mühlhausen. In the former place he seems to have drawn the wrath of the church officials upon himself because of the "strange harmonies" which he introduced into his organ playing.

Before proceeding to describe the three important posts which Bach held during his lifetime, the position of the musician during this period must be made clear. He was regarded merely as an employee whose duty it was not only to perform music, but also to create it. The music so created usually remained the property of his employer. Musicians were expected to furnish new music for all occasions, and such inspiration as might accompany the composition of a new work was entirely incidental. Writing for small courts rather than for a large public, composers wrote only such music as was demanded of them. Music was a commodity supplied by the court-composer in precisely the same manner that food was supplied to the princely table by the cook.

Wilhelm Ernst, Duke of Saxe-Weimar, took Bach into his service as court organist and chamber musician in 1708.   Since the Duke was an intensely religious man, Bach's duties were confined entirely to the services held in the ducal chapel; and most of his major works for organ and a few cantatas were composed during this nine-year sojourn in Weimar.   Failure to receive an expected promotion to the post of Kapellmeister caused Bach to resign, and his audacity in demanding his release from ducal service earned him one month's arrest.

From 1717 to 1723 Bach was at Anhalt-Cöthen at the court of Prince Leopold, a young man fond of chamber music but not at all concerned with religious music.   Accordingly, almost all of Bach's secular works were composed while he was in the service of this nobleman.

Chiefly because of a desire to give his numerous progeny the educational advantages of a large city, Bach accepted his third and last post, that of Cantor of St. Thomas' Church in Leipzig in 1723.   Besides being responsible for all the music required by the four churches included in the parish of St. Thomas', Bach was charged with the musical instruction of the choirboys in the church school.   The products of his Leipzig period include the greater part of the choral music and some works for organ and clavier.   He died on July 28, 1750.

Bach was recognized in his day merely as a performer on the organ. Most of his compositions remained unprinted during his lifetime, and many have been lost.   Felix Mendelssohn, who conducted the *St. Matthew Passion* in Berlin in 1829—the first performance of the work after the death of the composer—started the movement which has culminated today in world-wide recognition of Bach's singular genius.

With the exception of the opera, there is hardly an aspect of the music of the seventeenth and eighteenth centuries with which Bach did not concern himself.   All of the numerous forms in which he wrote were brought to such heights by him that they overshadow entirely the works of contemporaries.   And again, Bach has had no successors, no imitators.   Such was the unique quality of his inspiration that, like almost every other genius in the history of art, he founded no school.

The Keyboard Stringed Instruments of Bach's Day

Before passing on to a discussion of the forms used by Bach, the various keyboard stringed instruments in use during his lifetime must be described.   These instruments can be divided into two classes: (a)

JOHANN SEBASTIAN BACH

those whose strings were struck, and (b) those whose strings were plucked.

The first class is represented by the *clavichord,* an instrument which at Bach's time had a range of about four octaves:

Ex. 1

The striking mechanism consisted of brass tangents which were placed in the ends of the key-levers. When a key was depressed, the tangent struck the string and set it in vibration. A peculiar feature of the clavichord, however, was the fact that the tangent remained in contact with the string as long as the key was depressed, and consequently determined its pitch. A much more important consequence of this continued contact of tangent and string was the degree of control exercised by the player over both the dynamic value and the quality of the sound produced. Although the clavichord produced a tone which was somewhat thin and lacking in brilliance, it possessed a much greater expressive power than any other keyboard instrument of its day. Its responsiveness caused Bach to prefer it for certain types of music.

To the second class belongs an instrument with several names. The English knew it as the *harpsichord,* the French as the *clavecin,* the Germans as the *Flügel,* the Italians as the *clavicembalo* or *cembalo.* Bach usually used the Italian term *cembalo.* The harpsichord was wing-shaped, resembling the form of a modern grand piano. This accounts for the German name *Flügel* (wing), a designation still employed in Germany for the grand piano. The strings of the harpsichord were actuated by plectra, fashioned from either crow quills or pieces of hard leather, and placed in short upright pieces of wood known as jacks, fastened to the ends of the key-levers. When the key was depressed, the jack was forced upward and the plectrum twanged the string. Harpsichords were often provided with two keyboards (manuals), one producing a brilliant tone and the other a soft tone. The instrument also possessed couplers (stops), mechanical devices which caused corresponding notes on a different manual or in a different octave to sound simultaneously. By means of the two manuals and the couplers, players could obtain a degree of dynamic alteration which was limited in scope and confined largely to contrasts between the larger divisions of a work. The harpsichord's deficiencies in subtlety of nuance were amply atoned for by its preciseness, power, and brilliance.

The harpsichord should not be regarded as a crude ancestor of the modern piano. It reached a high plane of mechanical perfection during Bach's lifetime, and it was not until the beginning of the nineteenth century that it was supplanted completely by the piano. While the piano may have ousted the harpsichord, it has not taken its place entirely; and modern times have witnessed a revival of interest in this instrument.

Bach became acquainted with one of the precursors of the modern piano when he visited King Frederick the Great in 1747; but he found the tone of this as yet unperfected instrument unpleasant. It is difficult to generalize about the performance of Bach's harpsichord and clavichord works on the modern piano. Many of the clavichord works are benefited by the transference; certain harpsichord pieces which demand the two keyboards of the older instrument lose in clarity.

The German word *Clavier* is a general term which embraces all of the keyboard stringed instruments—clavichord, harpsichord, and piano. In order to avoid confusion the common practice of designating compositions for these instruments as clavier music will be followed.

CLAVIER MUSIC

The Suites

We encounter one of the most typical of the eighteenth-century instrumental forms in Bach's six *French Suites* and six *English Suites* written at Anhalt-Cöthen, and in the seven *Partitas* written at Leipzig. Various explanations have been set forth concerning the origin of the terms *English* and *French* as applied to these clavier suites. None is satisfactory, however, and the question is only of academic interest.

A well-marked differentiation between vocal and instrumental idioms was not found in the music of the sixteenth century; compositions often bore the indication, "Apt for voices or viols." Thus many of the first attempts at instrumental music were merely transferences to instruments of music conceived along vocal lines. Composers of instrumental music soon found better models in dances with their well-defined rhythms and symmetrical construction. Although composers retained the titles and rhythmic characteristics of these dances, the artistic manner in which they treated them soon lifted them out of the category of mere dance music and made of them self-sufficient media of artistic expression. A piece so composed is therefore better described as an idealized dance, or a piece in dance form.

An important step in the development of modern instrumental music was taken in the early part of the seventeenth century when composers discovered that they might construct larger instrumental works by arranging these pieces in a well-contrasted series. For such a series of pieces the designation *suite* slowly came into use. The national origin of the term seems to indicate the important part played by France in the development of this form. The dances of many other European countries were taken up and cultivated by the French, only to be exported later on with Gallicized names, such as *allemande, polonaise, anglaise,* and so forth. Other designations in use at the time for a series of pieces in dance forms were *Lessons* or *Suite of Lessons* in England, *Ordre* in France, *Partita* in Italy and Germany.

The only uniform characteristic of the suite of Bach's day was that all of the pieces comprising it were usually in the same key. Although the conventions with regard to the nature and number of the pieces were not particularly rigid, the following forms usually appeared in the order given: *allemande, courante, sarabande, gigue.* When other forms were introduced it was customary to place them between the *sarabande* and the *gigue.* It is important to notice that almost all the movements of Bach's suites are in two-part form, each of the movements being divided into two nearly equal halves. Commencing in the tonic key, the first half gradually modulates and comes to a well-defined point of rest with a perfect cadence, usually in the key of the dominant; the second half commences in the key of the dominant and gradually returns to the tonic. There is usually a marked degree of correspondence between the opening and closing measures of each half.

FRENCH SUITE NO. VI IN E MAJOR

The sixth of Bach's French Suites will serve as a typical example of the suite form. The work consists of eight movements, all of which are in the tonality of E major. Bach retains the conventional *allemande-courante-sarabande* sequence and introduces four light, gay movements before the final *gigue*.

Ex. 2   1. Allemande.

The allemande is in quadruple rhythm. Commencing with an up-beat, that is, an unaccented note or group of notes leading up to a strong beat, it is moderate in speed and exhibits a quick and easy flow.

Ex. 3   2. Courante.

The courante is a lively animated movement in triple rhythm. Like its predecessor, it also commences with an up-beat.

Ex. 4   3. Sarabande.

The sarabande, in contrast with the two movements that have pre-ceded it, is a slow, dignified, inherently serious dance. It is in triple rhythm, characterized by a tendency to accentuate the second beat. The sarabande, as opposed to all the other movements of the suite, is essentially harmonic in style.

Ex. 5   4. Gavotte.

The gavotte is a moderately fast dance in quadruple rhythm. It almost always commences on the third beat.

Ex. 6   5. Polonaise.

The polonaise, as treated by Bach, is a simple, unpretentious movement in triple rhythm. Despite its name, the Bach form shows no Polish tendencies and should not be confused with the polonaise as found in the works of Chopin.

Ex. 7   6. Bourrée.

The bourrée is a lively, animated dance in quadruple rhythm, occasionally in duple.

Ex. 8   7. Minuet.

The minuet of Bach's time was a graceful, courtly dance in a moderately fast triple rhythm. The minuet possesses special interest inasmuch as it was the only element of the suite to become a member of that series of movements of later development which comprise the sonata and the symphony. Like the polonaise, the minuet took on different characteristics in the hands of later composers such as Haydn and Mozart.

Ex. 9   8. Gigue.

The gigue, the final movement of the suite, is a lively, rollicking dance employing triple rhythm or some multiple of it, that is, $\frac{3}{8}, \frac{6}{8}$, or $\frac{12}{8}$. The gigue is always written in a polyphonic manner with considerable imitation in the various parts.

Listening to a suite such as the one just discussed should serve to contradict irrefutably the old belief that the music of Bach is cold, impersonal, and mathematical. The clavier suites demonstrate, above all, Bach's ability to arrive at the true nature of these apparently stiff dance forms and, within their limitations, to create the profundities of the sarabandes and the gay, witty repartee of the gigues.

The first *Passepied* (a graceful dance in triple rhythm, commencing on the third beat) of Bach's fifth English Suite is written not in the usual two-part form, but in *rondo* form. The arrangement of the thematic material of the rondo (French *rondeau*) can be represented schematically as follows: A B A C A D A. The plan of the rondo is thus merely an extension of the principle of construction shown by three-part form (statement—digression—restatement) to include several digressions each followed by a return to the principal idea, often called the *refrain*. The digressions are written in a contrasting style and are usually called *episodes*. The *Rondeau* of Bach's second Partita is an excellent example of this procedure. The rondo scheme might be applied to any dance form, and pieces so written bore the designation *en rondeau* in addition to their usual title; for instance, *minuet en rondeau* and *passepied en rondeau*. The rondo of Bach and his contemporaries should not be confused with the form as remodelled and made into a movement of the sonata by Haydn, Mozart, and Beethoven.

Not all of the movements found in Bach's clavier suites are dance-like. The second French Suite contains an *Air;* all six English Suites and the seven Partitas commence with prefatory pieces having titles such as *Prélude, Sinfonie,* and *Fantaisie*. In his third and sixth English Suites Bach writes a pair of gavottes to be played in this order: Gavotte I—Gavotte II—Gavotte I. In this way two two-part forms were arranged so as to produce a three-part form. Inasmuch as Gavotte I was repeated literally, Bach followed the custom of merely writing *Da capo* at the end of Gavotte II. This Italian designation meaning "from the beginning" was an indication to the player to return to the beginning and play the first gavotte once more. Bourrées and minuets are also found grouped in this manner. It often happened that the second of such a pair of minuets was written in three-part harmony, thereby causing the second minuet to be called a *Trio*. The custom of writing this second minuet in three parts died out with Bach, but the name *Trio* has persisted as a designation for the middle section of such three-part forms as the minuet, the march, and the scherzo.

The term *suite* can be said to refer to a definite form—a series of idealized dances—only insofar as it is restricted to the works of seventeenth- and eighteenth-century composers. Later composers have used the term with great freedom, and it is frequently used as a designation for works such as the following:

1. A series of extracts from the incidental music written for a drama:

> Bizet—Suite from *L'Arlésienne* (Daudet)
> Grieg—Suite from *Peer Gynt* (Ibsen)

2. A series of extracts from the music for an opera or ballet:
> Bizet—Suite from *Carmen*
> Tchaikovsky—Suite from *The Nutcracker*

3. A series of narrative or descriptive pieces:
> Rimsky-Korsakoff—*Scheherazade*
> John Alden Carpenter—*Adventures in a Perambulator*

The Inventions

Bach gave the name *Inventions* to a collection of fifteen short two-part (two-voiced) clavier pieces which he wrote as exercises for his sons. A corresponding set of fifteen pieces in three parts he called *Symphonies,* an illustration of the loose way in which the term *symphony* was used for instrumental music during the seventeenth and eighteenth centuries. The Symphonies are now universally known as the Three-Part Inventions. The inscription with which Bach prefaced the collection of Inventions describes them for us: "A sincere guide wherein lovers of the clavier and especially those anxious to learn are shown a clear method for playing with facility in two parts, and, after suitable progress, in three parts; and wherein they may also learn how to create good ideas (*inventiones*), to develop them and above all attain a *cantabile* (singing) style in playing and acquire a strong predilection for composition." The mention of "cantabile" playing in this preface indicates that the Inventions were written for the clavichord. The Inventions are *études,* pieces designed as exercises for the development of technique. But as the composer tells us, these études are also models of the art of composition, having as an additional purpose the development of artistic discernment. The Inventions are short pieces written in a polyphonic style, but the contrapuntal ingenuity displayed in them is unobtrusive. Many of them possess the freshness and spontaneity of improvisation.

The Well-Tempered Clavichord

Bach gave the title *The Well-Tempered Clavichord* to a series of twenty-four preludes and fugues, in each of the twenty-four major and minor keys, which he completed at Anhalt-Cöthen in 1722. A second set was composed at Leipzig twenty-two years later, and the two sets are now referred to as Part I and Part II. Like the Inventions, the preludes and fugues of *The Well-Tempered Clavichord* were designed for "the use and benefit of young musicians who are anxious to learn."

In describing the clavichord, on which these works were to be played, as "well-tempered," the composer was referring to the system in which its strings were tuned. A tempered or well-tempered scale is one whose pitches are so tuned as to permit their forming a part of the scale of any key. It is the use of this system of tuning which enables the notes B-sharp, C-natural and D-double flat, for example, to be sounded by one and the same string instead of by the three different strings theoretically necessary. In the tempered system of tuning, the octave is divided into twelve equidistant semitones; and, while as a result of this, certain tones are somewhat higher and others lower than their acoustically correct values, the deviations are not appreciable to most ears.[1] Bach was not the inventor of this system, but inasmuch as *The Well-Tempered Clavichord* could only be per-

---

[1] The only instruments capable of producing scales that are acoustically correct are the string instruments, the trombone, and the human voice; although when these are used with other instruments they must perforce employ the tempered system. A string quartet suffers from no such restrictions and the beauty of tone of which such an ensemble is capable is attributable in large measure to its purity of intonation.

formed on an instrument which was tuned to it, this work served as a strong incentive to its ultimate universal adoption.

The Prelude

The term *prelude* is one of the most loosely used designations in the entire vocabulary of music. Composers have employed this title in many ways; it would be impossible to coin a definition that would cover a Bach prelude, a Chopin prelude, and a prelude to a Wagner music-drama. Discussion of the term must therefore be restricted to a particular composer's concept of it. As used by Bach, the label *prelude* describes a manner of writing rather than a set form. The general style of the preludes of *The Well-Tempered Clavichord* is one of improvisation. They may be brilliant or sombre, impulsive or restrained; some are rhapsodic songs in a homophonic style, others are worked out along polyphonic lines. Each of the forty-eight preludes is a law unto itself. All of the preludes are coupled to fugues in the same key; but despite the implications of their title, they are not merely prefaces to the fugues. The preludes are complete in themselves and may conceivably be played as independent pieces.

A Bach *Prelude and Fugue* is therefore a work whose two movements may be regarded as compeers, contrasting in mood and style, but joined through the use of a common key.

The Fugue

The chief characteristic of a *fugue* consists in the polyphonic elaboration of a melodic idea, called the *fugue-subject,* by several voices, fixed in number for a given work. Fugues may be written for instruments or for voices. A vocal terminology is used in either case and the various parts are always referred to as "voices."

The interplay of the voices in a rapid fugue will often give the effect of flight, whence the use of a word derived from the Latin *fuga* (flight) as a title; but fugues may be written in slow tempi as well, and the origin of the term should, therefore, not be taken too literally. From the standpoint of the listener, a fugue comprises two parts—the *exposition* and the *development*.

The exposition consists of successive presentations of the fugue-subject by each voice in turn. The order of entry of the voices is not subject to any fixed rule. The compact exposition of the fugue in C major, Part 1, No. 1 of *The Well-Tempered Clavichord* will serve as an example:

Ex. 10

In this particular fugue the subject is given out by the alto voice. At the conclusion of this enunciation of the subject, the soprano voice presents it, but in the key of the dominant. This second entry is called the *answer,* though in truth this second appearance of the subject is not to be construed as only a reply to the first. While the soprano gives out the subject, the alto voice continues with a new and subordinate melody in contrapuntal combination with it. In some fugues this new melody attains a degree of importance and is then known as the *counter-subject.* Similarly, when the subject is announced for the third time in the tenor voice, the two upper voices continue in contrapuntal combination. The same procedure is followed when the fourth and last voice, the bass, enters. There are several features of the exposition worth pointing out:

1. The fugue-subject has appeared in all of the voices and has therefore been heard as many times as there are voices.

2. The voices enter successively and at different pitches; the effect is thus cumulative.

3. The exposition is the most regular part of the fugue—the only part that can be described with some degree of statistical accuracy.

4. For the listener the most important section of the work is the exposition; and to fail to apprehend its content is like missing the first act of a play—one is ignorant of the situation.

In a few fugues the exposition is followed by one or more entries of the subject; if these entries occur in all the voices they constitute what is called a *counter-exposition*. Counter-expositions are to be found in Fugues I and IX of *The Well-Tempered Clavichord,* Part 1.

The succeeding section of a fugue is called the *development* and, as its name implies, is that part of the fugue in which the composer reveals the potentialities of the subject in any manner his imagination may suggest and his contrapuntal technique permit. In writing the development the composer is governed by no rigid conventions; it is evident, however, that the process of development must conform to the inexorable demand that every art work possess an organic unity. The development of the fugue consists of numerous entries of the subject in various tonalities, and in many cases with significant melodic and rhythmic alterations. The various entries are separated from each other by *episodes*—truce-like sections of great psychological effectiveness, in which the subject as an entity temporarily drops out of sight. The successive entries of the subject and the intervening episodes thus constitute an elaborate scheme of repetition and contrast.

There are three conventional methods of altering the subject during the course of the development. These procedures are called *inversion, augmentation,* and *diminution.* In inversion, the fugue-subject is turned upside down; that is, the directions of the constituent intervals are reversed, upward movement becoming downward and vice versa; for example, Bach—*The Well-Tempered Clavichord,* Part I, Fugue No. VI:

Ex. 11
(a) Subject.

(b) Inversion of subject.

Augmentation is the process of enlargement; that is, the lengths of all the constituent notes are multiplied, usually by two. Inasmuch as the relative time values remain undisturbed, the contours of the subject remain unaltered; for example, Bach—*The Well-Tempered Clavichord,* Part I, Fugue No. VIII:

Ex. 12
  (a) Subject.

  (b) Augmentation of subject.

Diminution is the converse of augmentation; the notes of the subject are now decreased in value, producing an effect akin to compression; for example, Bach—*The Well-Tempered Clavichord,* Part II, Fugue No. IX:

Ex. 13
  (a) Subject.

  (b) Diminution of subject.

Another method of elaboration of the subject is a device called *stretto,* a procedure wherein the entries of the subject overlap; that is, the subject is announced in one voice before the completion of the previous entry. The various voices apparently pile up on each other in a well-planned confusion productive of telling emotional effect. It can not be too strongly emphasized that the devices herein described do not exhaust the possible methods of development and that all, some, or none of them may be found in any given fugue. The fugue concludes with the *coda* (Italian for "tail") in which the subject, after all its tonal wanderings, finally returns to the home key—the original tonality. In many fugues, this return of the subject to its tonic will have about it an air of conquest and victory, much as if the subject were expansively proclaiming its triumph over the vicissitudes of the development.

The *sine qua non* for proper appreciation of a fugue is the ability to recognize the subject in its numerous repetitions, no matter how it may be disguised or transformed. This ability can be achieved only by concentration on the part of the listener. An excellent preliminary step in the acquisition of this habit is to count the entries of the subject.

There is a widely prevalent belief to the effect that the fugue is an essentially intellectual musical form, devoid of emotional appeal. The mechanism of the fugue is such that it can be used by composers who possess craftsmanship but lack inspiration. On the other hand, this same mechanism may be made to serve as a means of artistic communication which is not only forceful and direct but, as the fugues of Bach so well demonstrate, also capable of expressing every shade of human emotion.[1]

The possibilities of polyphonic elaboration inherent in the fugal style have caused many composers to employ it for portions of larger works. A section so written is called a *fugato*; it usually embodies only the exposition of a fugue. Examples are to be found in works far removed from Bach, such as many of the symphonies of Beethoven, the overture to Smetana's opera *The Bartered Bride,* the prelude to the third act of Wagner's opera *Die Meistersinger von Nürnberg, Through the Looking Glass* of Deems Taylor, and many others.

Like the Inventions, the preludes and fugues of *The Well-Tempered Clavichord* show amazing variety not only in the character of their thematic material, but also in the method in which this material is

[1] Within certain limits the fugue can even be used for descriptive purposes. An American composer, Philip James, concludes his *Suite for Strings* with a fugue depicting a scene in a university classroom. The professor, impersonated by the eminently respectable double bass, announces the topic of the day. This is taken up joyfully by the students by means of the fugal exposition; the discussion is described in the development; and the jolly coda is rudely terminated by strident chords suggesting the closing bell.

employed. While the composition of all of these works demanded great contrapuntal skill, they give the listener the impression of being essentially improvisational music. But free as the flow of Bach's fancy may seem, closer examination will show that his works are the product of splendid musical logic. Even his ostensibly theoretical treatise, *Die Kunst der Fuge* (The Art of Fugue), a collection of seventeen fugues and four canons on the same fugue-subject, possesses an expressive power which wholly overshadows the didactic aim of the work.

The Chromatic Fantasia and Fugue is one of Bach's larger works for the clavier and one of the few not part of a collection. Written in a majestic style with a long and impulsive fantasia, it closely approaches the idiom of the organ compositions. The work takes its name from the chromatic nature of the fantasia as well as of the fugue-subject:

Ex. 14

One of Bach's most brilliant pieces for the clavier, this work was among his first compositions to win popularity.

The *Italian Concerto,* written for the harpsichord, bears a title illustrative of the loose way in which musical works were labeled during the eighteenth century, even by so great a master as Bach. The title which Bach bestowed upon this harpsichord piece was *Concerto, after the Italian Manner.* The designation "concerto" derives from the practice then current in Germany of writing works for clavier solo in the style of the Italian concertos for violin and orchestra. This also explains "after the Italian Manner." The contrasts of *tutti* and *solo* which characterized the orchestral concerto[1] are realized in these solo concertos for harpsichord through changes of manuals. The *Italian Concerto* with its three movements—*Allegro, Andante,* and *Presto*—strongly prefigured the sonata form which was to occupy the center of the musical stage after the death of Bach.

[1] See page 82.

ORGAN MUSIC

The organ works of Bach may be divided into two groups: (1) the larger works such as the preludes and fugues, toccatas and fugues, fantasias and fugues; and (2) the shorter, more intimate chorale-preludes. Bach's organ works form only a small part of his total creative accomplishment[1]; but they constitute the very foundation of the repertory of the modern organist.

The organ of Bach's day appears as a crude affair when compared with the mechanical marvels of the present. But despite the limitations of his organ, Bach has written his most majestic instrumental music for it. It was, it should be recalled, the instrument which he himself played, and unlike the uncertain orchestral resources of which he could avail himself, it offered him a reliable medium for the performance of larger instrumental works. It is interesting to note that although Bach was the greatest organ virtuoso of his day, if not of all time, only a very small proportion of the works which he composed for this instrument falls into the category of music that exists simply to allow a performer to demonstrate his mechanical dexterity. The organ works of Bach are difficult, but these difficulties are incidental to a higher musical purpose and are not merely quasi-artistic hurdles.

Most of the fugues for organ are monumental works based on subjects of much originality, treated in a manner from which a dramatic note is seldom absent. Bach exploits to the full the organ's ability to provide effective contrasts and thrilling climaxes.

Like the fugues, whatever differences that exist between the organ preludes and the clavier preludes have their origin in the nature of the instrument for which the works were designed. Two other forms, the *fantasia* and the *toccata,* are also found in combination with the organ fugues.

The term *fantasia,* like the term *prelude,* has had a somewhat checkered career in the service of the world's great composers. As employed by Bach, it is a freely constructed work giving the impression of being an extemporization. It differs from the prelude in that it often displays many moods and styles. One of Bach's finest fan-

---

[1] Four of the sixty volumes of the complete edition issued by the Bach Gesellschaft.

tasias is to be found in the Fantasia and Fugue in G Minor, one of the most famous of Bach's organ works. The fugue subject is:

Ex. 15

The *toccata* derives its name from the Italian *toccare* (to touch). The toccata is a "touch piece," brilliant in style, rapid in tempo, and abounding in spectacular effects. It, too, is cast in the free style of improvisation. Its original purpose was merely to serve as a vehicle for virtuoso display, but in the hands of Bach the form was elevated to a position of true musical value. A typical Bach toccata is the celebrated one in F major:

Ex. 16

Neither the prelude, nor the fantasia, nor the toccata should be considered subordinate to the fugues which they preface. Acquaintance-ship with any larger work will prove conclusively how indissolubly its two sections are bound together.

It is difficult to generalize about these monumental compositions. To a great majority of individuals they remain almost unknown because of the infrequency of performance on the instrument for which they were composed. Such is their musical worth, however, that other musicians have not been content to allow them to remain the exclusive property of organists. Pianists have adapted several of them for their instrument; notable arrangements have been made by Liszt, Tausig, von Bülow, and Busoni. Many have also been arranged for orchestra, usually with happy results. Among those who have made orchestral transcriptions of Bach's organ works may be listed the composers Sir Edward Elgar, Ottorino Respighi, and Arnold

Schoenberg, and the conductors Leopold Stokowski and Sir Henry Wood.

PASSACAGLIA AND FUGUE IN C MINOR

As one of Bach's most important organ works, the Passacaglia and Fugue in C Minor merits detailed discussion. The *passacaglia* is descended from a slow Spanish or Italian dance in which a short bass melody was repeated incessantly. Although the passacaglia is almost identical with the *chaconne,* theorists have attempted to establish a difference between the two forms by stating that the theme of the passacaglia remains continually in the bass, while that of the chaconne may wander into the upper voices. Composers, however, do not seem to have been guided by consideration for such niceties of definition; Bach in his Passacaglia has not hesitated to introduce the theme in the upper voices.[1]

In the passacaglia we encounter a new application of the basic principles of musical form as displayed by works which are classified as *variations.* Variations are a series of melodic, harmonic, or rhythmic transformations of some self-contained theme; these transformations may follow each other without pause, or they may be in themselves self-contained pieces terminating with a full close. The variation form satisfies in a very simple manner our desire for repetition and contrast in a musical composition. Variations are often grouped in order of complexity and brilliance, thus producing an additional effect of organic growth. There are many different types of variations. These will be described as we encounter them in the works of the great composers.

The passacaglia is a variation form characterized by the use of a short bass phrase as its theme, and by the construction of numerous variations above successive repetitions of this phrase. A phrase so employed is often called a *ground,* a *ground bass,* or *basso ostinato* (Italian for "persistent bass"). In many passacaglias the ground bass remains substantially unaltered; but in some instances it may be either

---

[1] Bach was above all a practical musician. The description of him to be found in an obituary notice published by a Leipzig musical society includes the following: "Our late friend Bach never entered into deep theoretical discussions about music, and was all the more proficient in art." (Bernhard Friedrich Richter—"Der Nekrolog auf Sebastian Bach von Jahre 1754." *Bach-Jahrbuch 1920.*)

inverted or broken up into smaller figures, or placed in an upper voice.

Bach's passacaglia utilizes a solemn ground bass of eight measures, borrowed from a composition by a French organist, André Raison:

Ex. 17

On this melody Bach proceeds to construct twenty variations. Two variations are quoted here to demonstrate the technique employed:

Ex. 18
(a) Variation I.

(b) Variation XIV.

The variations follow each other without pause and with continually increasing complexity. By the end of the twentieth variation, the listener might suspect that the possibilities of the ground bass had been exhausted; but Bach, in very dramatic fashion, takes its first four measures, alters them slightly and combines them with a new theme:

Ex. 19

and proceeds to cap his magnificent tonal structure with a tremendous *double fugue*.[1]

The Chorale-Preludes

The larger organ works represent Bach, the organ virtuoso, who delights in the creation of towering edifices in sound. There is, however, another aspect of his creativeness—his ability to frame the hymns of the Lutheran Church in imaginative musical settings.

The expressive congregational hymns of the German Lutheran Church are known as *chorales*. To aid in the work of the Reformation, Luther himself wrote the melodies for eight chorales as well as texts for many melodies already in existence. In attempting to understand the nature of the *chorale-prelude,* it must be borne in mind that the chorales were sung by the entire congregation in its own language and with true devotion. The beautiful melodies of the chorales as well as their fervid texts were therefore known to all and could be employed by the organist in a manner which his listeners would find meaningful.

During the principal service of worship of the Lutheran Church it was customary for the organist to play a prelude on the appointed chorale before the congregation sang it. Hence the name *chorale-prelude* (*Chorale-Vorspiel*) for a form which may be defined as a free setting for organ of the melody of a chorale. These settings are more than mere transcriptions, however. Examination of Bach's chorale-preludes will show that the composer has utilized his harmonic and contrapuntal technique as well as his melodic invention in the creation of what are essentially new versions of the chorales, versions which are sensitive interpretations of a highly subjective nature. Furthermore it will be found that Bach derived his inspi-

---

[1] A *double fugue* is a fugue on two subjects. In this particular double fugue, the subjects are announced simultaneously and remain inseparable throughout.

ration for many of these settings from the chorale texts. True
appreciation of the chorale-reludes demands possession of the self-
same equipment as that of the parishioners of Bach's church, namely,
a knowledge of both the text and the melody of the chorale on which
the chorale-prelude is based.[1]

Of the several diverse styles employed by Bach in his treatment of
the chorale melodies, the simplest and at the same time most effective
may be described as follows: the melody of the chorale is preserved
almost intact and appears in the soprano voice; to this melody are
added new melodies of a descriptive or symbolic nature, inspired
by the text of the chorale.

CHORALE-PRELUDE—"ICH RUF' ZU DIR, HERR JESU CHRIST"

A typical example of such a setting is the prelude on the chorale
Ich ruf' zu dir, Herr Jesu Christ (I cry to Thee, Lord Jesus Christ)
from the collection of forty-five chorale-preludes called by Bach
Orgelbüchlein (Little Organ Book).[2] The original melody of this
chorale is:

Ex. 20

Ich ruf' zu_ dir, Herr Je - su Christ, ich bitt', er - hör' mein Kla - gen
Ver - leih' mir_ Gnad' zu die - ser Frist, lass mich doch nicht ver - za - gen:

Den rech - ten weg, O_ Herr ich mein', den woll - est du mir ge - ben,

Dir zu le - ben, mein' Nächsten nutz zu sein, dein wort zu hal - ten· e - ben.

(*Prose translation of the text:* I cry to Thee, Lord Jesus Christ, hear my plaint,
I pray! Incline Thy Grace to me at this moment, do not let me lose heart!
Grant me the True Faith, O Lord, to live for Thee, to help my neighbor and
to keep Thy Word holy.)

[1] All of the ninety-odd chorales which served Bach as the source for his one hundred and
forty-three chorale-preludes are to be found in Vol. XX of the Novello edition of his organ
works.

[2] There is no better key to the musical language of Bach than a study of the
imaginative musical miniatures comprising the *Orgelbüchlein*; nor is there any better way
to approach Bach than by actual performance of them. They can be played on the piano

The fervid supplication of the text finds its musical embodiment in two motives, an undulating figure in the middle voice combined with a pulsating figure in the bass:

Ex. 21

ORCHESTRAL MUSIC

The orchestral music of Bach may be conveniently classified as follows: (1) the four orchestral suites, (2) the six Brandenburg concertos, and (3) the concertos for violin, or for clavier, and orchestra. The infrequency of performance of many of these works should not be construed as in any way indicative of their artistic worth as compared to that of the relatively few Bach compositions which have been singled out for regular presentation. There is an enormous amount of truly inspired music by Bach which is heard all too seldom.

Although these compositions are classified as orchestral music today, the designation is something of a misnomer for, according to modern usage, the term implies music to be played by a symphony orchestra at a public concert.

Bach took but little interest in the attempts which were made during his lifetime to establish public concerts in Leipzig. It was not until 1781, thirty-one years after his death, that a series of regular public concerts was started in that city. During the greater part of Bach's lifetime the art of music as practiced by professional musicians was restricted to the church, the opera house, and the salons of the nobility. Various musical activities were also undertaken by the *Collegia musica,* organizations composed of amateur performers. Bach's

with pleasure and profit by dividing the three staves employed for organ music between two players in an impromptu piano duet. An excellent American edition of the *Orgelbüchlein,* edited by Albert Riemenschneider and published under the title *The Liturgical Year,* includes not only the chorale-preludes, but also the equally important chorales as well as translations of their texts.

orchestral works therefore fall into the category of chamber music—music to be played in the salon or drawing room. At Anhalt-Cöthen, where much of his orchestral music was composed, performances were given by an orchestra of sixteen players for the delectation of Prince Leopold and his guests. In Leipzig Bach was director of the *Collegium musicum* of the University for seven years, and both he and his two sons, Karl Philipp Emanuel and Wilhelm Freidemann, frequently took part in its activities.

All of the music of this period, which was written for combinations of instruments, or of instruments and voices, demanded harmonic completion by an accompanying harpsichordist or organist playing a part called either *basso continuo, continuo,* or, by a curious error of translation, *thorough-bass.* The harpsichordist not only served as a sort of leader for the other performers, but also "filled in" the harmonic structure of the work from a description of it written in a musical shorthand and called a *figured bass.* This figured bass consisted of the bass forming the harmonic substructure and numbers describing the chords to be constructed upon it. The method of elaboration of the figured bass was left to the discretion of the harpsichordist, who extemporized his part from this shorthand version of the required chords. It was not until the era of Joseph Haydn that instrumental music finally dispensed with the use of the continuo as an agency for harmonic "filling in."

The Orchestral Suites

Of the four orchestral suites only two are heard today, the second, in B minor, for flute, strings, and continuo, and the third, in D major, for trumpets, oboes, kettledrums, strings, and continuo. In each of these four works we find a long preparatory piece called an *overture* [1] written in a form which had become a convention in the works of French operatic composers. This so-called French overture is another addition to our collection of three-part (A B A) forms. The first section is slow, dignified, and majestic in character and almost invariably employs dotted rhythmic figures of this type:

$$\text{♫ ♩. ♫ ♩. ♫}$$

[1] Bach called his four orchestral suites "overtures."

It is followed by a lively animated fugue. The third section may either be a literal repetition of the first, or a slightly altered version; for example, the overture from the Suite in D major (No. 3).

Ex. 22
  (a)

The other numbers of the suite are all pieces in dance form with the exception of the celebrated *Air* for strings from the third suite. An inartistic arrangement of this Air as a G-string solo for violin with piano accompaniment was made over a century after the composer's death, and Bach's work is therefore erroneously known as the *Air for the G-string.* In the orchestral suites, the conventional *Allemande* and *Courante* have been supplanted by other dance forms. The second suite, for example, contains a *Polonaise* and a *Badinerie* (French for "fooling," "trifling").

The Concertos

The remaining orchestral works of Bach are examples of another important instrumental form of the early eighteenth century—the *concerto.* The name *concerto* or *concerto grosso* was given during Bach's time to a composition for many players in which certain passages were played by all of the instrumentalists while others were assigned either to a solo performer or to a small group of solo performers. The larger group consisted almost exclusively of string instruments and was known as the *ripieno* or *concerto grosso* (large concerto). The smaller group was called the *concertino* (little concerto), and often consisted of two violins and a violoncello; the solo performers were for the most part violinists.

The preponderance of string instruments is a direct result of the high degree of perfection which they had already attained. It is interesting to observe that Bach was one of the first composers to write concertos in which the harpsichord was used either as a solo instrument or as a member of the concertino.

No strict demarcation can be made between the concerto and the concerto grosso of the early eighteenth century. The former term, preferred by Bach, was more inclusive; the latter was apparently reserved for works with a concertino of three or more instruments. There is, however, a marked difference between the concerto of Bach and his age and the more familiar one of Mozart and his contemporaries and successors. Of the earlier type, which is now being discussed, the most celebrated masters were Corelli, Vivaldi, Bach, and Handel. The first of these composers is known today largely for his Concerto Grosso in G minor (No. 8), which because of its descriptive last movement entitled *Pastorale* is called the Christmas Concerto. It was Corelli who first demonstrated the effectiveness of a concertino composed of two violins and violoncello. Vivaldi, some of whose concerti grossi were transcribed for the organ by Bach, composed many brilliant solo concertos for violin, several of which bear fanciful titles such as *La Caccia* (The Hunt) and *La Tempesta di Mare* (The Storm at Sea). Before proceeding to a discussion of Bach's concertos, it should be observed that the underlying principle of the early eighteenth-century concerto was that of contrast between passages alternately delivered by groups differing in strength and in tone-color. Although those passages which were allotted to the solo performers were frequently more difficult than those assigned to the ripieno, the concerto of the period was more than simply a medium for the display of virtuosity.

About sixteen solo concertos by Bach may be heard today. Of these, the best known are the concertos in A minor and in E major for solo violin, the concerto in D minor for two violins, and the concerto in D minor for clavier. There are also two concertos for two pianos, two for three pianos, and a concerto for four pianos. The last was transcribed from a work by Bach's model in concerto composition—the Italian composer Antonio Vivaldi.

Many of the clavier concertos are transcriptions of violin concertos whose original scores have been lost. Bach probably made these occasionally ineffective transcriptions for performance at the meetings of the *Collegium Musicum* of the University of Leipzig.

It has already been observed in the suite and in the prelude and fugue, for example, that large musical works are frequently constructed by arranging in series a number of shorter works which are entities in themselves. From a theoretical standpoint the individual movements of most of the larger works written before the advent of Beethoven may be regarded as independent; the only objective demonstration of their affinity consists in pointing out their common source and their ties of tonality. But independent as individual movements may be, they are only parts of a larger artistic whole, a unique federation in which the degree of autonomy enjoyed by the members is somewhat limited. Composers have on occasion not been loath to revamp a movement from some earlier work and to insert it in some new composition. In this respect Bach was a chronic offender, a circumstance which is easily understood when one recalls his obligation to supply music for so many diverse occasions.

Most of Bach's concertos consist of three movements, the first and last of which are in a fast tempo. Both the first and the last movements are in the same key, and it is by this key that the concerto is designated. The middle movement offers a contrast in style and in tonality; it is slow and serious in vein and is in a related key. The usual characteristics of the individual movements are described below.

The first and the last movements consist of passages delivered alternately by the soloist or soloists and the ripieno. A passage played by all the instruments is called a *tutti* (Italian for "all"); similarly a passage for the soloist is called a *solo*. In the solo sections the ripieno merely furnishes a discreet background which is, however, more than a mere accompaniment. In many concertos there is a strong division of thematic material between the tutti and the solo parts. In others, however, the solo episodes are based on motives derived from the tutti. The tutti section will reappear from time to time much like a refrain, hence the name often given to it, *ritornello* (Italian for "refrain"). These successive reappearances of the ritornello can be likened in many respects to the behavior of the subject in a fugue; the solo episodes are also analogous to the episodes of a fugal development. In some of the finest of Bach's concertos the fast movements open and close with powerful tuttis.

The slow middle movements of Bach concertos are wonderful

demonstrations of his genius. They are constructed in a manner which while extremely simple is also extraordinarily effective. Bach habitually built these movements on an expressive bass melody akin to a ground bass, but modulating freely. Over this bass the solo instrument sings an elaborate melody in a rhapsodic manner.

No technical description, however, does justice to the vitality and robustness of the Bach concertos. The concerto is a form which Bach seems to have handled with great zest, never losing sight of the etymology of the term (Latin *concertare*—to strive). A Bach concerto is a concerted effort on the part of several performers, each of whom is entrusted with an important part in the lively contrapuntal interplay.

CONCERTO FOR VIOLIN IN E MAJOR

As a typical work in this form we may investigate briefly Bach's Concerto for Violin in E major. The first movement begins with this animated tutti:

Ex. 23

The solo episodes consist of very elaborate passages for the violin. It will be noticed, however, that a motive drawn from the ritornello, that is, its first three notes, appears in all of the episodes. The middle movement, in the related key of C-sharp minor, is built on this profound bass melody.

Ex. 24

The final movement is an interesting combination of the rondo [1] and the concerto forms. The ritornello:

Ex. 25

[1] See page 65.

is heard five times, each time in the same key. Between these appearances of the ritornello four different episodes are to be found. The organization of this movement may thus be represented schematically as A B A C A D A. All of these divisions are sixteen measures long with the exception of D, which is enlarged to thirty-two measures.

The six *Brandenburg Concertos,* which take their name from their dedication to Christian Ludwig, Margrave of Brandenburg, are really concerti grossi. They demonstrate, above all, Bach's ability to take the conventional forms of his day and bring them to a state of perfection in which they not only outstripped the works of all his predecessors and contemporaries, but also brought the form in question to its zenith for all time. Thus the Brandenburg concertos represent the highest point of development of the concerto grosso. Bach is content with neither the conventional form nor the conventional instrumentation. Retaining the fundamental idea of contrast between tutti and soli, these concerti grossi possess a wealth of polyphonic texture and dramatic development. In a similar manner, Bach has not been content to employ merely string instruments for the concertino; he introduces such groupings as trumpet, flute, oboe, and violin (Concerto No. II), violin and two flutes (Concerto No. IV), or violin, flute and clavier (Concerto No. V). With the exception of the first concerto which contains some dances usually associated with the suite, and the third which consists of two fast movements joined by two chords, the order and character of the movements of the Brandenburg concertos are in accordance with the convention of the period.

OTHER INSTRUMENTAL MUSIC

No discussion of Bach's instrumental music is complete without mention of the six sonatas for unaccompanied violin. The most celebrated single movement from these sonatas is the great *Chaconne* with its sixty-two variations on the bass of this four-measure theme [1]:

Ex. 26

[1] See the discussion of the passacaglia, page 76.

The Chaconne is a worthy compeer of the great organ works. It, too, has been transcribed for piano solo. Bach has also written six suites for unaccompanied 'cello as well as several sonatas for flute and clavier, and for violin and clavier.

CHORAL MUSIC

Bach's choral music constitutes the major part of his creative accomplishment. It was in music of this type that he reached his greatest heights of inspiration. With the exception of a few secular works, all his choral music is liturgical and was written to be used in the various Lutheran churches, the music for whose services he was expected to supply.

We may thus include these works in the category of functional music—music written for some specific occasion. A knowledge of the circumstances which brought these works forth will therefore be of aid in the understanding and appreciation of them. The more important choral works are (1) the church cantatas, (2) the *St. Matthew Passion,* and (3) the *Mass in B minor.*

The chorale plays an important part in all of Bach's sacred works based on German texts. These devout and expressive hymns sung in the vernacular in the Lutheran Church had a strong attraction for Bach. He created inspired interpretations of them in his chorale-preludes and used them freely in his larger choral works. He himself wrote only a few original chorale melodies. His great contribution consists of the new harmonic settings which he devised for these traditional melodies, transformations which add immeasurably to their expressiveness.

The Church Cantatas

The term *cantata* (Italian *cantare*—to sing) was initially used to differentiate a work designed to be sung from the *sonata* (Italian *suonare*—to play), a work to be played. The long history of this form which, like all the others treated by Bach, reached its apotheosis at his hands, need not concern us here. The church cantata will be discussed in this section solely as treated by Bach; for while he was far from being the only German composer to write church cantatas, his works in this form are practically the only ones performed today.

The cantata was one of the musical parts of the principal service, the service for Sundays and holidays, of the Lutheran Church. The liturgical usage of St. Thomas' Church in Leipzig specified fifty-nine occasions during the year for which Bach had to supply music—either works from his own pen, or such works as were already in the church library, or which could be obtained from other composers. For these fifty-nine annual occasions Bach composed sets of works for five full years—two hundred and ninety-five cantatas, of which about one hundred and ninety-five have been preserved.

In the Leipzig service the cantata not only followed the reading of the appointed Gospel, but was in itself a setting of a text based on the self-same Gospel extract. It usually comprised several numbers for chorus, soloists, and orchestra. The cantatas of Bach are descriptive works, in which the composer strove continually to drive home to the listener the implications of the Gospel text, as he saw them. The vividness of presentation, both vocal and instrumental, and the mastery of combination of word and tone which the cantatas display place them in the same category as the music-dramas of Wagner. They represent, in their multiplicity of moods and in the wealth of subjects they portray, the most intimate, the most personal of all of Bach's works. They reveal for us his theology, his world outlook, his faith. The great Bach critic Albert Schweitzer has aptly observed: "In comparison with the cantatas, everything else that Bach has done appears as hardly more than a supplement." [1]

The texts of most of the cantatas were supplied to Bach by various writers in Weimar and Leipzig. Over thirty were written by the composer himself. They consisted of verses based on the Gospel for the day and usually divided into six or seven numbers suitable for choruses, recitatives,[2] arias, duets, and so forth. There was no prescribed order. Most of the cantatas opened with a chorus of large dimensions followed by recitatives and arias, and usually closed with a chorale, in the singing of which the congregation joined. They ranged in duration from twenty minutes to half an hour.

[1] Albert Schweitzer—*J. S. Bach,* Vol. I, page 264.
[2] See page 90.

The resources available to Bach for the production of these works were indeed pathetic, and it is not surprising that the cantatas made no impression when they were performed. Bach had to content himself with a chorus of about seventeen voices and an orchestra of about twelve players, many of whom were poor performers. Only one of the cantatas was printed during Bach's lifetime [1]; and it was not until 1821, seventy-one years after Bach's death, that publication and dissemination of these musical treasures were begun.

Inasmuch as the available recordings of the cantatas are neither complete nor adequate, and since opportunities for hearing these magnificent works are rare indeed, no cantata can be singled out for discussion here. The neglect which continues to be the lot of these masterpieces is most unfortunate. Until such time as they achieve their due measure of public performance, Bach will remain a composer of whom our picture is woefully incomplete.

The Secular Cantatas

For weddings, ceremonies honoring university professors, civic ceremonials, and various functions in honor of visiting royalty, Bach composed some twenty secular cantatas. Of these, three have become well-known to modern audiences: *The Contest between Phoebus and Pan* (*Der Streit zwischen Phoebus und Pan*); the *Coffee Cantata* (*Schweiget stille, plaudert nicht*); and the *Peasant Cantata* (*Mer han en neue Oberkeet*). The last two works are examples of a comparatively unknown aspect of Bach, namely, Bach the humorist in music. The *Coffee Cantata* deals with the comical situation which develops when a father tries to break his daughter of the habit of drinking coffee [2]; the *Peasant Cantata* was written to felicitate an official of the city of Leipzig on his acquisition of some land. After the villagers have congratulated their new master they retire to the inn for free beer. For this work Bach writes an overture employing peasant tunes and finishing with a waltz. The text must have appealed strongly to Bach, for the entire *Peasant Cantata* is filled with jolly tunes of a rustic nature.

---

[1] An early cantata, written in 1708 for the inauguration of a *Bürgermeister*.
[2] See C. v. d. Borren—"Tobacco and Coffee in Music," *The Musical Quarterly,* July, 1932.

Passion Music

The Passion, one of the oldest of musical forms, arose from the practice of reading publicly during Holy Week those sections of the Gospel dealing with the sufferings and crucifixion of Jesus. In its aim to dramatize biblical events for the laity, the Passion claims relationship to the medieval mystery play.

As brought to its highest point of development by Bach, the Passion consists of a setting for soloists, chorus, orchestra, and organ of a text based on the portions of the Gospels describing the agony and sufferings of Jesus.[1] It was performed in the church as part of the vesper service for Good Friday, the anniversary of the Crucifixion. Bach is said to have composed four Passions, of which two, the *St. John Passion*, and the *St. Matthew Passion* have survived in their entirety.

Of these two settings of the Passion, that according to St. Matthew, composed in 1729, is universally regarded as the finer. It is a work similar in spirit to the cantatas and possessing the same fundamental aim: a vivid presentation of a text based on the Scripture lesson for the day, in this instance one of sadness and suffering.

The text of the *St. Matthew Passion* consists of (1) rhymed paraphrases of excerpts from the Gospel, and (2) verses of a devotional or commentative nature interpolated at salient points in the unfolding of the narrative. Of the several soloists, the most important is the "Evangelist" to whom the greater part of the Biblical text is entrusted. Other soloists either portray characters such as Jesus and Pontius Pilate, or sing the commentative verses. The chorus has the same duality of function: it participates as a dramatic protagonist, for example, the crowd at the trial before Pontius Pilate; or it serves as a medium for the expression of devotional commentary. The whole is arranged in a series of scenes consisting of recitatives, arias, duets, and choruses. Of these types of vocal expression, only the first demands explanation.

The *recitative* (Latin *recitare*—to recite) is a musical setting of a text in either prose or verse, the words of which are not sung but

[1] St. Matthew xxvi–xxvii
  St. Luke   xxii–xxiii
  St. Mark   xiv–xv
  St. John   xviii–xix

rather declaimed. The performer is usually not held to any prede-
termined rhythm; music serves here as an agency to heighten the
declamatory accents of speech. In the simpler styles of recitative the
accompaniment consists of a succession of supporting chords. During
Bach's day these were usually played from a figured bass by the harpsichord or the organ, assisted by a violoncello and a double bass. In
the *St. Matthew Passion* the recitatives of Jesus are always declaimed
to a soft, limpid accompaniment played by the strings. Like many of
the other elements of the Passion, the recitative was operatic in origin.

The musical idiom of the *St. Matthew Passion* is one of intense
piety and devotion. In this work, as in the cantatas, we find many
examples of Bach's ability to characterize and to depict in a manner
remarkable even today. One of the finest examples of this art of
tonal painting is the aria for soprano, *Aus Liebe will mein Heiland* aria
sterben, which forms a part of the trial scene. The combination of
dramatic and devotional elements in the *St. Matthew Passion* can be
shown by the recitatives which precede the aria. These, in translation, are:

The Evangelist: (as narrator)	The Governor said:
Pilate: (as participant)	What evil hath He done?
Soprano: (as devout commentator)	He hath done good to us all. He gave the blind their sight, He made the lame walk; He spoke His Father's Word to us, He drove the devil away; He consoled the downcast; He lifted up the sinful and embraced them; nought but this did my Jesus do.

The aria which follows these recitatives is a setting of this text:

> Aus Liebe will mein Heiland sterben,
> Von einer Sünde weiss er nichts.
> Dass das ewige Verderben
> Und die Strafe des Gerichts
> Nicht auf meiner Seele bliebe,
> Aus Liebe will mein Heiland sterben, *etc.*

(Prose translation: For love would my Saviour die, He knows nought of
sin. So that eternal ruin and the punishment of the Last Judgment do not rest
on my soul, for love would my Saviour die.)

Bach describes the innocent Jesus in the instrumental introduction
to the aria. He employs only three instruments, a flute and two
oboes da caccia (obsolete instruments closely related to the modern
English horn) in the presentation of this gentle phrase:

Ex. 27

The vocal soloist then enters as a fourth voice in this plaintive discourse. The aria is cast in Da Capo form,[1] the instrumental introduction being repeated.

The *St. Matthew Passion* also contains many magnificent choruses.
Outstanding among them are the opening movement depicting Christ
on the road to Calvary, and the final movement in which the chorus
cries down to Christ in His tomb. This last chorus is one of the
world's great masterpieces of devotional music. In the *St. Matthew
Passion* Bach again makes effective use of the Lutheran chorale. One
of the most moving of these chorale interpolations occurs in the prison
(Praetorium) scene (St. Matthew xxvii). The Evangelist has declaimed "and they spat upon Him, and took the reed and smote Him
on the Head." Bach then introduces this chorale, one of his numerous
harmonizations of a melody which although secular in origin, had
taken on a funereal character:

Ex. 28

O   Haupt voll Blut und Wun - den, voll Schmerz und voll - er   Hohn!
O   Haupt, zu Spott ge - bun - den mit ei - ner Dor - nen - kron!

[1] See page 65.

O Haupt, sonst schön ge - zie - ret mit höch-ster Ehr' und Zier, Jetzt

a - ber hoch schimp - fi - ret: ge - grü - sset seist du mir!

(Prose translation of the text: O Head covered with blood and wounds, O Head tortured and despised! O Head mocked by a crown of thorns! O Head once adorned with highest honor, and now abused: I bow before Thee!)

The Mass in B minor

Bach's Mass in B minor is only one of thousands of musical settings of a text which has attracted composers since its final formulation as part of the extensive liturgy of the Roman Catholic Church in 1014. The Mass is the very core of the Catholic liturgy; it is the chief act of Catholic worship and in its symbolic representation of the Last Supper, a liturgical drama. The text of the Mass cannot be said to be the product of any one individual or any one church conference; it was the result of a long process of development and evolution. The text of the Mass may be divided into two parts: (1) the *Proprium Missae*—the Proper; and (2) the *Ordinarium Missae*—the Ordinary. The Proper contains those elements of the Mass which vary according to day or season. The Ordinary, however, is composed of a text which has been invariable since it took final shape. The Ordinary consists of five parts bearing these designations: (1) *Kyrie Eleison,* (2) *Gloria,* (3) *Credo,* (4) *Sanctus,* (5) *Agnus Dei.* As a musical term, the title *Mass* indicates a setting of the Ordinary. No other text has been set to music so frequently.

The question immediately arises: What caused Bach, a Lutheran, to set a text so closely identified with the Catholic Church? This is easily answered. The Lutheran Church had preserved many of the elements of the Catholic ritual, and while the Ordinary of the Mass was not utilized as an entity, each of its five parts might be heard at different times during the church year. The so-called Lutheran Mass, for example, was composed of the *Kyrie* and *Gloria*. In 1733, Bach forwarded such a *Kyrie* and *Gloria* to his sovereign Augustus III, Elector of Saxony and a Roman Catholic. A petition asking that he be appointed Court Composer accompanied the music. The title was conferred upon Bach in 1736; but there is no record of any Dresden performance of the Lutheran Mass.

Bach's nature was apparently such as to compel him to complete a work. Movements were added to this Lutheran Mass, so that by 1737 an entire Roman Catholic Mass had been created. Eight movements, seven of which are choruses, were adapted from church cantatas.

Bach's setting of the Mass is scored for chorus, soloists, and orchestra. It consists of twenty-four movements of which fifteen are choruses, six are arias, and three duets. Bach conforms to Catholic tradition in not admitting recitative. The comparatively large orchestra comprises strings, two flutes, two oboes, two oboes d'amore (obsolete lower-pitched relatives of the oboe), two bassoons, one horn, three trumpets, tympani, and the indispensable continuo.[1] (Not all of these instruments are used in every movement.) The designation Mass in B minor indicates that B minor is the basic tonality; but the work does not remain in this key throughout, and use is made of the more closely related keys. Only five of the twenty-four movements are in the key by which the Mass is known.

While the Mass in B minor was inspired by a liturgical text, it cannot in any sense be regarded as liturgical music except insofar as portions of it are suitable for the rites of the Lutheran Church. Its length alone renders it unusable in the church from whose ritual its text was borrowed.

The idiom of the Mass in B minor is precisely like that of the cantatas and the *St. Matthew Passion*. In this work we find the same grasp of the implications of the text combined with an ability to give utterance to this interpretation by means of realistic music.

In his setting of this ancient text Bach has revealed his own inner-

[1] See page 81.

most faith. A beautiful illustration of the intensely subjective nature of the Mass is afforded by the *Crucifixus,* a part of the *Credo.* Here Bach describes the Crucifixion for us in a choral movement whose mood is one of awe and terror. For this chorus Bach has chosen one of the most direct of musical forms, the passacaglia.[1] The words, *Crucifixus est etiam pro nobis sub Pontio Pilato, passus et sepultus est* (And was also crucified for us under Pontius Pilate, suffered and was buried), are sung in anguished accents over this *basso ostinato* heard thirteen times:

Ex. 29

SUGGESTED READINGS

One of the outstanding authorities on Bach was the late Professor Charles Sanford Terry of the University of Aberdeen. His *Bach, a Biography* (Oxford University Press) is the best work dealing exclusively with Bach's life. His *The Music of Bach* (Oxford University Press) is a convenient guide to the more important works. Professor Terry also made four important contributions to *The Musical Pilgrim* (Oxford University Press), a series of handbooks describing the classics; these are *The Magnificat, The Mass in B Minor, The* [*St. Matthew*] *Passions, The Cantatas.* He also wrote a fine article on Bach for *Grove's Dictionary of Music and Musicians.* The two-volume work of the Alsatian organist, theologian, and medical missionary, Albert Schweitzer, entitled *J. S. Bach* (Black) is the best critical discussion of Bach's art; Schweitzer's analysis of the elements comprising Bach's tonal language is most revealing. The three-volume *Life of Bach* (Novello) by Philip Spitta is somewhat verbose, but contains valuable information not to be found in other works. For additional technical information concerning the various forms employed by Bach, the following should be consulted: Vincent d'Indy—*Cours de composition musicale* (Durand); Ebenezer Prout—*Applied Forms* (Augener); R. O. Morris—*The Structure of Music* (Oxford University Press), the most concise of all these treatises; and Hugo Leichtentritt—*Formenlehre* (Breitkopf und Härtel). There are also many compendious articles in *Grove's Dictionary of Music and Musicians* (Macmillan).

[1] See page 76.

Chapter VII

GEORGE FRIDERIC HANDEL

O F THE numerous significant contemporaries of Bach, thé most outstanding was George Frideric Handel,[1] born only a few weeks before Bach on February 23, 1685 in the town of Halle, not far distant from Eisenach. Both the careers and creative accomplishments of these men stand in sharp contrast to each other. Handel seems to have been ignorant of Bach's attainments, but he cannot be reproached for this inasmuch as Bach was an obscure Cantor in a provincial city. Bach, on the other hand, always the zealous student of the works of other composers, studied some of Handel's compositions, as copies of them in his own hand attest. The two men never met.

Unlike Bach, Handel could claim no musical heritage; no traces of any musical proclivities are to be found in his ancestry. His father was a barber-surgeon, the stern head of a typical German middle-class family, who desired nothing more of his son than that he also embark upon some respectable professional career.

The father's hopes received their first jolt when his son gave evidence of marked musical talent; and it was only at the insistence of a local ruler, the Duke of Weissenfels, that Handel was permitted to receive systematic musical instruction. The lad was placed under the tutelage of Zachow, the organist of the Liebfrauenkirche in Halle, and received from him a thorough grounding in the technique of composition as well as training in playing the violin, the oboe, the clavier, and the organ. Handel developed rapidly as a virtuoso performer on the harpsichord, and even made two trips to Berlin to appear as a prodigy before the Prussian court. Inasmuch as Handel's father had planned a legal career for him, none of this musical activity was

---

[1] The original German form is *Händel*; this has now been Anglicized as *Handel*.

GEORGE FRIDERIC HANDEL

allowed to interfere with his academic training. He was graduated from the local *Gymnasium* and in 1702 he enrolled as a student at the University of Halle. In the same year he was given the post of organist at the Domkirche (Cathedral) in Halle. But Handel was not attracted by the prospect of life in a smug commercial town, and in 1703 he resigned from both the University and the Domkirche. The prime cause for this decision was the attraction exercised upon him by the glamorous musical life of Hamburg, and it was to this thriving seaport that he now betook himself.

Hamburg was at that time the leading musical center of Germany. Bach had visited it in the previous year to hear the playing of its famous organist, Reincken. But Handel had been attracted not by the music to be heard in Hamburg's churches, but rather by the productions of its celebrated opera house then at the height of its fame. He quickly found a place for himself in the opera orchestra. His initial engagement was as a violinist, but his talents were such as to win him promotion to the position of harpsichordist, a post of great importance. It was at Hamburg that works from Handel's pen were first heard by a large public. These were a *St. John Passion* and four operas. One of these operas, *Almira,* was successful enough to warrant its being performed over twenty times in one season. But Handel was drawn to yet another focal point of musical life, Italy, and towards the end of 1706 he left Hamburg.

The years which Handel spent in Italy were profitable indeed. Here he came into close contact with the oratorios of Giacomo Carissimi (1604–1674), and became personally acquainted with the great opera composer Alessandro Scarlatti and his son, the harpsichordist, Domenico Scarlatti, as well as with an important figure in the development of violin music and the concerto grosso—Arcangelo Corelli. The talented Handel was enthusiastically fêted by the art-loving princes of Italy. He also wrote two operas for Italian theaters. One of these, *Agrippina,* was given twenty-seven successive performances. The three years which Handel spent in Italy were filled with such triumphs that, although only a young man of twenty-five, he had already become famous.

He left Italy to assume the post of Kapellmeister at the court of the Elector George of Hanover. A short time after entering the Elector's service, Handel received permission to visit London. This journey proved to be a turning point in his life. Opera in Italian had become firmly established in the English capital, and a magnificent opportunity now presented itself to a composer of Handel's attainments. Shortly after his arrival in London he was introduced to the manager of the Haymarket Theater. Within fourteen days he had composed the music for *Rinaldo,* performed on February 24, 1711 with great acclaim.

Handel's first stay in London was cut short by his obligation to Hanover. But Hanover had no opera house, and the autumn of 1712 found Handel back in London composing more operas. From 1712 until his death, England was his home; he became a naturalized British subject in 1726. The Elector of Hanover, from whose service Handel had been playing truant, became George I of England in 1714. Handel was forgiven by the king, a pension was conferred upon him, and he was appointed music master to the two princesses. In the meanwhile opera had fallen into desuetude in London, and for a period of time Handel served as music director to the Duke of Chandos.

In 1719 a new operatic venture, the Royal Academy of Music, was started in London. Handel turned out opera after opera for this institution until its bankruptcy in 1728. An important factor in the downfall of the Royal Academy was the popularity of *The Beggar's Opera* of Gay and Pepusch, a parodic and somewhat licentious work, the music of which was largely a compilation of popular songs coupled with several purloinings from the operas of Purcell and Handel.

Handel resumed the composition of operas in 1730 and continued to produce works in this form until 1741, although the enormous expenses and the dwindling proceeds from operatic performances had forced him into bankruptcy in 1737. A curious combination of events served to turn his attention to another type of dramatic music, a form in which he scored his greatest triumphs—the *oratorio.* While in the service of the Duke of Chandos, Handel had composed a masque, *Haman and Mordecai,* for presentation in the Duke's private theater. In 1732 he proposed to mount this twelve-year-old work at one of the London theaters. This plan to present Biblical incidents on a public stage met with much opposition and the Bishop of London banned the performance. The stubborn Handel added a few scenes to the masque, changed its name to *Esther,* and performed it as *The Story of Esther, An Oratorio in English.* A note in the advertisement announcing the performance read as follows: "There will be no action on the stage, but the House will be fitted up in a decent manner for the Audience." [1]

The success of this presentation served to awaken Handel's interest in the artistic potentialities of the oratorio, and a notable series of works in this form now commenced to flow from his facile pen. They met with varying sorts of receptions and the composer's status in the musical life of London remained uncertain until the triumphant performance of his oratorio *Judas Maccabaeus* in 1747. From this time on he was the undisputed master of English music. No other composer arose to contest his supremacy. He became totally blind in 1753; but this neither prevented his appearing in public as organ soloist at performances of his oratorios, nor kept him from composing. A musical secretary, Christopher Smith, took down his last works as he dictated them. Handel died in 1759. The choice of Westminster Abbey for his final resting place indicates the esteem in which the British held this remarkable foreigner.

The list of compositions by Handel includes forty-six operas, thirty-two oratorios, and many instrumental works, of which the more important are the *Water Music* for orchestra, the concerti grossi for strings, the organ concertos, a few harpsichord pieces, and the sonatas for violin and piano. But Handel has shared the fate of his contemporary, Bach: only a small fraction of his creative accomplishment is known to the musical public of today.

The Early Opera

The opera, a form which Handel so assiduously cultivated, had been in existence hardly a hundred years when he was born. It owed its origin to one of the characteristic aspects of the Italian Renaissance—interest in the civilization of ancient Greece. Between 1580 and 1589 a group of Florentine gentlemen met regularly at the home of Count Giovanni Bardi, an accomplished scholar and mathematician. In their discussions, which were concerned with the nature of Greek drama, the Florentines maintained that the dramas of classical an-

[1] Newman Flower—*George Frideric Handel*, page 196.

tiquity were sung in a declamatory manner, and that the style of Greek music was more fitted for dramatic expression than the complex polyphony of the sixteenth century. In an endeavor to restore what they deemed to be the style of Greek drama, this group of Florentine gentlemen created the modern opera. The earliest operas were plays whose texts were declaimed in a recitative-like style to the accompaniment of a few string instruments. While these earliest operas would hardly be interesting to modern ears, their advent marked a well-defined turning point in the history of music. Through their emphasis on one voice they served to accelerate the development of a homophonic style, and through their employment of instruments, to aid in the formulation and growth of the orchestra. But above all it should be observed that the first operas were conceived primarily as dramatic works, in which music was regarded merely as a medium for heightening the effectiveness of dramatic poetry. The earliest opera that has been preserved is the *Euridice* of Jacopo Peri, performed in 1600. The new form immediately found many adherents. The first truly great opera composer was Claudio Monteverdi (1567–1643), whose *Arianna* (Ariadne) given at Mantua in 1608 contains the celebrated *Lament*.

The first public opera house was opened in Venice in 1637, less than fifty years before Handel's birth. It was not long before the initial dramatic purpose of the opera was obscured by the various extravagances which the populace came to demand from it. Works were performed with magnificent settings and spectacular stage effects which frequently included wild animals, representations of storms, and aerial flights. The stage machinist often outranked the composer. The dramatic recitative gradually disappeared, and in the works of Monteverdi's pupil, Francesco Cavalli (1602–1676), tuneful melodies written in a popular vein became an important feature of the opera. The rapidly increasing musical public soon developed an appreciation of fine singing and was prompt to bestow its patronage upon its favorite performers. These favorites, on the other hand, were not loath to make capital of their attainments. Fabulous fees were earned by them and such was their position that they tyrannized managers and composers with impunity. Our modern "star" system with all its abuses probably traces its history back to the early days of opera.

The diverse trends of early Italian opera are summed up in the work of Alessandro Scarlatti (1659–1725), with whose compositions Handel was familiar. Scarlatti, composing for the royal opera at Naples, introduced several devices in the Italian opera of the eighteenth century, which through persistent use in his own works became established conventions. Of these the most important were: (1) the Da Capo form (A B A) as a pattern for the organization of arias; (2) the employment of a series of three instrumental movements as an introduction to an opera. The Da Capo form[1] became a somewhat deadly stereotype. The three short instrumental movements were called by Scarlatti *Sinfonia.* The first movement was fast, the second slow, the third again fast. It is from this Italian type of introductory piece (overture) that our modern symphony evolved.

Handel's Operas

Handel was the direct successor of Scarlatti. All of his operas employed Italian texts and followed the Italian tradition. The libretti of these works were usually based on classical history or medieval romance. Typical operas were *Rinaldo, Flavio, Giulio Cesare, Orlando,* and *Alcina.* The literary value of most of the texts was almost negligible. The cast was usually confined to a few characters, and the chorus played a very unimportant part. The male parts were sung almost exclusively by *castrati,* male sopranos, the pitch of whose voices had been preserved from boyhood by a brutal and dangerous operation. Solo music predominated, and a Handel opera might well be described as a series of recitatives and arias, designed to permit singers to display their ability and at the same time to regale the audience with attractive melodies. Handel strove to make his musical settings as faithful to their texts as the conventions of his epoch allowed and a surprising degree of dramatic verisimilitude may often be found in them. Original and effective passages were also entrusted to the orchestra. But the Handel operas are primarily collections of beautiful melodies of all shades and types. The conventions which governed the composition of these works have stood in the way of their performance today. The male parts in particular present difficult problems.

[1] See page 65.

The most widely known piece of music by Handel, the celebrated *Largo,* is operatic in origin. Thoroughly typical in its breadth, it was originally an aria (*Ombra mai fù*) in the humorous opera *Serse* (Xerxes), sung by King Xerxes as he thanks a plane tree for its welcome shade. Many of the present-day transcriptions of this simple melody amply merit the condemnation "monstrous perversion" meted out to them by an eminent critic, Philip Hale.

The Oratorio

The *oratorio* may be defined as an extensive setting for solo voices, chorus, and orchestra, of a text derived from or based on the Bible.[1] The oratorio is performed without scenery, costumes, or action. The earliest oratorios were descended from the allegorical mystery plays which were presented in the church. With the advent of the opera at the time of the Renaissance, these plays became to all intents and purposes sacred operas, produced in the church with orchestra, action, and costume. The name given these works was in reality the name of the chapel in the church in which they were performed, the *oratorio* (oratory). The operas of Handel were written with due deference to the conventions established by his predecessors; his oratorios, on the other hand, while showing some influence of the early Italian composers, are far removed from all other earlier works in this category. The oratorio, in the modern sense of the word, is largely Handel's own creation.

The Handel oratorio, unlike the Bach cantata, was not part of a liturgy. It was designed for performance on the stage of the theater and not in the choir loft; it was written for an audience and not a congregation. Its text, written in the English language and based on familiar selections from the Scriptures, was infinitely superior to the stilted and artificial libretto of the opera. The members of the chorus, with the music before their eyes, were freed from the necessity of memorizing their parts and could therefore be utilized in a manner so effective as to compensate amply for the absence of action, scenery, and costume. The raising of the chorus to the role of principal dramatic protagonist constitutes Handel's most significant contribution to

---

[1] An oratorio may occasionally employ a text of secular origin and then be designated as a "secular oratorio."

the oratorio. The other features of the Handel oratorio are shared by his operas—the profusion of expressive melodies, the ability to make a text dramatically effective by simple means. As has been observed, the Handel oratorio is an "entertainment." Although based on Holy Writ, these Handel oratorios cannot be considered truly religious music. They were designed not to stimulate piety and devotion, but rather to furnish a full evening of vocal music utilizing the dramatic potentialities of Biblical episodes. No matter what type of text he employed, Handel remained an eminently practical composer of music for the theater, and like most theatrical composers, he always had his audience in mind. His oratorios, like his operas, are conceived along broad lines such as would be easily appreciated by the public. In this respect he and Bach represent opposite poles of musical thinking.

THE MESSIAH

Of Handel's oratorios the better known are *Israel in Egypt, Samson, Judas Maccabaeus,* and *The Messiah.* The last-named work is performed with great frequency today by choral bodies everywhere with consequent neglect of the other oratorios. The unique appeal of *The Messiah* has been responsible for the continued existence of many choral organizations, for the character of the music has always served to attract both participants and auditors.

Handel composed *The Messiah* in 1741 in the incredibly brief space of twenty-four days. His fertility was extraordinary, even for an epoch in which composers were expected to toss off music for any occasion at a moment's notice. The work had its first performance in Dublin in 1742. It was given in London the following year; but it met with such a storm of protest from the clergy that Handel was forced to advertise it without its name, as "A Sacred Oratorio." It was not until 1750 that *The Messiah* was accepted by Londoners. Since that date it has probably been sung more often than any other choral work.

The text of *The Messiah* was compiled by a British clergyman, Charles Jennens. It consists of a series of Biblical excerpts telling of the second coming of the Redeemer, drawn from the Psalms, the Prophets, and the Gospels. These excerpts are arranged as a series of episodes which possess little dramatic continuity.

The orchestra which Handel demanded for *The Messiah* consisted

largely of strings; wood-wind and brass instruments found only occasional employment. As in the choral works of Bach, many of the
recitatives were accompanied from a figured bass. The organ was
also utilized, either for the accompaniment of recitatives or to lend
support in the choral numbers. *The Messiah* contains two celebrated
purely instrumental movements—the overture and a *Pastoral Symphony.* The overture follows the customary French pattern,[1] but
without repetition of the opening *Grave.* Its concise fugue is based
on this robust subject:

Ex. 1

Like all of the overtures written at this time, the overture to *The
Messiah* bears no dramatic relationship to the work which it prefaces.
The *Pastoral Symphony* is played by the orchestra immediately before
the recitative for soprano: "There were shepherds abiding in the field,
keeping watch over their flocks by night." The title "Symphony" was
used freely for instrumental music at this time and should not be
interpreted in the more modern sense. The *Pastoral Symphony* is a
charming orchestral intermezzo which in its use of $\frac{12}{8}$ rhythm and its
drone-bass recalls the tunes played by Italian shepherds, tunes Handel
must have heard during his stay in Italy.

The Messiah is replete with beautiful arias, of which the greater
number are happy fusions of Handel's melodic and dramatic gifts.
Two of the more outstanding arias are the solo for the bass, "The
People that Walked in Darkness," and the solo for the alto, "He Shall
Feed His Flock Like a Shepherd." In the former aria Handel creates
an atmosphere appropriate to the text by muting all the strings and
having them play the following groping figure in unison with the
soloist:

Ex. 2

The peo-ple that walk-ed in   dark   -   ness, that walk-ed in dark   -   ness.

[1] See page 81.

The alto aria describes the Lord as the Protector of His flock by means of this expressive melody written in the manner of a *pastorale*:

Ex. 3

The choral writing, in four parts throughout the work, reveals Handel as a consummate master of vocal idiom. The choral numbers abound in passages which, although difficult, are nevertheless thoroughly vocal in style and offer no insurmountable obstacles to executants of only moderate attainments. Hence *The Messiah* is invariably performed with gusto by amateur choral groups. The choruses vary from the simple massive style of, for example, "Surely He Hath Borne Our Griefs":

Ex. 4

(The vigorous orchestral part is not shown.)

to the expressive polyphony of the fugal chorus, "And With His Stripes We Are Healed" constructed on this dramatic subject:

Ex. 5

King George II rose from his seat when he heard the imposing *Halle-lujah* chorus, thereby establishing a custom which has now become universal.

Instrumental Music

Handel's best-known instrumental work is a set of variations which ends a harpsichord suite in E major (No. V). The five essentially simple variations are based on a broad, robust theme called *The Harmonious Blacksmith*. The title was not given to the music by Handel, and it did not make its appearance in association with his work until long after his death. The set of twelve concerti grossi for string orchestra was composed in October 1739. As usual Handel composed these works with amazing facility; so quickly did his crea-tive processes operate that the composition of each concerto grosso consumed about a day. The concertino employed for these works consists of two violins and 'cello, an indication of Handel's familiarity with the works of Italian masters, notably Corelli. The number of movements to be found varies, and dance forms such as the sarabande and the minuet make their appearance. The twelve concerti grossi are not of equal worth; several betray the haste with which they were composed, others bear the stamp of genius. The style of these works differs markedly from the Brandenburg concertos of Bach. The Handel movements give a continual impression of improvisation, and more than one movement which starts out as a fugue tarries joyfully by the wayside as its composer toys with his material in brilliant fashion.

For a concert on the river Thames given for King George I in 1715, Handel composed what is now called the *Water Music*. This con-sisted of twenty-one pieces which were rendered by an orchestra of fifty musicians playing on a barge adjoining that of the King. There is a traditional tale to the effect that King George had been angry with Handel as a result of the latter's failure to return to Hanover; but deeply impressed by the wonderful music which reached the Royal Barge, he summoned Handel and bestowed his forgiveness upon him. The story has been discredited, however, by a Handel biographer, Newman Flower. Extracts from the *Water Music* are played today in a modernized version. A lovely *Air* and a vigorous *Hornpipe* are notable features of the score.

Of the world's great composers, Handel spoke in the simplest and most direct musical language. It is indeed regrettable that so little of his music is well known.

Suggested Readings

Handel's life and times are interestingly described by Newman Flower in his *George Frideric Handel* (Houghton Mifflin). The *George Frideric Handel* of Romain Rolland (Henry Holt) is also valuable. The most complete discussion of Handel is the *Händel* of Hugo Leichtentritt (Deutsche Verlags-Anstalt), an important work not yet translated into English.

Chapter VIII

CHRISTOPH WILLIBALD GLUCK

THE VARIOUS abuses which had crept into the opera have been described in the previous chapter.[1] Handel accepted these abuses and later turned his attention to the oratorio. While the artificialities of the opera had been the object of many bitter and satirical literary attacks, no attempt was made at a return to the principles of dramatic propriety laid down by the Florentine composers who had brought the opera into being, until three years after the death of Handel. The epoch-making opera was *Orfeo ed Euridice* (Orpheus and Eurydice), composed by Christoph Willibald Gluck and produced in Vienna in 1762. It is the oldest opera to retain a firm place in the repertory of the world's great opera houses.

Gluck was the son of a gamekeeper on the Bavarian estate of Prince Eugene Lobkowitz, a music-loving nobleman whose son later became one of the important benefactors of Beethoven. He was born in the small town of Erasbach in the Upper Palatinate in 1714. Most of his early musical education was acquired at a Jesuit school in Bohemia, and he became tolerably proficient as a vocalist and as a performer on the violin and the violoncello. In 1736 he came to Vienna, and through his association with the Lobkowitz family met a wealthy musical amateur, Prince Melzi, who defrayed the cost of further musical study in Italy. Seven operas were composed by Gluck for Italian audiences, and he met with a success sufficient to warrant his traveling to London in 1745. His attempts at operatic production in London were utter failures, however, and Gluck returned to Vienna and devoted himself to supplying conventional Italian operas for the court theater.

[1] See page 101.

The break with the old tradition occurred with the mounting of *Orfeo ed Euridice* in 1762; this was followed by the equally daring *Alceste* in 1767. An attaché of the French embassy in Vienna now became interested in Gluck and his operatic theories, and prevailed upon him to set to music the *Iphigénie en Aulide* of Racine. The composer was called to Paris to superintend the first performance of his work, and *Iphigénie* was presented there in 1774. The partisans of the old-style Italian opera were outraged by the success of this new-comer, and rallied around the now forgotten Italian composer Niccola Piccinni. The acrimonious squabble which ensued between the Gluck-ists and Piccinnists assumed the dimensions of warfare. The Gluckists emerged victorious, and after the successful presentation of his *Iphigénie en Tauride* Gluck returned to Vienna where he passed his last years in ease and comfort. He died in 1787. He had been made a member of the Order of the Golden Spur by Pope Benedict XIV, in 1756, and from that time on had always called himself "Chevalier (or Ritter) von Gluck."

Gluck's Reform of the Opera

Gluck was a reformer and possessed a true reformer's temperament. He was unyielding in his belief that the prime purpose of the opera was a dramatic one, and that every aspect of the opera was to be sub-ordinated to the accomplishment of this goal. Gluck's ideas were not new; but he was the first individual with the courage and the energy to bring them to fruition. Like all reformers he was intolerant and often tyrannical. As a conductor of his own works he was merciless with singers, dancers, stage-machinists, and scene-painters. He was one of the first of the world's great orchestral conductors. Nor did he hesitate to resort to the pen in defense of his ideas. His opera *Alceste* is prefaced by this *credo*:

When I undertook to set this poem, it was my design to divest the music entirely of all those abuses with which the vanity of singers, or the too great complacency of composers, has so long disfigured the Italian opera, and ren-dered the most beautiful and magnificent of all public exhibitions, the most tiresome and ridiculous. It was my intention to confine music to its true dra-matic province, of assisting poetical expression, and of augmenting the interest of the fable; without interrupting the action, or chilling it with useless and superfluous ornaments; for the office of music, when joined to poetry, seemed to me, to resemble that of coloring in a correct and well-disposed design, where the lights and shades only seem to animate the figures, without altering the outline.

I determined therefore not to stop an actor, in the heat of a spirited dialogue, for a tedious *ritornel*; nor to impede the progress of passion, by lengthening a single syllable of a favorite word, merely to display agility of throat; and I was equally inflexible in my resolution, not to employ the orchestra to so poor a purpose, as that of giving time for the recovery of breath, sufficient for a long and unmeaning cadence.

I never thought it necessary to hurry through the second part of a song, though the most impassioned and important, in order to repeat the words of the first part, regularly four times, merely to finish the air; where the sense is unfinished, and to give an opportunity to the singer of showing that he has the impertinent power of varying passages, and disguising them, till they shall be no longer known to the composer himself; in short, I tried to banish all those vices of the musical drama, against which, good sense and reason have in vain so long exclaimed.

I imagined that the overture ought to prepare the audience for the action of the piece, and serve as a kind of argument to it; that the instrumental accompaniment should be regulated by the interest of the drama and not leave a void in the dialogue between the air and recitative; that they should neither break into the sense and connection of a period, nor wantonly interrupt the energy or heat of the action.

And lastly, it was my opinion, that my first and chief care, as a dramatic composer, was to aim at a noble simplicity; and I have accordingly shunned all parade of unnatural difficulty, in favor of clearness; nor have I sought or studied novelty, if it did not arise naturally from the situation of the character, and poetical expression; and there is no rule of composition, which I have not thought it my duty to sacrifice, in order to favor passion and produce effects. [1]

Gluck commenced his operatic reform with an examination of the conventional libretto. Here he was fortunate to have the association of an Italian man of letters, Ranieri Calzabigi. In *Orfeo* and *Alceste* they produced jointly libretti of classical simplicity from which the traditional intrigues and counterplots were entirely excised. The old laws governing the number of characters and types and sequence of arias were cast to the winds.

The musical setting of these simple texts aimed continually at dramatic truth. Such stereotypes as the Da Capo aria were dispensed with. Singers were afforded no opportunity whatsoever for vocal acrobatics, and were permitted to take no liberties with the composer's music. Arias were simple and comparatively short, and evolved

---

[1] Burney—*The Present State of Music in Germany*, Vol. I, page 265.

naturally from the drama. Recitatives were conceived not as dull
interludes between arias, but rather as highly realistic declamatory
passages, accompanied by full orchestra rather than by the harpsichord. The chorus took on a wholly new importance in the unfolding of the drama and such a work as *Orfeo* may well be described as a
choral opera. Gluck was superb in the writing of pathetic music.
No finer example can be given than the celebrated lament of Orpheus
for his dead Eurydice:

Ex. 1

Che fa - rò senza Eur - i - di - cel   dove an - drò senza il mio   ben?

(*Translation:* What shall I do without Euridice!   Where shall I go without my
beloved?)

Of equal importance was Gluck's concept of the role of the orchestra. The orchestra plays no subordinate part in his operas. As Gluck
himself has written in the above-quoted preface to his *Alceste,* he considered the overture to be in the nature of an introduction to the opera;
his overture to *Iphigénie en Aulide* is one of the world's great pieces
of dramatic music. Gluck banished the harpsichord from the opera
orchestra, and with it went the older custom of "filling in" the orchestral harmonies from a figured bass. [1]   Gluck was also one of the first
composers of dramatic music to utilize the possibilities of dramatic
expression latent in the various orchestral timbres. His works abound
in usages of the orchestral instruments, which were highly original in
their day. Berlioz in his *Treatise on Instrumentation* (1844) quoted
many examples from Gluck's operas. The scores of Gluck ushered
many instruments into a permanent place in the modern orchestra:
the piccolo, the harp, the trombones, the bass drum, the cymbals, the
side-drum, and the triangle. Gluck was not only a reformer of the
opera; he was also one of the first great masters of orchestration.

The reforms which Gluck advocated and whose artistic validity he
so successfully demonstrated in his own works were short-lived and
did not take firm hold until almost a hundred years after the compo-

[1] See page 81.

sition of *Orfeo,* when another reformer, Richard Wagner, took up the cudgels in defense of dramatic truth in opera.

Only two works of Gluck may be heard today: the opera *Orfeo* and the celebrated overture to the opera *Iphigénie en Aulide* (Iphigenia in Aulis). The latter work is always performed with a concert-ending written for it by Richard Wagner. (In the opera the overture proceeds without pause into the opening scene.) It is a perfect example of the nobility, the grandeur, and the classically restrained pathos of Gluck's style. The following motives serve as thematic material:

Ex. 2

SUGGESTED READINGS

An excellent article on Gluck by Sir Donald Tovey is to be found in *The Heritage of Music,* Part II (Oxford University Press). Martin Cooper's *Gluck* (Oxford University Press) includes discussions of the operas and a chapter on Gluck's position in the history of music.

Chapter IX

THE VIENNESE SCHOOL: JOSEPH HAYDN

URING the second half of the eighteenth century there occurred
what may well be called a revolution in the art of music.
The forms and the style employed by Bach and Handel disappeared
entirely and new forms and a new style, both of which had been
slowly evolving from the opera, commenced to dominate the musical
scene.

This revolution in the art of music coincided with other revolutions,
political and economic. The French Revolution (1789–1799), the
American Revolution (1775–1783), and the Napoleonic Wars (1804–
1815) brought forth new nations and established new political ideas.
The invention of the steam engine, the spinning-jenny, the cotton-gin,
the steamboat, and the locomotive altered the entire course of civilization. Equally significant activity was to be found in the sphere of
arts and letters. In Germany Lessing (1729–1781), Schiller (1759–
1805), and Goethe (1749–1832) were creating the great classics of their
national literature; in England the celebrated literary figures were the
poets Burns (1759–1796), Blake (1757–1827), Coleridge (1772–1834),
Wordsworth (1770–1850), Shelley (1792–1822), and the playwright
Sheridan (1751–1816). England's greatest painters were also active
at this time—Gainsborough (1727–1788), Reynolds (1723–1792),
Turner (1775–1851), and Constable (1776–1837).

The form whose cultivation brought about the revolution in music
was the symphony and its related forms—the sonata, the string quartet, the overture, and the concerto; and the new style was a homophonic one with a strong emphasis on melody. Simultaneously, public
orchestral concerts commenced to flourish; orchestras composed of
both professionals and amateurs were formed in many of the towns

JOSEPH HAYDN

and cities of Germany; and orchestras and wind-bands were maintained by many members of the nobility. The piano came to the fore as a keyboard instrument, displacing the clavichord and the harpsichord; the virtuoso performer appeared on the scene. In the midst of all this activity most of the few works of Bach that had been published seem to have been entirely forgotten. While some of the composers of the period were acquainted with his music and had occasionally expressed some admiration for it, no strong influences can be traced. Polyphony had reached its second high point in the compositions of Bach. Thenceforth a new idiom was to become paramount.

With the mechanical perfection of instruments, instrumental music now came into its own and the orchestra evolved from a miscellaneous collection of instruments into a well-defined body; but interest in the opera was by no means dormant, and hundreds of operas were written and produced.

Precisely as Bach and Handel were not pioneers but rather individuals who utilized to the full the rich heritage left to them by the efforts of hundreds of predecessors, so the great instrumental composers of this period, Haydn, Mozart, and Beethoven, were indebted to a great number of composers of lesser talent who had conducted the preliminary explorations for them. Their works were rather the culmination of a movement than the movement itself.

The activity of these composers was confined for the most part to Vienna and its vicinity and while no one of them was actually born in the city, they are frequently referred to as the "Viennese School" and their epoch as the "Viennese Period," the most significant period in the development of modern instrumental music. Ostensibly the chronological limits of the period would extend from the birth of Haydn (1732) to the death of Beethoven (1827). In truth, however, it was not until 1781 that Haydn gave the world his Opus 33, six quartets which mark his maturity as a composer.

Vienna at the Close of the 18th Century

Vienna, at that time the third largest city in Europe (population in 1800, 231,050), was the capital of a large and heterogeneous empire containing many racial groups. Strategically located on the Danube and long the seat of the Holy Roman Empire, the city was an important commercial and political center. The Hapsburgs and many of the nobles attached to their court had huge and luxurious palaces within the city walls. A strict censorship was in operation to prevent the infiltration of "revolutionary" ideas engendered by the French Revolution.

Vienna had long been famous as a center of musical activity. The principal feature of its musical life, however, was the number of private orchestras maintained by members of the nobility. These orchestras were composed of musicians who not only wore the livery of their princely employer, but also performed other household duties. It was customary for the conductor of the orchestra, the Kapellmeister, to compose music for it; and all music so composed was the property of the individual in whose employ the Kapellmeister was, unless express permission could be obtained for its sale to some other private individual or to a publisher.

Musical tastes were exactly the reverse of those of today—the Viennese nobles demanded a continuous supply of *new* music. Inasmuch as the private concerts were quite long, there was a tremendous demand for new works. Curious ways of securing music prevailed. Princes would frequently commission composers to supply their establishments with music and would order their musical needs in batches, usually dozens or half-dozens, so that we find Haydn, for example, writing six symphonies for some concerts in Paris, or six quartets for a wealthy Viennese wholesale merchant who was eager to have some Haydn quartets for the delectation of prospective purchasers of his goods.

While these proprietary rights of the nobles to the music produced by their various Kapellmeisters may seem a bit odd today, it must be borne in mind that the system was not without its benefits and advantages. The incentive to musical creativeness afforded by the incessant demand for new music greatly accelerated the progress of the art; and the composer of the period was liberally compensated for whatever social inferiority he was made to feel, by having the pleasure of knowing that everything that he wrote would be performed, usually before select and discriminating audiences.

Music-making, however, was not confined entirely to professionals. Many members of the nobility were themselves competent instrumentalists or vocalists, and frequently participated in the musical events which were given at their palaces. The middle classes were also extremely musical, and orchestras composed almost entirely of amateurs gave concerts at the homes of the more prosperous merchants.

JOSEPH HAYDN

The first composer to play an important part in all this activity was (Franz) Joseph Haydn. He was born in 1732, in the small village of Rohrau, in Lower Austria. His musical aptitudes as a small boy caused his parents to send him to school at the not far distant town of Hainburg where he received instruction in voice, clavier, and violin. His fine singing ultimately won for him a place in the choir of the famous cathedral of St. Stephen's in Vienna. During the nine years that Haydn served as choirboy at St. Stephen's his academic studies included reading and writing, religion, and Latin; his musical studies, clavier, violin, and singing, and a scant amount of harmony and counterpoint. When his voice broke St. Stephen's had no further use for him and he was dismissed in 1749. Occupying a drafty garret and possessing only an old decrepit clavichord, the penniless youth eked out an existence by playing the violin in the nocturnal serenades then so popular in Vienna, and by giving lessons. The most important aspect of this period in Haydn's life was the rigorous discipline of self-instruction which he imposed upon himself. The guides which he took for himself were Karl Philipp Emanuel Bach, whose sonatas for clavier he studied assiduously, and Johann Joseph Fux, to whose theoretical work, the *Gradus ad Parnassum,* Haydn applied himself with great thoroughness. Like almost every other composer of genius, Haydn was practically self-taught.

After making the acquaintance of several of the important musical personages of Vienna and for a time holding the post of music director at the court of Count Morzin at Pilsen, in Bohemia, Haydn was engaged as assistant Kapellmeister at the palace of Prince Paul Esterhazy (1761). The Prince maintained an excellent orchestra of fourteen performers at his estate at Eisenstadt, not far from Vienna. The contract which Haydn signed when he entered into the service of the Esterhazy family gives us an excellent description of the status of the musician at that time. Haydn agreed to take charge of the music, conduct himself in a sober manner, see that the musicians appeared in white hose and with their wigs thoroughly powdered, preserve peace between the musicians, "compose such music as His Highness shall order, divulge these new compositions to no one—and compose nothing for anybody without His Highness' knowledge and gracious permission." He agreed, furthermore, to take zealous care of the musical instruments, instruct the singers, play upon the various instruments of which he had command, and so on. [1]

Prince Paul died in 1762 and was succeeded by his brother, Prince Nicholas, who gave Haydn full direction of his musical forces in 1766. Prince Nicholas, an enthusiastic patron of music, was very kind to Haydn and valued his musical gifts highly. The situation was a fortunate one for the composer as is shown by the great number of works composed while Haydn was in the employ of the Esterhazy family. His name now began to be known in all of the musical circles of Europe. His works were brought out by various publishers, and commissions for new compositions came from places as far away as Paris and London. On one of his sojourns in Vienna Haydn came in contact with Mozart. A fast friendship was formed between the older master and his youthful contemporary, which was interrupted by the untimely death of Mozart in 1791.

On the death of Prince Nicholas in 1790, Haydn accepted an invitation to appear at a series of concerts in London under the management of the violinist-impresario, Salomon. His fame had preceded him to England, and he was received there with much enthusiasm; all of his concerts were heavily patronized, dinners were given in his honor, and Oxford University bestowed upon him the degree of Doctor of Music. Haydn returned to Vienna in 1792, but he went back to London for another series of equally successful concerts in 1794. For these London performances he composed twelve new symphonies. Returning to Vienna in 1795, he commenced the composition of an oratorio, *The Creation*. The first performance (1798) of this work was a virtual triumph. All the nobility of Vienna were present and the composer was the object of universal acclaim. The next oratorio to appear was *The Seasons* (1801). The closing years of Haydn's life were spent in retirement in Vienna. Musicians came from far

[1] C. F. Pohl—*Joseph Haydn*, Vol. I., pages 391–394.

and wide to visit him. He was made an honorary citizen of the city, had many medals and decorations bestowed upon him, and was elected to membership in many honorary societies. He died of old age in 1809.

Haydn was a gentle, kindly individual who won for himself the affection and esteem of all with whom he came in contact. He was almost universally known as "Papa Haydn." A pious Catholic, he maintained that his mission on earth was merely to utilize to the full the gifts that God had given him.

Despite his devout nature, the important works of Haydn were not his masses and sacred music, but rather his instrumental music, particularly his symphonies and string quartets. Of the tremendous quantity of music Haydn wrote—seven hundred instrumental works alone, including one hundred and four symphonies and eighty-three string quartets—a comparatively small amount is played today. Only a few symphonies and about a dozen string quartets are heard with any degree of frequency; and all of these are works written in Haydn's later years.

The Historical Importance of Haydn

Historically Haydn is of tremendous importance. He has even been called "the father of the symphony," and "the father of the string quartet"; but these appellations, complimentary as they are, must be regarded as exaggerations. Both the symphony and the string quartet had existed long before Haydn. Nor did he invent any new forms. The true significance of Haydn lies in the fact that he crystallized these forms for all time, and by continually employing them, demonstrated their musical potentialities to the world.

Haydn was predominantly a composer of instrumental music, and his idiom, as opposed to that of Bach, was essentially a homophonic one. The outstanding characteristic of Haydn's music is the wealth of fresh and sparkling melody to be found in it—melody intrinsically instrumental in style. The composer also manifested a fondness for themes that are folk-like in character, occasionally even going so far as to employ actual dance tunes. Throughout all his music, however, there is a trend towards expressive melody—melody which may be gay and sprightly and occasionally almost naive, as in some of the symphonies, or profound and meditative, as in the slow movements of many of the string quartets. It is wholly erroneous to believe that Haydn wrote only "pleasant" music or that his own personality found no expression in his compositions.

One of the great contributions of Haydn was the standardization of the instrumentation of the orchestra. The one hundred and four symphonies of Haydn demonstrated the possibilities of the combination of instruments that he had chosen; and this particular orchestral grouping has remained substantially unaltered to the present day. Later composers have merely added more instruments. This "classical" orchestra was composed of the usual strings, one flute, two oboes, two bassoons, two horns and two trumpets (both *natural* instruments), and a pair of kettledrums; clarinets are found only in the last symphonies. Haydn handled his orchestra with consummate skill and with a fine appreciation for the idiom and tone-color of each particular instrument.

Haydn not only wrote for the orchestra with due regard for its coloristic possibilities, but also employed a harmonic idiom which was full and complete in itself so that it became unnecessary to employ a harpsichord to "fill in" the gaps caused by poverty of harmonic texture. Haydn's symphonies mark the disappearance of the harpsichord as a sort of crutch to support the harmonic structure.

THE SONATA FORM

The form which Haydn brought to its full definition appears under various names, depending entirely on the instruments or instrumental combination for which it is employed. For a solo instrument or for two instruments in combination, such as the piano and the violin, the term *sonata* is used; for the usual group of strings—two violins, viola, and violoncello—*string quartet* serves as the designation, while the name *symphony* is given to works for orchestra. No matter what the instrumental combination may be, the form is substantially the same. The evolution of the symphony from the early opera overture need not concern us here.

The sonata (or string quartet, or symphony) is an instrumental work, usually in three [1] or four movements, the first movement of

---

[1] If a work is in three movements, as often happens in the solo sonata, the middle movement may be either a slow movement or a minuet.

which is in the so-called sonata form. Inasmuch as this form is invariably associated with the first movement, it is sometimes known as the sonata first-movement form; and since the first movement is frequently in a fast tempo, it may occasionally be called the sonata-allegro form. The four movements of a typical Haydn symphony usually are:

I. A short, slow introduction followed without pause by a fast movement in sonata form.

II. A slow movement—either a set of variations or a song-like movement in three-part form.

III. A minuet.

IV. A fast movement in sonata form (occasionally in rondo form). The first and last movements are in the same tonality, and it is this tonality by which the symphony is known. The second and third movements are usually in closely related tonalities.

The sonata first-movement form may be schematically represented as follows:

A. EXPOSITION
  1. First Group
      One theme, or several themes, in the tonic key.

  2. Second Group
      One theme, or several themes, in a closely related key, usually that of the dominant. Frequently closes with some allusion to the first theme of the first group.

  The entire exposition may be repeated, the repetition being optional and at the discretion of the performer.

B. DEVELOPMENT
      Free development of the subject matter of the exposition. Modulation into remote keys with ultimate return to the tonic, leading to the—

C. RECAPITULATION
      Repetition of the entire exposition, the second group now not in the key of the dominant, but in that of the tonic.

D. CODA
      May be a short and cursory conclusion, or may occasionally be quite extended and partake of the nature of a second development. Brings the movement to a satisfying conclusion.

It should be borne in mind that the above scheme is merely an ideal form, a statistical representation. Few movements follow this form literally. It is, however, the basic skeleton upon which great composers have created hundreds of sonatas, symphonies, and string quartets.

The most striking characteristics of the sonata first-movement form are the division of the exposition into two sections in two different keys, and the presentation of at least two, and frequently more, themes. It is this duality of thematic material which sets the sonata apart from the fugue and which makes the sonata form such an ideal method of presentation of musical thought. Besides the inevitable contrast of key, a contrast of style may occasionally occur. The first group, for instance, may open with a theme of a forceful and dynamic nature, while the second group may commence with a theme which is lyrical or song-like. The end of the second group, that is, the close of the exposition, is usually vigorous and conclusive and often contains allusions to the opening theme of the first group. It is in the development section that the musicianship and imagination of the composer make themselves manifest. The composer may choose to work with only one, some, or all of the themes presented in the exposition. Restrained by no convention except that of good taste, he is free to do as he pleases with his subject matter. Needless to say, appreciation of the development presupposes a knowledge on the part of the listener of the thematic content of the exposition.

The manner in which the development is joined to the recapitulation is always an interesting detail of any movement in sonata form. The term *recapitulation* is somewhat of a misnomer, for this section is largely a restatement of the exposition and not a summation of the movement. The French designation *réexposition* is more accurate. To avoid the monotony of literal repetition of the exposition, composers have frequently made certain changes in harmonization or instrumentation. Since the recapitulation remains in the tonic key, the transition section joining the first and second groups affords composers their best opportunity to avoid conventional restatement.

The coda is the true summing-up or epilogue of the movement. It varies in length and importance, depending on the composer. Those of Haydn and Mozart are usually short, while those of Beethoven are often quite extensive.

SYMPHONY NO. 94 IN G MAJOR ("THE SURPRISE")

As a typical example we may take one of the most celebrated of the Haydn symphonies—the Symphony in G major (No. 6 in the old catalogue of the publishers Breitkopf and Härtel, No. 94 in the new and correct numbering). This work, written for the first series of London concerts, bears the title *The Surprise* because of a wholly unexpected loud chord which appears in the second movement. All the names attached to Haydn symphonies, such as *The Clock, The Bear, The Hen,* and so forth, were not given to the works by Haydn himself, but were supplied by well-meaning admirers.

The symphony opens with a slow and somewhat solemn introduction of sixteen measures:

Ex. 1

The first group of the first movement presents the following sprightly and thoroughly typical themes:

Ex. 2

This leads to the key of the dominant and to the second group, which commences with a waltz-like theme:

Ex. 3

and also includes this rustic melody:

Ex. 4

The terse development confines itself almost exclusively to the first of the two themes quoted in Example 2. The recapitulation presents no striking points of departure. The coda commences with this charming allusion to the principal subject given out by a solo flute:

Ex. 5

The second movement of a Haydn symphony is frequently a theme and variations, although occasionally the movement may be in three-part form. The presence of a variation form in the symphony or sonata can be traced back to the practices of the suite. Using the *Surprise* Symphony again as an example, we find a theme consisting of an extremely simple, almost child-like melody commencing as follows:

Ex. 6

This is then repeated very softly only to be interrupted by the loud chord which has given the symphony its name.[1] On this theme Haydn proceeds to construct variations of much charm and originality. The third variation

Ex. 7

in which the theme is entrusted to the oboe, and the fourth, in which it is given out by the strings and combined with two new melodies in the flute and oboe, are excellent examples of Haydn's command of the orchestra.

---

[1] There is a widely prevalent story to the effect that Haydn inserted this chord to awaken sleeping members of the audience. This symphony was written for London and was performed before audiences so enthusiastic and so appreciative that the second movement of every symphony invariably had to be repeated. We may interpret the loud chord merely as a bit of pleasantry on Haydn's part.

Ex. 8

The third movement of a Haydn symphony is invariably a minuet —the sole dance form to survive from the suite. The minuet is in triple rhythm and is performed in a moderate tempo. As found in the symphony it is a three-part form, another A B A. The B section, which is usually in another key, is called the *Trio*.[1] The fresh and lively minuets to be found in the Haydn symphonies represent one of the most characteristic features of his art. That of the *Surprise* Symphony opens with this robust figure:

Ex. 9

The Trio, in this instance in the same key, affords an effective contrast.

Ex. 10

The fourth movement of a Haydn symphony is usually a fast, breezy affair. The last movement of the *Surprise* Symphony is in sonata form and commences with this lively theme:

Ex. 11

The second group begins with this laconic subject:

[1] For the origin of this term see page 66.

Ex. 12

The development is a masterpiece of terseness and condensation. Almost very symphony of Haydn is brought to a close by a brisk, sparkling movement of this type.

The four movements of the Haydn symphony have no relationship other than that of key. It was not until Beethoven that the four movements of the symphony were fused into one organic whole.

Of the one hundred and four symphonies which Haydn composed, the following, all late works, and with one exception composed for his London concerts, are likely to be heard today:

1. Symphony in G major, No. 88 (Breitkopf u. Härtel old No. 13), composed for the *Concerts Spirituels* in Paris
2. Symphony in G major (*The Surprise*), No. 94 (Breitkopf u. Härtel old No. 6)
3. Symphony in D major (*The Clock*), No. 101 (Breitkopf u. Härtel old No. 4)
4. Symphony in E-flat major (with the Drum-roll), No. 103 (Breitkopf u. Härtel old No. 1)
5. Symphony in D major (*London*), No. 104 (Breitkopf u. Härtel old No. 2)

The String Quartets

The string quartet, like the symphony, had been in existence long before the time of Haydn. But little music of consequence had been written for it and, as an instrumental medium, it had frequently been associated with nocturnal serenades. (Haydn called his earliest quartets *divertimenti*.) It was his set of six quartets, Opus 33 published in 1781, which established the form on a high artistic level.

To the string quartet Haydn brought the same sense of instrumental color and the same power of development that had made his symphonies so outstanding. Writing for the string quartet demands an intimate knowledge of the innate idiom of string instruments. Each of the four parts must have equal musical interest; no one may be allowed to dominate the others. Goethe happily described the string quartet as "the serious conversation of four individuals." It was Haydn who established the principles of writing for this combination of instruments. Every contemporary musician praised his quartets highly; and Mozart said, "I learned string quartet writing from him."

It is in his string quartets that we find the true Haydn. The intimate nature of this medium as compared to the symphony gave him opportunity to express his own most personal emotions. Particularly is this true in the slow movements. Here Haydn does not employ the variation form, but rather writes slow song-like movements of great profundity and intensity.

The string quartet employs the same form as does the sonata or symphony. Occasionally the positions of the slow movement and the minuet are reversed; that is, the second movement will be a minuet and the third a slow movement.

Two quartets, the Opus 33, No. 3 in C major and the Opus 74, No. 3 in G minor will serve as typical examples.

STRING QUARTET IN C MAJOR, OPUS 33, NO. 3

The String Quartet Opus 33, No. 3, is one of a set of six dedicated to the Archduke Paul of Russia. An interesting feature of this set is the appearance in each quartet of a movement marked *scherzando* (Italian for "humorously")—the forerunner of the *scherzo* of Beethoven. The Opus 33, No. 3 quartet is filled with figures which suggest the sounds of birds, and consequently it has been given the name "Bird Quartet" (*Vogelquartett*) though, to be sure, Haydn had no such descriptive intent.

The first movement opens, after a preliminary measure, with this theme:

Ex. 13

The second group, in G major, begins with some pleasant twitter:

Ex. 14

The second movement, marked *Scherzando,* is an ABA form, and has an interesting middle section, a duet for the two violins.

The third movement, a slow movement, is one of the few Haydn slow movements written in sonata form.

The last movement is in rondo form, which is frequently used for last movements by the Viennese school. The designation "rondo" has been freely and, on occasion, misleadingly used by composers. Many types of rondo exist, but a thorough explanation of the form is beyond the scope of this volume. As used by the Viennese masters the rondo is a fast movement, usually witty and epigrammatic. It is characterized by the successive reappearance between digressions, or episodes, of the rondo subject.[1] For the last movement of this quartet Haydn employs a combination which may be graphically represented as follows:

A	—	B	—C(Development)—A—B—A—Coda.
(Tonic)		(Relative minor)	(Tonic)

The rondo theme, A, is:

Ex. 15

Theme B is:

Ex. 16

STRING QUARTET IN G MINOR, OPUS 74, NO. 3

The Quartet in G minor, Opus 74, No. 3, was written in 1792 when Haydn had returned to Vienna after his first series of concerts in London. Like the Quartet in C major, Opus 33, No. 3, it too has certain characteristics which have caused a name to be attached to it. This particular quartet is usually called the "Horseman's Quartet" (*Reiterquartett*) because of certain jogging figures which

---

[1] See page 65.

appear in the first and last movements; but again it must be borne in mind that this appellation was not bestowed upon the work by Haydn.

The figures which have given the quartet its name are heard in an introduction which is unusual in that it is very brief and is in the same tempo as the first movement proper:

Ex. 17

After two measures of silence, this expressive subject opens the first group:

Ex. 18

The second group strikes a cheerful note with this exuberant theme:

Ex. 19

etc.

The development is an elaboration of the themes set forth in Examples 17 and 18. The coda is unusually short.

The outstanding feature of each of the late Haydn quartets is the slow movement, and the slow movement of this quartet is no exception. Haydn has chosen to write it in a very remote tonality, E major, thereby anticipating the methods of Beethoven. Like most of the slow movements of the Haydn quartets, this movement is in three-part form, the A section of which is varied and embellished on repetition. The thematic material of both the sections is profound and reflective:

Ex. 20

(a)

(b)

The minuet is in the usual cheerful vein. The fourth movement, in sonata form, commences with a capricious subject whose characteristic features are sudden alterations between forte and piano, and jogging after-beats:

Ex. 21

The second group establishes a more confident mood with one of Haydn's most optimistic melodies:

Ex. 22

The development disports itself with the theme of Example 21. The coda is a humorous trifle into which this motive from Example 21 insists on intruding:

Ex. 23

CHORAL MUSIC

Haydn's two oratorios, *The Creation* and *The Seasons,* for a long time rivalled those of Handel in popularity, but they are performed comparatively seldom today. The first of these two works is not without historical significance. As Arnold Schering has pointed out in his *Geschichte des Oratoriums, The Creation* was one of the great moving forces which brought our modern concert life into being. A desire to perform this celebrated work was responsible for the formation of choruses and orchestras in many of the smaller cities and towns of Europe. While a few of the choruses and arias in these oratorios merit praise, and although the orchestral writing is masterful and ingenious, lack of a dramatic sense prevented Haydn from becoming a great writer of choral music. In the field of the oratorio he is definitely overshadowed by Handel, a hearing of whose works in London had prompted Haydn to compose in the same form.

The composition of Haydn which is best known and most often performed is neither a symphony nor a string quartet, but a simple heart-felt song, *Gott erhalte Franz, den Kaiser,* composed for the birthday celebration of Kaiser Franz II in 1797. So enthusiastically was the song received that it became a national hymn spontaneously. Haydn, who played the hymn almost daily, always spoke of it as his favorite work and used it as a theme for the set of variations which comprise the third movement of the quartet in C major, Opus 76, No. 3, known consequently as the "Emperor Quartet" (*Kaiserquartett*). This beautiful melody has not remained the exclusive property of Austria. In 1841 a German poet, Hoffmann von Fallersleben, wrote the text, *Deutschland, Deutschland über alles* to be used with Haydn's melody, thereby creating what is now one of the national hymns of Germany. The melody has also been employed for church hymns and is to be found in combination with various texts in the church hymnals of England and America.

SUGGESTED READINGS

The standard work on Haydn, the Pohl-Botstiber *Joseph Haydn* (Breitkopf und Härtel), is in German. The most concise English treatment of Haydn is Michel Brenet's *Haydn* (Oxford University Press). The *Musical Quarterly* for April 1932 is given over entirely to papers on Haydn, of which the article "Haydn in England" is especially valuable. An illuminating study of the string quartets is to be found in the compendious article on Haydn written for *Cobbett's Cyclopedic Survey of Chamber Music* (Oxford University Press) by Sir Donald F. Tovey. Volume I of Sir Donald's *Essays in Musical Analysis* (Oxford University Press) includes some lively analyses of the well-known symphonies.

Chapter X

THE VIENNESE SCHOOL:
WOLFGANG AMADEUS MOZART

WOLFGANG Amadeus Mozart, like Haydn, was not a native of Vienna. He was born in Salzburg on January 27, 1756, the son of Leopold Mozart, vice-Kapellmeister and court-composer to the Archbishop of Salzburg. Although Mozart was twenty-four years younger than Haydn, the two men must be regarded as contemporaries; and it should be observed that the majority of the works of Haydn which are heard today are of later origin than those of Mozart.

The phenomenal musical capacities of Mozart made themselves manifest when he was very young. He played the harpsichord when only three years old, and by his fifth year he was already composing short pieces. His studies in clavier, violin, and composition were all carried out under the direction of his able and sympathetic father. Mozart's sister Marianne was also a proficient harpsichordist, and in 1763 the father took the two child prodigies on a tour of the principal European cities. The travelers spent much time in Paris and in London. Fourteen days were spent at Versailles where the young Wolfgang amazed the members of the court by his performances on the harpsichord, the violin, and the organ, by his ability to accompany songs and transpose them at sight and, above all, by his skill at improvisation. While there Mozart also composed a violin concerto for the Princess Adelaide. The London appearances were also highly sensational.

The Mozart family returned to Salzburg in 1766, but two years later father and son set out on another series of artistic journeys, this time in Italy. The Italian tours were another succession of triumphs. The young Mozart was fêted everywhere and honors were heaped upon him. It was during this Italian trip that the boy accomplished

WOLFGANG AMADEUS MOZART

his celebrated feat of copying down from memory the *Miserere* of Gregorio Allegri, a work for nine voices in two choirs, after having heard it sung only once at the Sistine Chapel in Rome. Up to the year 1773 the account of the life of Mozart is largely the chronicle of his travels, of his meetings with the important musicians of the day, and of his achievements as a performer and a composer.

In taking his son on a tour of the larger European cities, Mozart's father had as his prime purpose the publicizing of the boy's name and talents so that, when he came of age, he might be offered an appointment commensurate with his gifts. In this the father was unsuccessful. To make matters worse, the new Archbishop of Salzburg, Hieronymus, was unimpressed with Mozart's abilities, but, following the custom of the times, was partial to Italian musicians. The Archbishop was an efficient though despotic administrator, who regarded the Mozarts merely as names on a payroll. Father and son, now grown accustomed to acclaim and adulation, found his attitude unbearable and much hard feeling ensued. The Archbishop had appointed Mozart to the posts of concertmaster (principal violinist) and court organist, but the remuneration was small and the conditions of employment far from congenial. By 1781 the strained state of affairs developed into an open breach. Mozart petitioned for a discharge and was rudely dismissed from the Archbishop's service.

From 1781 till his death in 1791 Mozart was a free-lance in Vienna. He earned a miserable living by giving lessons and appearing as composer and soloist at concerts managed by himself. Important compositions flowed from his pen in a steady stream, but the financial results were disappointing. The Austrian Emperor did go so far as to appoint Mozart *Kammerkompositeur* (chamber-composer); but the duties of this position were confined to the writing of dances for the Imperial masked balls, and the compensation was small. Continued overwork coupled with financial worry brought about Mozart's complete physical collapse, and he died in 1791 in his thirty-fifth year. He was given a third-class funeral and was buried in a potter's field.

Mozart was one of the most gifted composers that the world has ever known. Yet through an unfortunate combination of circumstances his extraordinary creative talent was cut off before it had blossomed into full flower. With few exceptions, the world's greatest musical works have been written by composers who were in their forties or fifties. Bach, Beethoven, and Wagner were creative artists whose finest compositions were written in their later years. It is interesting to speculate on what course of development the art of music might have taken if Mozart had found a kindly and sympathetic master such as Prince Esterhazy, or if the Austrian Emperor had offered him a post commensurate with his talents, or if he had had the tenacity and aggressiveness of a Beethoven or a Wagner.

Some of the happiest moments of Mozart's brief life were spent in the company of Haydn. The two men had met in Vienna in 1781 and a fast friendship combined with a sincere mutual admiration had resulted. The comments made by both of these great composers about each other's works are touching indeed. Haydn, on hearing some of Mozart's quartets performed, turned to the composer's proud father and said: "I assure you before God, as an honorable man, your son is the greatest composer that I know personally or by reputation; he has taste and in addition the greatest knowledge of the technique of composition." [1] Mozart in turn inscribed this group of six quartets with a heart-felt dedication to his "caro amico Haydn." [2]

Mozart was a short, slight individual whose head seemed too large for his body and whose outward appearance would not have led anyone to suspect his artistic capacities. He was exceptionally proud of his small, ultra-refined hands. Socially, Mozart might have been called "a good fellow"; he was fond of conversation, dancing, and billiards. Despite the critical nature of his times, he seems to have manifested no interest in politics; nor was he well read. He was highly impractical, especially as far as his finances were concerned, and this impracticality combined with his kindly disposition made him an easy prey for designing friends. A pious Catholic, he had always longed for a position in a church, and one of his greatest works is his last composition, the *Requiem Mass.*

Characteristics of Mozart's Music

Unlike Haydn, Mozart was versatile in all types of composition, and made significant contributions to the world's store of operas,

[1] Pohl—*Joseph Haydn,* Vol. II, page 211.
[2] Pohl—*op. cit.* page 212.

orchestral music, chamber music, and choral music. He was a composer whose compositions flowed effortlessly from his pen. It was his custom to work out the details of a composition mentally, and the actual writing, regarded by him as an unpleasant mechanical task, was frequently delayed to the last moment. He was one of the world's greatest masters of melody, yet he did not restrict himself to a homophonic style of writing and on occasion would write with great fluency in a complex polyphonic idiom.

Mozart's harmonic technique was singularly advanced for its time, and in many instances it definitely anticipated nineteenth-century procedures. The following semitonal progression from the second movement of the Quartet in E-flat major, K. V. 428, is a fine example of the chromaticism to be found in Mozart's works, as well as a striking foreshadowing of a passage in Wagner's *Tristan und Isolde*:

Ex. 1

(a)

(b)   Wagner—*Tristan und Isolde*.

The opening of the C major Quartet, K. V. 465, with its strongly dissonant A-natural in the first violin and its chromatic melodic progressions, represents a Mozart so far ahead of his age that some conservative musicians were moved to "correct" it.

Ex. 2

The formal perfection of Mozart's works has become proverbial; they are continually cited as true examples of classic art—works in which form and content are inseparably united and are co-existent. Mozart's compositions give no evidence of fussy over-attention to detail; spontaneity is one of their chief characteristics. The emotional content of Mozart's finer works will elude the casual listener. The unhappy circumstances of his life found but little reflection in his music; and while gayety and vivacity characterize many of his compositions, it must be emphasized that passionate utterance was not foreign to Mozart's temperament and that he has, on occasion, spoken in tragic accents. Notable examples of this aspect of Mozart's art are the symphony in G minor, K. V. 550, and the quintet in G minor, K. V. 516.

Mozart's records of his productivity were fragmentary—it was not until the day of Beethoven that composers began to make systematic numbering of their works a regular practice. To eliminate confusion, a German scholar, Ludwig von Köchel, compiled a catalogue of Mozart's works in 1862, and they are now known by their numbers in this catalogue. The letters K. V. are the abbreviation of its German name, Köchel Verzeichnis. Over 600 works by Mozart are listed by Köchel.

DRAMATIC MUSIC

It was but natural that the melodic attainments of Mozart should find their most congenial outlet in the opera. Bastien und Bastienne, his first important dramatic work, was composed in 1768 when he was only twelve years old. This charming little one-act pastoral opera is still an effective and thoroughly captivating stage piece. Mozart wrote twenty-two operas in all, of which the following, all written during the last decade of his life, are significant:

Die Entführung aus dem Serail (The Abduction from the Seraglio), 1782
Le Nozze di Figaro (The Marriage of Figaro), 1786
Don Giovanni, 1787
Così Fan Tutte (So Do They All), 1790
Die Zauberflöte (The Magic Flute), 1791

As the first and last titles on this list indicate, the distinction of having written the first great operas in the German language instead of the conventional Italian belongs to Mozart.

The texts for which Mozart composed music seem decidedly inferior when compared to those set by Gluck. If these operas seem vivid and effective on the stage today and if the characters in them appear genuine and valid, it is only because of Mozart's music. The operas of Mozart show a strong admixture of the Italian tradition, and unlike Gluck, Mozart has not hesitated to introduce so dramatically questionable a procedure as elaborate coloratura. With the exception of *Die Zauberflöte*, the chorus is either entirely absent or plays a very minor role. Mozart's outstanding virtue as a composer of operas was his ability to create convincing personalities by means of musical characterization. This characterization can be attributed to two of Mozart's unique faculties—his ability to write expressive melody, and his skill in treatment of the orchestra.

One of the finest examples of Mozart's skill at characterization is the page Cherubino of *Le Nozze di Figaro*. This adolescent, in the throes of his first love, sings an impassioned aria which tells of his new experiences, so pleasant and yet so distressing. Mozart's setting is an excellent description of Cherubino's agitation:

Ex. 3

(*Prose translation of the text:* I no longer know what I am or what I do; first I am hot as fire, then cold as ice. Every woman makes me blush, every woman makes my heart palpitate. Etc.)

The overtures to *Le Nozze di Figaro* and *Die Zauberflöte* are often played in the concert hall. The overture as written by Mozart and his operatic successors, Beethoven and von Weber, was an orchestral movement in sonata form, the exposition of which was not repeated. Mozart's overtures have a limited degree of musical affiliation with the works they preface. The effervescent overture to *Le Nozze di Figaro* opens with this merry subject:

Ex. 4

Clavier Music

The majority of Mozart's clavier works cannot be numbered among his great compositions. Most of them are early works, and many were written for students. One of the most popular of the seventeen clavier sonatas is the attractive one in A major, K. V. 331, of whose three movements not one is in sonata form. The first movement is a set of simple variations on this folk-like melody:

Ex. 5

The second movement is a minuet. The third, marked *Rondo alla Turca*, is an attempt to use the clavier to imitate the Turkish effects so common in the orchestral and operatic music of the period.

One of Mozart's greatest clavier works is the solemn Fantasia in C minor, K. V. 475, a late work which in many respects recalls the style of Bach. Its basic mood is established by the opening measures:

Ex. 6

Mozart later published this fantasia as an introduction to the great Sonata in C minor, K. V. 457.

CHAMBER MUSIC

The prolific Mozart composed a large amount of chamber music during his brief lifetime. Of this vast quantity of music the greater part consists of earlier works, many of which were written to order. The significant chamber-music compositions, all products of Mozart's maturity, are: the six quartets dedicated to Haydn (K. V. 387, 421, 428, 458, 464, 465); the three string quartets dedicated to King Friedrich Wilhelm II of Prussia (K. V. 575, 589, 590); and four string quintets (with second viola) (K. V. 515, 516, 593, 614). With the exception of the quartets dedicated to the King of Prussia, none of these works was commissioned and each may be considered the result of a genuinely artistic urge for expression. All were written after Mozart had made the acquaintance of Haydn, and show the influence of the older master. The later works have two striking features, an originality in harmonic method and a subjectivity in mood, which are comparable to the methods and idioms of composers of a much later period. A decided melancholia pervades most of them; and the Quintet in G minor, K. V. 516, in many respects Mozart's most profound composition, is surcharged with an emotional intensity and a spirit of tragic foreboding that place it in the same category as the last quartets of Beethoven. It seems worthy of note that all of the great Viennese masters preferred the medium of the string quartet for the communication of their most personal utterances and that they all made important contributions to its literature.

The string quartets, together with the later symphonies, exhibit the most prominent characteristic of Mozart's instrumental style—the cantabile nature of his themes. His inexhaustible melodic invention found the limitations of instruments to be no barrier, and in writing for them he had no difficulty in making them sing with a fervor usually associated with the voice. Mozart does not reserve this songlike idiom for slow movements only, but introduces it in fast movements as well. This infusion of a cantabile style into the two fast movements of the string quartet and symphony was highly novel and constituted an important contribution to the development of these forms.

STRING QUARTET IN D MINOR, K. V. 421

The String Quartet in D minor, K. V. 421, the second of the Haydn group, serves as an excellent example of Mozart's accomplishments in the sphere of chamber music. The mood of the entire composition is established in the first few measures by one of Mozart's most moving subjects:

Ex. 7

A note of melancholy pervades the two subjects which comprise the second group:

Ex. 8
(a)

(b)

The development commences with a dramatically sudden modulation and contains some striking dissonances.

The second movement, an *Andante* in three-part form, offers only a change of key and of tempo; the melancholy mood remains. The first theme

Ex. 9

contains a short rhythmic motive (marked *m*) which pervades all but the middle section.

The Minuet is a fine study in contrasts: Its main section is written in a thoroughly polyphonic style; its Trio, on the other hand, consists of a suave melody played by the first violin to a simple rhythmic accompaniment furnished by the rest of the quartet.

The last movement is a set of five variations on a dance-like theme:

Ex. 10

The fourth variation, in D major, is the only one of the series to offer any relief from the gloom in which the entire quartet is enveloped.

THE SYMPHONIES

Of the forty-nine symphonies which Mozart has written, only four appear regularly in the repertoire of modern symphony orchestras. These are:

The Symphony in D major, K. V. 385
The Symphony in E-flat major, K. V. 543
The Symphony in G minor, K. V. 550
The Symphony in C major, K. V. 551

The three last-named symphonies, written for a projected series of subscription concerts which never took place, were composed in 1788 within the space of six weeks. It should be noticed that all these symphonies antedate the well-known ones of Haydn.

The most important point of departure between the symphonies of Mozart and those of Haydn is to be found in the style of their thematic material. The Haydn themes are lively and fresh; those of Mozart are broad cantabile subjects from which a pathetic note is seldom absent. While Haydn occasionally builds his second group on themes similar in style to those heard in the first group, Mozart invariably secures an effective contrast between the two sections. Like the string quartets, the last symphonies contain many original harmonic progressions, particularly in the development sections. The orchestration of these works is masterly; the wind instruments, in particular, are treated with a thorough understanding of their capabilities. The texture of the symphonies, thanks to Mozart's polyphonic fluency, is always full and rich. The C major Symphony, for example, concludes with a celebrated movement which, although in sonata form, is worked out in a complex fugal manner and with a technical facility which enables the composer to accomplish the feat of combining in the coda all of the five themes he has employed during the course of the movement. This C major Symphony is often called the *Jupiter Symphony*. The origin of the name is not known.

SYMPHONY IN G MINOR, K. V. 550

The Symphony in G minor, K. V. 550, is the quintessence of all that is Mozartian. The cantabile first theme, of singular beauty and grace, and, like many of Mozart's melodies, characterized by a certain wistful quality, is announced by the violins in octaves over a restless rhythmic accompaniment in the violas. The piano is quite incapable of reproducing the atmosphere of these initial measures. The notes themselves are:

Ex. 11

The first three notes of this theme (marked *m*) constitute a motive which finds frequent employment throughout the movement. The second group, in the related key of B-flat major, presents a song-like subject, the chromaticism of which is typical:

Ex. 12

Toward the end of the exposition motive *m* is again heard as a clarinet and a bassoon toss it back and forth; then the entire orchestra turns into the emphatic

Ex. 13

The exposition concludes with the usual stock cadences. By means of a few abrupt chords the tonal center of the work is shifted bodily from G minor over to the remote F-sharp minor. The composer then proceeds to develop the first theme (Example 11), which is thoroughly dismembered, carried through many keys, placed in various registers of the orchestra, and finally, by means of a beautiful chromatic passage in the wood-winds based on motive *m*, allowed to emerge unscathed into the comparative calm of the recapitulation. The coda is very brief.

The *Andante,* which serves as the second movement, is in sonata form. It abounds in chromatic progressions and colorful and original passages for the wood-wind instruments, and achieves a high degree of unity through Mozart's persistent use of a tiny motive composed of only two thirty-second notes, which makes its first appearance in the seventh measure.

Ex. 14

The robust Minuet is another instance of Mozart's polyphonic facility. An unusual feature of this movement is the division of its main section into phrases which are three measures long instead of the conventional four:

Ex. 15

The graceful Trio, of charming rusticity, contains a prominent passage for the horns.[1]

---

[1] Quoted on page 17.

The fourth movement, an *Allegro assai,* gets off to a cheerful start with:

Ex. 16

The second group, however, contains more than a hint of the melancholy mood of many of Mozart's last works:

Ex. 17

The development is extremely energetic and replete with all manner of harmonic audacities. Mozart concentrates his efforts on the first theme (Example 16) with a tenacity which can be compared only with Beethoven. The recapitulation is quite regular and the coda rather perfunctory.

THE CONCERTOS

The term *concerto* can be used to describe two types of works written for a solo instrument, or group of instruments, and orchestra. With the earlier form, the *concerto grosso,* whose formal design is based on the alternation of tutti and soli passages, we are already familiar. It will be recalled that concerti grossi were written predominantly for strings and that the form reached a high point in the works of Bach and Handel. It has been used but seldom since their day.

Mozart and his successors have used the term *concerto* for a work which may be described as a symphony for a solo instrument and orchestra.

Form of the Mozart Concerto

The form of the concerto, as brought to a state of perfection by Mozart, differs from the symphony in the following respects:

1. The concerto has three movements instead of four.[1] The first

---

[1] The Brahms Piano Concerto in B-flat major is in four movements.

movement is in sonata form. It will be recalled that the exposition of a symphony might be repeated at the discretion of the conductor. In the concerto, instead of this literal repetition of the exposition, there are two expositions. The first of these expositions is usually entrusted to the orchestra alone, which represents the thematic material of the movement in a somewhat abridged manner and without any substantial degree of modulation. The second exposition, on the other hand, is written for both the solo instrument and the orchestra and follows the usual procedure in regard to arrangement of thematic material and distribution of keys. The second movement is slow, usually in three-part form or in sonata form; and the last is a lively movement in either sonata or rondo form. The double exposition, however, is confined to the first movement.

2. The solo part calls for a virtuoso performer. Conversely, one of the incidental purposes of the concerto is to serve as a vehicle for the display of virtuosity.

3. A *cadenza* will occur in the first movement and often in the second and third as well. The cadenza is a brilliant unaccompanied passage for the soloist. Up to the time of Beethoven, the performer was expected to improvise the cadenza; Mozart in all his concertos merely indicated a pause for the orchestra at the point at which the cadenza was to be played. Nowadays cadenzas are no longer improvised; when presenting classical concertos, the performer plays one of his own choice which he has learned beforehand.

The peculiar nature of the concerto finds its explanation in the musical customs of the period in which it came to flower. The public concert was just starting to become a regular institution during Mozart's lifetime. He was in fact the first individual to play a piano concerto in public in Vienna (April 3, 1781).

Three things were demanded of the soloist at that time. He was naturally expected to be a finished performer. But the public also insisted that he be a composer as well, and when instrumentalists appeared in public they invariably played concertos of their own composition with an orchestra. The third faculty demanded was skill at improvisation. The performer was expected not only to extemporise the cadenzas for his concerto, but also to regale his listeners with an elaborate series of improvisations on themes from some of his other works, or occasionally from those of other composers. The performance of concertos was the only way in which an instrumentalist might attract an audience to a public concert. It was not until the day of Liszt that the solo recital came into vogue. In his attempt to keep body and soul together, Mozart gave concerts in Vienna at which he appeared as soloist, playing a concerto freshly composed for each occasion. Between 1782 and 1786 he produced no less than fifteen concertos for the piano, an instrument which was then beginning to find widespread acceptance. His total production in this sphere included twenty-seven piano concertos and six violin concertos. The latter were composed in 1775–1776 while he was at Salzburg.

Several of the piano concertos composed for the Vienna concerts rank with Mozart's finest works. He himself was rather proud of them; and the audiences that heard them as they first came into the world under the fingers of their creator appreciated them thoroughly. These audiences were drawn exclusively from the ranks of the musically cultured upper classes, a social group whose taste finds a reflection in the compositions themselves. In a letter to his father, Mozart wrote: "The concertos are neither too easy nor too difficult; they are very brilliant and pleasant to the ear, without, however, lapsing into the superficial." [1] The piano concertos owe their effectiveness to Mozart's exquisite sense of form and to his skill in writing for both piano and orchestra. He has maintained in them a balance of importance between the solo instrument and the orchestra, which, while meeting the legitimate demands of the virtuoso performer, does not relegate the orchestra to the menial task of acting merely as accompaniment. Other notable features are the skilful manner in which the entrances of the solo instrument are brought about and the originality in utilizing the wood-wind instruments of the orchestra. The concertos, like the symphonies and the string quartets, contain a profusion of beautiful melodies.

PIANO CONCERTO IN D MINOR, K. V. 466

One of the finest of Mozart's creations in this form is the Piano Concerto in D minor, K. V. 466, composed in 1785. This work was a favorite of Beethoven, who played it in 1795 at a concert given

---

[1] Jahn-Abert—*W. A. Mozart*, Vol. II, page 202.

for the benefit of Mozart's widow, and also wrote cadenzas for it. The first movement, an *Allegro*, commences with an orchestral exposition which, as was customary, is a purposely incomplete statement of the thematic material. The restless opening with its ominous bass figures casts a shadow over the entire movement.

Ex. 18

After the presentation of several expressive cantabile subjects, the first exposition is brought to an end by the entrance of the solo instrument, which introduces a new theme:

Ex. 19

Other themes make their first appearance in the course of the second exposition. The development commences with an orchestral tutti which after a *forte* statement of the theme quoted in Example 18 subsides to the level of a *piano* and ushers in the soloist. The development confines itself almost exclusively to the two themes quoted above. The manner in which they have been treated is significant: The first (Example 18) is given to the orchestra with rapid passages in the piano as embellishment; the second (Example 19) remains the exclusive property of the solo instrument and appears in three unaccompanied episodes of an improvisational character. The return to the recapitulation is brought about by a short and typically chromatic passage. Mozart has indicated that a cadenza be played just before the coda. The movement comes to a dramatic conclusion with a piano statement of the bass figures heard in the opening (Example 18). A strong resemblance may be observed between the mood of this first movement and that of Mozart's other great work in D minor, the String Quartet K. V. 421.

The second movement, which bears the title *Romanza,* provides in its delightful artlessness an effective contrast to its more serious predecessor. The designation which Mozart has employed is derived from the French *romance,* defined as *"un morceau de chant sur un sujet tendre et touchant."* [1] The term indicates, therefore, more a style of writing than a specific form, although most works which are labelled *Romanza* are in three-part form. The movement, in B-flat major, begins with the presentation of one of Mozart's most charming melodies by the solo piano:

Ex. 20

The middle section is in the related key of G minor and contains brilliant passages for the solo instrument.

Mozart calls the third movement a *Rondo;* but in this instance his use of the term, as is often the case, is more the result of its habitual use as a label for a last movement than an indication of a formal plan. In the strict sense this movement is not a rondo at all[2] but a brisk movement in sonata form, without optional repetition of the exposition and without a development section. To compensate for the lack of formal development the thematic material is subjected to some elaboration in the recapitulation; and there is a coda whose length (sixty-three measures) and treatment of the subject matter is highly unusual for Mozart. The movement, which returns to D minor, commences with this epigrammatic theme given out by the solo instrument:

---

[1] *Nouveau Petit Larousse illustré.*
[2] For the typical rondo of this period see page 129.

Ex. 21

The first group includes another subject, in a contrasting style though in the same key. It, too, is announced by the solo piano:

Ex. 22

But the most attractive feature of the entire movement is the appearance in the second group of a melody which would be difficult indeed to surpass in gayety and sparkle. Its first presentation is entrusted to the wood-winds:

Ex. 23

The composer himself was apparently fascinated by this melody, for he has permitted it to play an important part in the coda, which forsakes D minor for the brighter realms of D major. No finer example of Mozart's ready wit can be found than this final treatment of the theme with its unexpected pirouette in the third and fourth measures, followed by plaudits in the trumpets and horns:

Ex. 24

The entire episode is a splendid instance of Mozart's skilful use of the orchestra.

SACRED MUSIC

The list of sixty-eight sacred works to be found in the Köchel catalogue includes twenty masses, portions of which are occasionally employed in church services today. Of the many shorter pieces of church music the *Ave Verum Corpus*, K. V. 618, is the best known. Mozart's crowning achievement in this sphere is his *Requiem Mass*, K. V. 626, in the composition of which he was engaged when he died.

Mozart undertook to make a setting of the *Missa Pro Defunctis*, the Mass for the Dead, as the result of a commission placed with him by a mysterious stranger who demanded that the composer complete the work by a certain date and under no circumstances attempt to ascertain the name of the individual who had ordered it. Mozart was in failing health at the time, and during the composition of the work was obsessed with the idea that he really was composing his own Requiem. He died before the work was finished and his widow, fearful lest the anonymous individual who had commissioned the score might take advantage of the situation, besought Mozart's pupil, Süssmayer, to complete it. Süssmayer had not only been in close contact with his master, but had a handwriting so similar to his as to confuse even experts. Süssmayer filled in the gaps, completed the instrumentation, and added three choruses. Inasmuch as he was probably acquainted with Mozart's plans, the authorship of these choruses is open to question.

The identity of the individual who had ordered the Requiem was revealed after Mozart's death. He proved to be a Count von Walsegg, an amateur whose habit it was to purchase compositions, bind the composer to secrecy, and then palm them off as his own creations. In this instance, the Count had wished to have a Requiem Mass for performance in memory of his deceased wife.

The music of the Requiem Mass represents Mozart at the height of his powers. It emphasizes more than any other of his compositions the loss which the art of music sustained through his premature death. Throughout the work there is evidence of his study of the compositions of Bach and Handel. One of the subjects of the great double-fugue, *Kyrie Eleison—Christe Eleison,* seems to have been directly inspired by "And with His Stripes We Are Healed" from *The Messiah.*[1]

Ex. 25

Ky - ri - e   e   - le - i - son

SUGGESTED READINGS

The standard work on Mozart, the two-volume *W. A. Mozart* by Hermann Abert (Breitkopf und Härtel), is as yet untranslated. Abert's work was initially a revision of the earlier biography by Jahn, of which an English translation was made in 1882 (Novello). The *Life of Mozart* by Edward Holmes (Dutton), while originally published in 1845, is a thoroughly serviceable shorter treatise. *The Letters of Wolfgang Amadeus Mozart,* edited by Hans Mersmann (Dutton) constitutes an excellent selection. Detailed information about Mozart's chamber music may be found in H. Abert's article in *Cobbett's Cyclopedic Survey of Chamber Music.* The best study of the operas is E. J. Dent's *Mozart's Operas* (Chatto and Windus). The last symphonies are treated by A. E. F. Dickinson in *A Study of Mozart's Last Three Symphonies* (Musical Pilgrim Series, Oxford).

[1] Quoted on page 106.

Chapter XI

THE VIENNESE SCHOOL:
LUDWIG VAN BEETHOVEN

L UDWIG van Beethoven's compositions mark one of the most decided turning points in the evolution of the art of music. Appearing in Vienna at the close of the eighteenth century, Beethoven was not in anyone's employ, and composed only such music as he was compelled to create through the force of his own unique personality. The infusion of his own ego into the traditional forms of his time paved the way for most of the music of the nineteenth century. It was Beethoven who sired the romantic movement in music.

Ludwig van Beethoven was, as the prefix *van* indicates, of Flemish ancestry. He was born on December 16, 1770, in the Rhine town of Bonn, the son of Johann van Beethoven, a tenor in the chapel choir of the Elector of Bonn. His musical gifts made themselves manifest during his early boyhood, and the father, seeing in the lad a second Mozart and hoping to reap financial gain thereby, cruelly forced him to practice an inordinate length of time, much to the neglect of his general education. His musical training was for a time under the supervision of his ne'er-do-well father and later under Tobias Pfeifer, a wandering actor-musician who boarded with the family. These youthful influences were of great significance in the formation of Beethoven's character. Maltreated and abused, with no one in whom he might confide or trust, it is small wonder that he felt himself isolated and excluded from the world. Deprived of the rudiments of a general education, suffering because of the social inferiority of his family and the degradation brought upon it by his drunkard father, Beethoven developed a character and personality for which artistic expression served as the sole means of relief. The few benevolent forces that operated upon Beethoven during his youth in Bonn were the chapel organist, Neefe, who gave him conscientious and sympathetic instruction, and the cultured von Breuning family, at whose home he was a frequent visitor. Eventually he became Neefe's assistant. In 1787 Beethoven journeyed to Vienna. He played before Mozart, who is said to have been impressed by his ability to extemporize, but the illness of his mother brought the youth back to Bonn before anything materialized from this artistic contact.

Two events, both of great importance in Beethoven's artistic development, occurred after his return to Bonn. The first was the beginning of his acquaintanceship with the young Count Ferdinand von Waldstein, the earliest of the many cultured, art-loving members of the nobility who through their interest and magnanimity aided in the unfolding of Beethoven's talents. The second was the formation in 1788 of an opera company at the Electoral Court. Beethoven became a member of the opera orchestra, playing viola. The significance of this activity on his part cannot be overestimated. As a youth in his late 'teens, he was enabled to become intimately acquainted with the mechanism of the orchestra and, through participation in performance, to learn the important works of the time, notably the operas of Mozart. In July 1792 Haydn, returning from the first series of his London concerts, stopped at Bonn. Beethoven was introduced to him and showed him some of his compositions. It has often been surmised that Haydn invited him to be his pupil, although direct evidence is lacking. In November of the same year Beethoven again set out for Vienna, to remain there for the rest of his life.

After his arrival in the Austrian capital Beethoven immediately busied himself with study. His teachers were Haydn, with whom his relations were neither happy nor fruitful; Albrechtsberger, who gave him over two years of instruction in counterpoint; and Salieri, under whom he studied dramatic composition. Mozart had been dead for a year and the stage was now set for the appearance of a pianist of Beethoven's abilities. It was not long before his phenomenal pianistic talents were known to most of the nobility of Vienna. His services were much in demand and so rapidly did his fame increase that he appeared as soloist at several benefit concerts. During these early years he also came in contact with other princely patrons and

LUDWIG VAN BEETHOVEN

counselors—Prince Karl Lichnowsky, Baron van Swieten, and Prince Lobkowitz.

For some time Beethoven's proficiency as a pianist obscured public recognition of him as a composer. One of his first public successes was won by his Septet in E-flat major, Opus 20 (for violin, viola, 'cello, double bass, clarinet, bassoon, and horn), which with its piquant instrumentation and attractive melodies immediately became popular. On the same program in which the Septet was first performed publicly (there had been prior private performances at the Schwarzenberg Palace), the First Symphony also had its première (April 2, 1800). This work was not well received and, like many of the other works which followed, was at first deemed eccentric and perverse by the Viennese. These initial condemnations, however, were almost invariably short-lived and were quickly supplanted by general approbation and enthusiasm.

The period 1799–1814 is an astounding record of artistic creativeness. During this comparatively short time Beethoven composed eight symphonies, three concertos for piano, a concerto for violin, seven sonatas for piano, eleven string quartets, much other chamber music, the opera *Leonore,* and the music for Goethe's *Egmont,* as well as many shorter works. The Viennese public quickly came to appreciate the unique genius living in their midst; and at one time (1808–1809), when it seemed as if he might be lost to the city because of an offer of the post of Kapellmeister at the court of Jerome Bonaparte at Cassel, the Archduke Rudolph and the Princes Lobkowitz and Kinsky came forward and guaranteed him an annual income if he would remain. Unfortunately, the intrinsic value of this financial settlement was much reduced afterwards by monetary inflation. Nevertheless this magnanimous act is a clear indication of Beethoven's importance in the musical life of Vienna as well as of the artistic discernment of his patrons.

Beethoven's success, however, was marred by the greatest misfortune that could possibly befall a musician—deafness. The disease had made itself manifest as early as 1799, and in a most moving document, a letter to his brother written in 1802,[1] Beethoven pathetically described

---

[1] This letter, known as the *Heiligenstadt Will,* may be found in Thayer's *Life of Beethoven,* Vol. I, page 352.

his own despair at the life of isolation that lay before him. By 1814 the deafness had become so complete that he was prevented from making any further appearances as a soloist. At the first performance of the great Ninth Symphony in 1824, the composer, who sat on the stage, had to be turned around so that he might see the tumultuous applause which the second movement had brought forth.

Yet another cause for unhappiness was the composer's disappointment in love. Several ladies of the upper classes were the objects of his affection, but his uncouthness and personal unattractiveness coupled with the rigid class distinctions of the period caused his aspirations to end in bitter frustration.

A nephew, the son of his brother Kaspar, became his ward in 1815. Beethoven, seeking some outlet for the abundant store of affection pent up within him, lavished all manner of care and attention upon the unworthy youth. Much to his uncle's dismay he turned out to be a weak individual, unsuccessful even in an attempt to commit suicide (1826).

Because of his deafness, Beethoven became quite detached from the active musical life of Vienna; but so great had his fame become that individuals came from far and wide to see him. Inasmuch as the composer could not hear, remarks had to be addressed to him in writing. Fortunately, these "conversation books" have been preserved. A commission to compose music even came from so distant a point as Boston, Massachusetts. The English piano manufacturer Broadwood presented Beethoven with one of his new grand pianos; another English admirer sent him a forty-volume set of the works of Handel.

All this attention, however, must be regarded as superficial. The last decade of Beethoven's life was spent in complete spiritual isolation. But this isolation bore magnificent artistic fruit—the *Missa Solemnis,* the Ninth Symphony, and the last string quartets—works which in their intense subjectivity, vastness of dimensions, and absolute freedom from convention, present serious problems to the listener.

In December 1826 signs of dropsy made themselves manifest, and after much suffering Beethoven died on March 26, 1827.

In appearance Beethoven was a short, stocky individual with a swarthy face, ugly but expressive. The facial features which betrayed the artist underneath were the strong brow and the small, penetrating eyes. In dress Beethoven often attempted to affect the grand manner, but carelessness in his attire, coupled with fantastic gestures, often caused onlookers to regard him as a curiosity.

One of the most important aspects of his personality was his intense and occasionally almost exaggerated love of freedom, which was combined with an exalted estimate of his own personal position. On more than one occasion he acted towards members of the nobility in a fashion which can only be described as boorish. An inordinate pride made him particularly sensitive to anything that might be construed as condescending or patronizing. His irascible nature, combined with a strong temper, kept him from forming any fast friendships. Many individuals clustered about him, yet none of them affected him vitally in any way. His love of nature was exceptionally strong and he spent much time in the country about Vienna. In a letter, Beethoven wrote: "No one could possibly love the country as much as I do. Rocks, trees and forest supply the echo which man desires." [1] This appreciation of nature found musical expression in the Pastoral Symphony.

Almost all that we know about Beethoven's inner personality derives from his musical utterances. The deficiencies of his general education prevented his having any literary skill, and his letters are, as a whole, disappointing sources of information. He was a great admirer of the works of Goethe and Schiller, and no better proof can be given of his innate sensitivity to great literature than the music which he wrote for the former's tragedy, *Egmont*. But judged by the conventions of his time, Beethoven was not a cultured individual.

His compositions were the result of tremendous inner conflict and of great powers of concentration. It was the composer's custom carefully to work out the subject matter and general plan for his works over a long period of time before proceeding to their actual composition. The *Sketch Books,* in which Beethoven labored at the themes from which so many gigantic works were to spring, have been preserved. They serve not only as records of the various stages in the evolution of the great Beethoven melodies, but also as evidence of the searching self-criticism to which all of his compositions were subjected.

[1] A. C. Kalischer—*Beethovens Sämtliche Briefe,* Vol. I, page 204.

The key to the artistic and historical significance of Beethoven is to be found in his own personality. It was this personality which drove him to speak as he did and, in so doing, to change the course of musical art. Beethoven's music at no time aims merely to please the ear or to serve as tuneful entertainment. It is, however, fallacious to believe that his music is "personal" in the narrower sense. It is rather one man's expression of great universal concepts. One of the foremost of Beethoven's disciples and interpreters was Richard Wagner; and it was Wagner who has given us the tersest and, at the same time, most exact commentary on a work of Beethoven. After conducting the Third Symphony (the *Eroica*) Wagner autographed a program for his friend Liszt. Writing out the opening theme of the symphony, Wagner added these words: *"So dachte B. über heroische Dinge!"* (This was Beethoven's concept of the heroic!)

Most of Beethoven's works lack descriptive titles, but in each one of them the listener is aware of some programmatic content. Each and every one portrays a conflict of a dramatic nature. Beethoven himself has left us but few clues to the meaning of his works, yet by their very nature they have inspired a great mass of descriptive and interpretive commentary. Occasionally these commentaries, particularly those of Richard Wagner or of Romain Rolland, are provocative; but they serve more as revelations of the inner workings of the minds of their authors than of Beethoven. There is no guide to Beethoven's music other than the listener's own personal reactions to it.

It is difficult to speak of a specific Beethoven style, for one of the most prominent characteristics of his music is the unique quality of each and every work. While the external forms may frequently be similar, no two movements can be said to be alike.

Classification of Beethoven's Works

It is customary to divide the creative accomplishments of Beethoven into three groups and to assign a definite style to each. A knowledge of the style of each of these "periods" may prove helpful, provided that the lines of chronological demarcation are not drawn too rigidly. The "periods" should be considered merely as convenient groupings and not as successive metamorphoses of Beethoven as a composer. His development as a creative artist was continuous and the stamp of his genius is found in almost every work, no matter of what period. Unless they be done with caution and understanding, classifications of art works are destructive of their purpose—a better comprehension of the artist and his creations.

The "period of imitation" may be said to end with the Second Symphony (1802). This period may be described, with many reservations, as one in which Beethoven was under the influence of his great predecessors, Haydn and Mozart. The break with the traditions of the past commenced in 1803 with the Third Symphony. The second stage, or "period of realization," ends with the Piano Sonata in E minor, Opus 90 (1814). The last period, the "period of abstraction," commences chronologically with the Piano Sonata, Opus 101, in A major; but its most typical works are the last string quartets (Opus 127, 130, 131, 132, 135), the Ninth Symphony, and the *Missa Solemnis*. In the last stage we find Beethoven deviating from the traditional forms almost to the point of incoherence. Everything was rendered subordinate to content. J. W. N. Sullivan has aptly remarked that "language . . . is poor in names for subjective states, and this poverty becomes particularly apparent when we try to describe such works of art as the late quartets." [1]

Beethoven and the Sonata Form

The majority of the works of Beethoven that are heard today are works of the second period, whose style may therefore be discussed in some detail. Beethoven cast his musical expression in two forms— the sonata and the variation—and both were considerably altered by him in his search for adequate media of communication. The sonata was materially lengthened, the development section being considerably expanded and occasionally even containing new themes. The coda also took on added significance, frequently becoming so long and involved as to partake of the nature of a second development.

There is no better illustration of this expansion of the dimensions of the sonata form than the Third Symphony, written in 1804. Its performance lasts fifty minutes as compared to the twenty minutes required for the *Surprise* Symphony of Haydn, written in 1792.[2] But

---

[1] J. W. N. Sullivan—*Beethoven, His Spiritual Development,* page 226.
[2] Beethoven himself stated that this symphony was written "at greater length than usual."

hand in hand with this expansion of dimensions goes a concentration of subject matter, so that developments become even more concise and direct, and entire movements are based upon only one musical idea: for example, the first movement of the Fifth Symphony, dominated

throughout by . The recapitulation often

appears not as a mere repetition of the exposition, but rather as the culmination of the development. Beethoven also finds the old conventions of key relationship irksome, and frequently indulges in considerable freedom in choice of tonalities for the internal divisions of movements as well as for the various movements of a given work.

One of Beethoven's great achievements was his development of the *scherzo* out of the old shell of the minuet. While preserving the outward form and rhythm of the older dance form, he greatly accelerated its pace, and made it into a vigorous and forceful, sometimes almost explosive, movement. The Beethoven scherzos are characterized by their overwhelming and inexhaustible energy, their sudden contrasts, their unexpected outbursts. In them are to be found some of the most realistic examples of the composer's sense of humor. The term *scherzo* had been employed before Beethoven as a designation for a humorous piece (*scherzo,* Italian for "joke"); but the humor displayed by Beethoven in these movements is of cosmic proportions. The scherzo as employed by Beethoven is more a manner of expression than a form. The Scherzo of the Ninth Symphony, for example, is written in sonata form, while the Scherzo of the String Quartet in C-sharp minor, Opus 131 is written in duple rhythm. Beethoven himself was apparently conscious of this differentiation between an idiom and a conventional form. Many Beethoven movements which are universally referred to today as scherzos possess no titles other than the usual designations of speed.

One of the most conspicuous of Beethoven's innovations is his integration of the several movements of the sonata or symphony into one complete whole. The various movements present evidence of relationship and in later works are frequently joined one to the other without pause, the last movement appearing as a triumphant culmination. There is no better example of the internal coherence of the various movements of the works of Beethoven than the Fifth Symphony.

The idiom of Beethoven is essentially homophonic.[1] Contrapuntal sections appear frequently and with a certain degree of effectiveness, particularly in the symphonies; but the part-writing is often labored and the listener easily perceives that as a writer of instrumental polyphony Beethoven must yield place to Bach and Mozart.

Use of the Variation Form

In his treatment of the variation form Beethoven again broke away from the conventions of the past. He was not content merely to utilize the obvious features of the theme as did his immediate predecessors; but he minutely explored its every possibility and employed a rhythmic figure, a harmonic progression, a motive, or some other aspect as an idea on which to construct a variation. There are many magnificent sets of variations by Beethoven, his greatest work in this form being his set of "Thirty-three Variations on a Theme of Diabelli." More familiar variations are the thirty-two in C minor for piano (without opus number), the last movement of the Third Symphony, and the second movement of the Fifth Symphony.

Beethoven's Humor

Within the works of Beethoven is to be found an infinite variety of moods, situations and conflicts, ranging from profound sorrow to the most rapturous exaltation, and often introducing an element of humor. Many of his compositions abound in boisterous outbursts akin to gigantic laughs. Beethoven himself described the mood which characterizes such movements as the finales of the Seventh Symphony and the Eighth Symphony as *aufgeknöpft* (unbridled).

Directions for Performance

Beethoven was one of the first composers to insert in his works meticulous and specific indications concerning dynamics, shading, and interpretation. He employed German as well as the conventional Italian terms and at no time hesitated to utilize any phrase which he deemed necessary for proper performance. The second movement of

[1] In the *Sketch Books* none of the themes is accompanied.

the Quartet in E minor, Opus 59, No. 2 is headed *"Si tratta questo pezzo con molto di sentimento"* (This piece is to be played with much feeling); and one of the variations in the Quartet in C-sharp minor, Opus 131, is marked *Lusinghiero* (in a coaxing manner). The *Missa Solemnis* bears the inscription *"Vom Herzen, möge sie zu Herzen gehen"* (From the heart, may it go to the heart).

Typical works from every category will now be examined, though it should be continually borne in mind that while each work is typical of Beethoven, it differs markedly from any of its fellows and can therefore be regarded as representative only in a limited sense.

Piano Music

Beethoven's works for piano solo include thirty-two sonatas, several sets of variations, and about one hundred shorter pieces, many in dance forms. All of these compositions must be regarded as chamber music, since they were designed for the intimate atmosphere of the salon and not for the concert hall. Whenever Beethoven appeared in public as a pianist he followed the custom of playing a concerto of his own composition with orchestra. Inasmuch as the piano was Beethoven's own instrument, it is but natural to conclude that his more intimate thoughts were confided to it. As a performer, Beethoven occupied a unique position in Vienna. His style differed markedly from the refined *galant* manner which the Viennese had so admired in the playing of Mozart. He strove continually to extract new and more powerful sonorities from the instrument; and his impetuous and fiery style of playing was often considered crude by contemporaries. But in improvisation he was universally regarded as a master. At no time did he allow the limitations of the instrument to hamper or confine him. Beethoven himself was a great virtuoso; but none of his piano music, difficult as some of it may be, was written to serve merely as a vehicle for feats of virtuosity.

SONATA IN F MINOR, OPUS 57

One of the best-known sonatas is the one in F minor, Opus 57, universally known as the *Appassionata*. This name, although far from misleading, was not given to the composition by Beethoven, but by the publisher Cranz. The work, completed in 1806, is in three movements, and is an excellent example of Beethoven's integration of several movements into a unified whole. The composer is said to have called it his greatest sonata.

First Movement—*Allegro assai; Piu allegro* (F minor)

Preceded by no introduction, the first group commences with a portentous motive whose first two measures outline the chord of F minor:

Ex. 1

A short, repeated-note figure makes its appearance in the tenth measure:

Ex. 2

"Knocking" motives of this type are to be found in many of Beethoven's works—the Fifth Symphony, the Concerto for Violin, the Concerto for Piano in G major, the String Quartet in E-flat, Opus 74.

The second group commences in A-flat major with a short theme bearing a marked rhythmic resemblance to Example 1:

Ex. 3

This gives way to yet another theme, a tempestuous motive beginning in A-flat minor:

Ex. 4

It will be observed that the fourth measure of this theme also contains a repeated-note figure. The development consists almost entirely of an intense working out of Example 1 and Example 3 and concludes with dramatic pronouncements of the "knocking" motive, Example 2. The recapitulation contains two notable features: (1) the return of Example 1 over a throbbing pedal leading up to (2), an emphatic statement of the same theme in F major with sudden alternations of piano and fortissimo. The "knocking" motive figures prominently in the transition section which leads to the lengthy coda. This concluding section is in reality a second development of the thematic material of the exposition. The movement terminates with a last statement of Example 1 which finally disappears in a pianissimo chord of F minor.

Second Movement—*Andante con moto* (D-flat major)

This movement, comparatively short, serves as a breathing spell between the forceful outer movements. It consists of four essentially simple variations on this fervent theme:

Ex. 5

A deceptive cadence at the close does not permit the movement to end but connects it directly to the last movement.

Third Movement—*Allegro ma non troppo; Presto* (F minor)

The quiet of the second movement is cut short by a trumpet-like figure:

Ex. 6

This is followed by a preparatory passage which eventually becomes the first theme of the first group:

Ex. 7

The second group, in C minor, commences with:

Ex. 8

The development, in addition to disclosing the potentialities of Example 7, introduces an entirely new theme:

Ex. 9

Following the recapitulation, the coda introduces another new theme, a rapid march-like strain:

Ex. 10

which, however, finally yields precedence to the theme quoted in Example 7, with which the entire sonata is brought to an emphatic conclusion on reiterated chords of F minor.

THE SYMPHONIES

The nine symphonies of Beethoven are his best-known works. They form a considerable part of the orchestral repertoire and are played unceasingly, yet without any diminution in their artistic significance. Beethoven took the symphony at the point of development to which it had been brought by Haydn and Mozart, and made of it an art form in which he has never been surpassed.

Beethoven's innovations include not only the general alterations in form and style mentioned previously, but also a new and revolutionary concept of the orchestra, an instrumental medium with which he had become well acquainted during his period of service in the opera orchestra at Bonn. Utilizing for the most part the same orchestral equipment as did Haydn and Mozart, Beethoven employed the various instruments in a manner that was considered so unconventional and audacious at the time as to bring condemnation on his head. None of these new departures should be considered merely as innovations in instrumentation, for the musical thoughts which Beethoven had to deliver brought forth these instrumental settings as their natural concomitants. Among the more conspicuous new usages of the orchestra may be mentioned the novel use of the hitherto fettered double bass, as in the Trio of the Scherzo of the Fifth Symphony and in the celebrated series of recitatives which open the fourth movement of the Ninth Symphony; the expressive writing for the horns in the Trio of the Scherzo of the *Eroica* Symphony; the elevation of the kettledrums to the point where they are actually entrusted with thematic material, as in the Eighth and Ninth Symphonies; and, in the Ninth Symphony, the introduction of the human voice.

Three of the symphonies have programmatic connotations. The Third was originally dedicated to Napoleon; but when he elevated himself to the rank of Emperor in May, 1804, Beethoven angrily changed the title of his work to "Heroic Symphony, composed to celebrate the memory of a great man." Many individuals have attempted to elucidate in prose the contents of this great work, with results which have been none too happy. The Sixth Symphony, the *Pastoral,* has a plentiful store of descriptive titles: *Awakening of Joyful Feelings on Arriving in the Country, Scene by the Brook, Joyful Gathering of the Country Folk, Storm, Shepherd's Song, Glad and Grateful Feelings after the Storm.* But lest the listener regard the work as mere musical photography, Beethoven places this caption on it: *"Mehr Ausdruck der Empfindung als Malerei"* (More an expression of feeling than tone-painting). The programmatic nature of the work greatly influenced subsequent composers such as Mendelssohn, Liszt, and Wagner, and for some time Beethoven was erroneously regarded as the father of modern program music. The Ninth Symphony is dominated by a program which finds concrete expression in the last movement in which Schiller's *An die Freude* (Ode to Joy) is set for vocal quartet and chorus. One of the most significant features of this work is the manner in which themes from the first three movements are furtively recalled at the opening of the fourth movement and peremptorily dismissed by dramatic recitatives in the 'cellos and basses.

The six remaining symphonies are devoid of specific programmatic connotations. That they do possess some definite programmatic content cannot be denied, but the nature of this content must remain the concern of the listener.

SYMPHONY NO. 5, IN C MINOR

The most famous Beethoven Symphony is the Fifth, in C minor, completed in 1807. It is doubtful if any other orchestral composition has been performed more often than this great work, whose message is such as to bear endless repetition.

First Movement—*Allegro con brio* (C minor)

The most striking feature of this movement is its relentless concentration on one idea, a terse repeated-note figure which is announced at the very beginning in an attention-arresting fortissimo:

Ex. 11

One need only compare the forceful opening of this symphony with that of the *Surprise* Symphony of Haydn [1] to realize how Beethoven was molding the symphony to suit his own needs of expression. His first biographer, Schindler, claims that the composer made this statement about the opening: "Thus Fate knocks on the door." But the veracity of Schindler is open to question. Repetitions of this motive culminate in two emphatic chords which bring about a modulation into E-flat major and pave the way for the entrance of the second group. This commences with an emphatic passage in the horns followed by a cantabile subject in the violins, which Beethoven has meticulously marked *dolce*:

Ex. 12

[1] See page 124.

It will be noticed that the repeated-note motive is heard in the horns and continues to hover about in the basses (measures 7 and 8). The entire exposition is so brief and so terse that conductors usually exercise their option of repeating it.

The development contains an episode which illustrates one of Beethoven's characteristic procedures—the breaking up of a theme almost to the point of its complete demolition. Commencing with the first three measures of the second subject, into the last of which the trumpets insert an emphatically dissonant C,

Ex. 13

the composer proceeds to hack away until only these chords, given out in a hushed dialogue between strings and woodwinds, remain:

Ex. 14

The development, as is usually the case in Beethoven's mature works, debouches into the recapitulation, the course of which is halted by the celebrated passage for solo oboe.[1] The coda not only proceeds to cast new light upon what has already transpired, but also contributes a new theme.

Ex. 15

Second Movement—*Andante con moto* (A-flat major)

This movement is a series of variations with many interpolated episodic passages. Beethoven has followed a procedure to which

---

[1] Quoted on page 11.

Haydn was partial—the use of two themes instead of one. The first theme, one of Beethoven's most beautiful melodies, is given out by the violas and 'cellos:

Ex. 16

The second theme makes its first appearance in the clarinets and bassoons; but a modulation takes place en route, and it is transformed into a majestic tune solemnly intoned by the trumpets and horns:

Ex. 17

Beethoven's treatment of the variation form, as evidenced by this movement, again invites comparison with the methods of Haydn. The Beethoven variations wholly lack a formal note; the composer has given his imagination free rein both in treatment of subject matter and coloristic use of the orchestra. Some of the passages in this movement which seem admirable to modern ears were once deemed to be errors on Beethoven's part. This is another movement upon which certain nineteenth-century pedants were tempted to lay a "correcting" hand.

Third Movement—*Allegro* (C minor)

This movement is a typical Beethoven scherzo, though not designated as a scherzo by the composer. In contrast to the two preceding movements, it commences in a subdued, almost mysterious manner, with this theme assigned to the 'cellos and basses playing at the level of a pianissimo:

Ex. 18

The furtive atmosphere of these opening measures is suddenly dispelled by the horns, which blare out a repeated-note motive that can claim relationship to the one heard in the first movement:

Ex. 19

The Trio, written in a fugal style, is a fine example of that brand of musical humor which we associate with Beethoven. 'Cellos and basses perform lumbering acrobatics on:

Ex. 20

The return of the scherzo is not the familiar *Da Capo*, but an entirely new treatment carefully marked by the composer *sempre pianissimo*. An air of expectancy is thus created and it develops that Beethoven has purposely avoided a literal repetition so that he may lead the scherzo by means of a dramatic transition directly into the last movement. This union of two movements is another example of Beethoven's struggle to unify the hitherto independent movements of the symphony. A long period of suspense punctuated by a persistent repeated-note motive in the kettledrums culminates in the

Fourth Movement—*Allegro* (C major)

This movement is in sonata form and commences with a broad, triumphant tune given out by the entire orchestra, to which trombones have been added for the first time in symphonic music:

Ex. 21

The first group includes another theme which will become prominent in the coda:

Ex. 22

The second group consists of two important themes, the first of
which is:

Ex. 23

The short figure in half-notes, so unobtrusively presented by the
'cellos in the third measure of this example, assumes a very important
rôle in the development, becoming, in fact, its most prominent feature.
The other theme of the second group also employs repeated notes:

Ex. 24

The development carries the theme quoted in Example 23 through
many keys and rises to an impressive climax which normally would
lead to the recapitulation. But instead there is a hushed interpolation
of the scherzo, whose insistent "knocking" motives are finally dispelled
when the entire orchestra commences the recapitulation with the melody quoted in Example 21. The brilliant coda reaches its high point
with a canonic treatment of the opening theme of the movement:

Ex. 25

The close is an instance of another characteristic of Beethoven's style: the manner in which he emphasizes the tonality of a work. The last fifty-five measures of this movement never stray from C major, and the basic tonality is thus mercilessly impressed upon the listener.

It should be observed that Beethoven was the first composer to write a last movement of this type. The concluding movement of this symphony is not merely a pleasant termination to a series of pieces in contrasted tempi, but rather a summation of the entire work, a finale in the true sense of the word.

THE CONCERTOS

In this category are to be found five concertos for piano and one for violin. The thematic content, loftiness of inspiration, and sympathetic treatment of the solo instrument which characterize these compositions have given them a position of great prominence in the literature of the concerto. In his treatment of the concerto form, Beethoven has again revised traditional concepts. These works are not compositions for a soloist accompanied by an orchestra, but are full-length symphonies in which a solo instrument is entrusted with a prominent part which at no time is more important than that of the orchestra. The Fourth and Fifth Piano Concertos (in G major and E-flat major respectively) introduce the solo instrument at the very beginning instead of at the commencement of the second exposition. In the latter work, known in the English-speaking countries as the *Emperor* Concerto,[1] Beethoven has done away with the custom of allowing the solo performer to improvise a cadenza. At the point in the first movement where the cadenza would normally appear he has inserted a specific prohibition of its introduction, and has written a rather brief passage for piano solo to take its place. Since the day of Beethoven no com-

[1] This title did not originate with Beethoven.

poser, with the exception of Brahms, has left the cadenza of his concertos to the discretion of a performer. In both of the above-mentioned works the second and third movements are joined, in an attempt at unification similar to that which has already been observed in the Piano Sonata in F minor and in the Fifth Symphony.

The Violin Concerto, considered by many critics to be the greatest work of its kind, was written for and first performed by a Viennese violinist and conductor, Franz Clement. Beethoven, who always loved a joke, could not resist the temptation of making a pun on Clement's name, and the work bears the inscription *"Concerto par Clemenza pour Clement."* The outstanding feature of the composition is the persistent use of a "knocking" motive throughout the first movement in a manner which has its parallel in the Fifth Symphony. Beethoven introduces this figure in characteristically telling fashion by having it softly tapped out on a kettledrum:

Ex. 26

Particularly effective employment of this repeated-note motive is made in the development section when, during the earnest discourse of the solo violin, it is relentlessly intoned, first by the horns and then by the trumpets.

DRAMATIC MUSIC

Despite Beethoven's extraordinary powers of dramatic expression, he wrote only one opera, a work known today as *Fidelio.* His failure to write other operas may be attributed to his inability to find what he considered a suitable text. Many libretti were offered to him, and unfruitful discussions concerning possible opera texts took place with such literary figures as von Collin and Grillparzer; and like almost every other composer of the time, Beethoven considered the musical possibilities of Goethe's *Faust.*

The original title of the opera *Fidelio* was *Leonore*. Based on a melodramatic and somewhat obvious plot, the work deals with the last-minute rescue from death of an individual who had been illegally imprisoned—a favorite dramatic subject at the time. The first performance of the work in 1805 resulted in failure. After various deletions and revisions it was performed again the following year. Considerably altered and supplied with a new name and a new overture it was revived as *Fidelio* in 1814 with much success.

Judging by *Fidelio,* it cannot truthfully be said that Beethoven was a great opera composer. The direct demands made by the libretto could only be met by him in such scenes as he found congenial to his own temperament. His opera remains an uneven work with many dramatic episodes that fail to give a unified impression.

Beethoven's dramatic instinct found free play when he was unencumbered by the exigencies of a libretto, that is, when he could express himself in a purely instrumental manner; and in so doing he created yet another great medium of musical communication, the dramatic overture. For the various performances of *Fidelio* no less than four overtures were composed. Three are known and numbered as *Leonore* overtures and the fourth as *Fidelio*. Among the other overtures written by Beethoven for various dramatic works and festive occasions, two magnificent examples stand out: the overture for Heinrich von Collin's play *Coriolanus,* and that for Goethe's tragedy *Egmont*. For the latter play Beethoven also wrote some incidental music.

While Beethoven was not eminently successful in working out the details of a musical setting for a dramatic work, he showed an almost uncanny ability to extract from the libretto or play in hand the essence of its dramatic conflict, and to present this conflict in a musical condensation so vivid as to make the play which it preceded appear almost as an anti-climax.

OVERTURE TO "EGMONT"

Beethoven said that he wrote his overture and incidental music for Goethe's tragedy *Egmont* "purely out of love for the poet" [1]; but examination of the play will show that Beethoven himself must have

---

[1] Thayer-Krehbiel—*Life of Beethoven*, Vol. I, page 192.

been strongly drawn to the Dutch hero Egmont with his love of independence, his unlimited confidence in himself, and his general
high-spiritedness. The essential conflict of the play, based on incidents which occurred during the Spanish rule in the Netherlands,
is the struggle between liberalism and personal freedom as represented
by Egmont, and reaction and tyranny as represented by the cruel and
fanatical Alva, emissary of the King of Spain. Egmont was charged
with treason and was executed at Alva's command on June 5, 1568.

Beethoven's overture is a powerful portrayal of Egmont, his aspirations, his failure, and his ultimate victory in death. The work is in
three connected parts—a slow introduction, an *Allegro* in sonata form,
and a brilliant coda. After a measure in which the note F is sounded
by the entire orchestra, the strings emphatically announce this ominous
theme:

Ex. 27

Plaintive answer is made by the wood-winds. Another theme appears
in the violins accompanied by a bass motive based on the first two
notes of Example 27, also a "knocking" motive. After further repetition of this motive the tempo changes to an animated *Allegro,* the
first subject of which is assigned to the 'cellos, with a significant
concluding phrase in the first violins:

Ex. 28

This rises to a frenzied climax in which repeated-note motives play
an important part. The second group commences with a dramatic
dialogue between the strings and wood-winds:

Ex. 29

The first two measures of this theme, it will be observed, are derived from the opening (Example 27). Here again we find a "knocking" motive.

The development confines itself exclusively to the theme quoted in Example 28, fragments of which are heard in the wood-wind instruments, whose discourse is regularly interrupted by loud chords. The recapitulation exhibits no striking points of departure. The transition to the coda is based entirely on the repeated-note figure heard in Example 27, which is alternately hurled out defiantly by clarinets, bassoons, and horns, and played softly by the strings. A final fortissimo statement of this motive is followed by a pause from which these prayer-like chords emerge:

Ex. 30

Nothing could be simpler than the interpolation of this wood-wind episode, yet it is one of the most moving passages that the composer ever penned. The triple *piano* which he has demanded is seldom realized in performance.

The coda bears one of Beethoven's most frequently employed designations—*Allegro con brio.* The key is now F major, and the atmosphere changes from one of oppression to one of victory and triumph. The thematic material of the coda is entirely new. The explanation of the mood of this conclusion is to be found in Goethe's play, at the end of which Egmont is led to his execution while a *Siegessymphonie* (Symphony of Victory) is played. The coda of the overture thus reappears at the conclusion of the play, not merely as a carrying out of Goethe's directions, but as a significant epilogue to the entire drama.

CHAMBER MUSIC

The chamber music of Beethoven includes nine sonatas for violin and piano, of which the Kreutzer Sonata (Opus 47) is the best known; five sonatas for 'cello and piano; eight piano trios; many pieces for miscellaneous combinations; and seventeen string quartets. Of these works the string quartets are the most important and form the very core of the literature for this particular instrumental combination. A knowledge of them is indispensable for a true appreciation of Beethoven.

Quartets composed of professional players often performed at the houses of Beethoven's patrons, and in his opportunities for hearing his works performed he enjoyed facilities which rivalled those of Haydn. As is the case with all the other musical media which he employed, Beethoven greatly enlarged the expressive possibilities of the string quartet. Nor did he permit the grandeur of his conceptions to be constrained by mere mechanical limitations; the last quartets, particularly, makes severe demands on the players.

One of the most prominent of Beethoven's patrons was the Russian Ambassador to Vienna, Count Rasoumovsky, to whom he dedicated the three quartets, Opus 59, and whose name they bear. As a complimentary gesture to his benefactor, Beethoven employed a Russian folk song in a movement in each of the first two.[1] These quartets, completed in 1807, mark a new departure in chamber music. Beethoven has done away with the old habit of composing quartets in batches of six; and after the Opus 59, he does not even write in groups of three, but regards each quartet as a distinct entity. An important feature of the Opus 59 quartets is their monumental size, an attribute which can be explained in terms of grandeur of conception, richness of development, and mastery of form. These works are substantially longer than their predecessors, the Opus 18 quartets. The average length of a quartet from the latter group is twenty minutes; the first quartet of the Opus 59, however, consumes about forty-one minutes

[1] See page 329.

in performance. This lengthening of the traditional form can be attributed to Beethoven's need for an adequate medium of personal expression. The long movements which are encountered in his mature works are never diffuse; almost all exhibit that stupendous power of concentration which is so characteristic of his style.

SECOND MOVEMENT OF THE STRING QUARTET IN E MINOR,
OPUS 59, NO. 2

One of the most impressive movements of this group of works is the second of the Quartet in E minor, Opus 59, No. 2, a slow movement written in the intimate soul-revealing style which Beethoven reserved for his quartets alone. At its head there stands the characteristically Beethovenish direction to the performers already quoted on page 165, *"Si tratta questo pezzo con molto di sentimento."* But the music which Beethoven has written makes his request seem unnecessary. The movement commences with a contemplative melody of incomparable serenity:

Ex. 31

The second group introduces a fervid theme whose intensity is greatly increased through reversal of the usual positions of viola and 'cello and writing the latter above the former:

Ex. 32

The exposition comes to an end with an impassioned melody given

out by the violins over a characteristic repeated-note motive in the
viola and 'cello:

Ex. 33

etc.

The brief development is an intense working out of the motives
quoted in Examples 31 and 33. The recapitulation is not a literal
repetition of the exposition, but contains new figuration and important
changes in instrumentation. The coda commences with a fortissimo
statement of the opening theme, which soon gives place to the theme
of Example 33 considerably expanded.

VOCAL MUSIC

Beethoven composed many songs, a few of which are heard today.
One song of a religious character, *Die Ehre Gottes aus der Natur*
(The Glory of God in Nature) has become well known in a choral
arrangement which, however, is not the work of the composer.

An oratorio, *Christus am Ölberge* (The Mount of Olives), composed in 1801–1802, was a somewhat popular work during the
composer's lifetime, but is seldom performed today. His great masterpiece of choral music is the *Missa Solemnis,* a setting of the
Catholic Mass which, like that of Bach, extends far beyond the ritual
of a church; and like Bach's Mass, Beethoven's setting is a confession
of personal faith. So intense and so earnest was Beethoven in his
desire to formulate his *credo* in tones that in this work, as in the
choral parts of the Ninth Symphony, he has frequently disregarded
the physical limitations of the human voice. But the strained character of the vocal writing does not obscure the composer's fervidness
of utterance, and an episode such as the *Dona Nobis Pacem* with its
sound of distant trumpets may well be regarded as one of Beethoven's
highest peaks of inspiration. At this point in the score Beethoven has

revealingly written, *"Bitte um innern und äussern Frieden"* (Prayer for inner and outer peace).

SUGGESTED READINGS

The literature on Beethoven is being continually enriched by new publications. The standard biography is the three-volume treatise of A. W. Thayer, edited and revised by Henry Krehbiel, *The Life of Ludwig van Beethoven* (Schirmer). This monumental piece of scholarship does not include critical examinations of the works. The two-volume *Beethoven Handbuch* by Theodor Frimmel (Breitkopf und Härtel) is an indispensable encyclopedia. The best single treatise on the career, the man, and his compositions is the *Beethoven* of Paul Bekker (E. P. Dutton).

All of the following works are valuable:

Oscar Sonneck—*Beethoven, Impressions of Contemporaries* (Schirmer).

Karl Kobald—*Beethoven, Seine Beziehungen zu Wiens Kunst, Kultur, Gesellschaft und Landschaft* (Amalthea Verlag).

Romain Rolland—*Beethoven, The Creator* (Harpers).

J. W. N. Sullivan—*Beethoven, His Spiritual Development* (Knopf).

Sir Donald F. Tovey—*A Companion to Beethoven's Pianoforte Sonatas* (Associated Board of the R. A. M. and the R. C. M., London).

Sir George Grove—*Beethoven and his Nine Symphonies* (Novello).

Sir Donald F. Tovey—*Essays in Musical Analysis*, Vols. I, II, III, IV (Oxford University Press).

Sir William H. Hadow—*Beethoven: The Opus 18 Quartets* (Musical Pilgrim Series—Oxford University Press).

Paul Mies—*Beethoven's Sketches* (Oxford University Press).

Chapter XII

ROMANTICISM IN MUSIC

A T THE beginning of the nineteenth century a definite movement towards new modes of expression made itself manifest in all the arts. This trend has been called "the romantic movement," although the implications of the term "romantic" are somewhat vague. Examination of the works of the critical writers of this period will show that romanticism as an artistic tenet was expounded in various ways. Victor Hugo called it "liberalism in literature"; Heinrich Heine found in it "the reawakening of medieval poetry"; Jean-Jacques Rousseau emphasized the emotional individualism of the movement in these words: "I am different from all men I have seen. If I am not better at least I am different."

While it is customary to think of the terms *classic* and *romantic* as antonyms, closer consideration shows that, although certain generalizations can be made concerning each mode of expression, no hard and fast line of demarcation can be drawn between them. The "classical" style is characterized by its objectivity and by its emphasis on the universal, as opposed to the specific and particular. It is marked by mastery of form, clarity of presentation, and emotional restraint. Because of its objective nature, however, classical art tends to become stylized and encumbered with set forms and conventions.

The underlying spirit of romanticism, on the other hand, is one of discontent with the artistic formulae and conventions of its more immediate past. The romantic artists have, however, in their desire to find new modes of expression, created new forms which in their universality of acceptance have in turn become classic. The romantic spirit is essentially a progressive spirit and as such has always been present in all art epochs. Stendhal remarked that "all good art was

185

romantic in its day," and numerous examples from such works as the cantatas of Bach or the string quartets of Haydn could be cited as proof. But what sets the romantic period apart is its self-consciousness, its ever-present sense of a break with the past. A romantic mode of expression was verily demanded from the artist; and literary critics insisted that it was his duty to seek out the strange and unusual, and to emphasize his own self, his own emotions, his own experiences. In artistic as well as in political thought the importance of the individual was stressed.

It is interesting to notice the emphasis placed on music in the literary discussions and in the critical essays of the period. Amidst the exaltation of personal feelings and sentiments, music is always described as "the language of the emotions." The romantic movement in literature, particularly in Germany, was to affect the progress of music in many ways. The poems of Goethe, Schiller, Heine, Eichendorff, and others prompted such composers as Schubert, Schumann, and Wolf to find musical settings for them; and Goethe's *Faust* served as an almost universal source of inspiration. In their love for the poetry of the Middle Ages, and in their interest in the great mass of German mythology and folk-lore with its elements of the fantastic and the supernatural as well as the picturesque and sentimental, such writers as Tieck, Schlegel, and the brothers Grimm were important factors in the development of the romantic opera. Composers shared with writers an enthusiasm for the works of Shakespeare. Outstanding instances are Mendelssohn's music for *A Midsummer Night's Dream* and Berlioz' symphony *Romeo and Juliet*.

The romantic movement in music also found inspiration in the works of Beethoven, and it is the group of composers immediately following him who are conventionally designated as "The Romantic Composers." The outstanding ones were Franz Schubert, Felix Mendelssohn, Robert Schumann, Hector Berlioz, Carl Maria von Weber, Frédéric Chopin, Franz Liszt, and Richard Wagner. The musical aspects of romanticism are numerous and diverse, but several features stand out clearly and may be briefly surveyed.

Although all of the romantic composers were ardent worshipers of Beethoven, the nature of their musical utterances made the sonata form seem unsuitable for their purposes. While many of them actually did compose sonatas, symphonies, and string quartets, in no instance did their mastery of these forms approach that of Beethoven. Their true significance lies in the wealth of new forms which they created: the shorter lyrical pieces for piano, the art-song, the longer programmatic orchestral forms, the romantic opera, and the music-drama. In the manner characteristic of the period, their expressions of subjective states are occasionally lacking in restraint, and in some instances verge on the sentimental or the fantastic.

"Program music," music having a stated descriptive purpose, came to the fore during this epoch, and numerous works either bore poetic titles or were accompanied by detailed "programs." Poems inspired not only songs, but entire symphonic works. In much of this descriptive music no set form was employed, and the plan of a composition was determined purely by the nature of the poetic idea inspiring it.

Numerous improvements were made in the general design and mechanism of the piano, particularly by American manufacturers. Extension of the compass, acceleration of the action, introduction of steel strings, and perfection of the sounding-board greatly increased the sonority, dynamic range, and variety of tone-color of the instrument. Great piano virtuosi appeared on the scene, who, while not abjuring sensationalism, made significant contributions to the art of piano-playing. An important result of this improvement of the piano was the endowment of the instrument with a musical self-sufficiency. The manifold possibilities of the instrument, as unfolded by virtuosi, enabled the pianist to appear publicly as a solo performer without the assistance of an orchestra. The modern "piano recital" thus came into existence. The popularity of the piano as an instrument for public performance was paralleled by its widespread adoption as a domestic musical instrument in the households of the now emerging middle class. The nature of much romantic music, particularly of the shorter piano pieces, was such as to win for it ready popular acceptance. A growth of interest in music and an elevation in the general level of musical taste were also phenomena of the period.

Improvements in the wind instruments of the orchestra, particularly those of the brass section, were followed by a keen interest in the expressive possibilities of orchestral tone-color, motivated, no doubt, by the desire to find new and effective ways of using instrumental music for descriptive and dramatic purposes. The orchestra was enlarged, new instruments were added to it, and the standards of orchestral playing were considerably raised.

It was during this period, too, that the art of orchestral conducting came to life. The new style of the symphonic and operatic works made the presence of a conductor imperative, and his true function as an interpreter of orchestral music came to be realized. Composers such as Liszt, Berlioz, and Wagner were outstanding conductors of their day; and the latter two wrote fine treatises on the art.

Musicians also found it necessary to take to the pen in defense of their new ideas. Schumann founded and edited a critical musical magazine, von Weber and Liszt wrote numerous essays, while Berlioz was a regular contributor of *feuilletons* to the Paris papers and wrote extensively about his musical experiences. The most prolific literary musician was Wagner, with no less than ten volumes of prose to his credit. All of this literary activity is a further indication of the self-consciousness which pervaded the romantic movement.

SUGGESTED READINGS

One of the best treatises on the romantic spirit in music is the chapter on "The Music of the Nineteenth Century" in Cecil Gray's *A Survey of Contemporary Music* (Oxford University Press). *The Romantic Composers* of Daniel Gregory Mason (Macmillan) contains an essay on "Romanticism in Music." French aspects of the romantic movement are treated in *La Musique aux temps romantiques* by Julien Tiersot (Alcan) and *Music and the Romantic Movement in France* by Arthur Ware Locke (Dutton). A valuable article by André Coeuroy in the *Musical Quarterly* for January, 1927, is entitled "Musical Theory of German Romantic Writers."

Chapter XIII

FRANZ SCHUBERT

DURING the time that Beethoven was the dominant figure in the musical life of Vienna, a shy and retiring individual living obscurely in poor surroundings was composing literally hundreds of works in a form upon which he was to leave as vital an impress as Beethoven had on the symphony and string quartet. This younger contemporary was Franz Schubert, and the form with which his name is indissolubly connected is the *song*.

Franz Schubert, born in a suburb of Vienna on January 31, 1797, was the son of a schoolmaster. His first lessons in music were received from members of his musically inclined family; his father taught him to play the violin, an elder brother taught him the piano, and a local choirmaster gave him vocal instruction. Like Haydn, the young Schubert had a fine soprano voice which served as a stepping-stone to further his musical education. But the lad was taken not into the choir of St. Stephen's Cathedral, but into that of the Imperial Court Chapel which, with the school associated with it, the *Konvikt,* offered excellent opportunities for his musical development. Schubert not only sang in the chapel choir, but also played violin and viola in the student orchestra. Among the works performed by the youthful instrumentalists were symphonies of Haydn, Mozart, and Beethoven; and while still a boy Schubert regarded the works of Beethoven with awe and veneration. Other studies at the school were neglected in favor of musical composition, in which Schubert seems to have received some instruction from the Imperial Kapellmeister Salieri, who many years before had given Beethoven lessons in dramatic composition.

At the behest of his father, whose opinions of a musical career were none too high, Schubert entered a normal school in order to prepare himself for a schoolteacher's post. A desire to avoid the long period of compulsory military service also may have caused him to adopt a profession for which he was so unfitted. When he had finished his period of training he was given an appointment in his father's school. This was the only regular post he ever held. But hand in hand with the drudgery of the schoolmaster's lot went a vast amount of inspired musical creation, and some of the world's greatest songs were composed during this period.

Three impetuous young men who had become enthusiastic over Schubert's compositions finally prevailed upon him to drop his dull position at the school, and to join them in their somewhat bohemian mode of life in Vienna. They also undertook to win some recognition for him by attempting to bring his compositions to the attention of members of the upper classes and of various publishers.

Schubert now became a member of a group of writers, artists, and poets who met frequently in the coffee-houses of Vienna. Among his more celebrated associates at one time or another were the dramatist Franz Grillparzer and the painter Moritz von Schwind. An influential singer, Johann Michael Vogl, was the first artist to realize the worth of Schubert's songs, and the major portion of the limited recognition which Schubert received during his lifetime may be attributed to Vogl's sympathetic rendering of them.

It was not until 1818 that a publisher undertook to print any of Schubert's works; none of the important songs appeared in print before 1821. His relations with his publishers were most unfortunate. Unlike Beethoven, he lacked a strong belief in his own artistic superiority; and priceless works were turned over by him for ridiculously small honoraria. Inasmuch as the income from the sale of his works was his principal source of funds, the poverty in which he lived may well be imagined.

The blame for the neglect of Schubert cannot be squarely placed on either the public or the publishers of his time. Unlike Mozart and Beethoven, he was not a great virtuoso who could at once command public attention. He lacked the polish and finesse of the former, and the strong, indomitable will of the latter. Nor was he fortunate enough to find a Prince Esterhazy to take him into a musical

FRANZ SCHUBERT

establishment and allow his creative gifts to flower unimpeded by pecuniary worries. The song, the medium in which Schubert excelled, was as yet confined to the salon, and no public recognition could be won through works which were then regarded as belonging to the domain of chamber music. Schubert had appeared before the Vienna public primarily as a composer of opera—a form in which his talents did not appear at their best. To make matters worse, the Viennese had become infatuated with the melodious operas of the Italian, Rossini, and the dazzling virtuosity of the violinist, Paganini. While it is true that Schubert enjoyed a small measure of popularity during his lifetime, and that the solitary concert which he gave not long before his death was well attended, he never received even a fraction of the recognition and affection that the Viennese public had lavished upon Haydn and Beethoven.

The ultimate recognition of Schubert's genius took place long after his death. The great C major Symphony was discovered by Robert Schumann in a pile of old manuscripts in 1839, eleven years after Schubert's death. The celebrated Unfinished Symphony was not unearthed until 1865. The magnificent piano transcriptions of over fifty songs, which Franz Liszt made and performed at his concerts, served to popularize Schubert's name over the entire European continent.

The untimely death of Schubert at the age of thirty-one constituted a tragedy which in its artistic implications can be likened only to that of Mozart, with whose life that of Schubert exhibits many parallelisms. Like Mozart's, the brevity of Schubert's career is no index of his creative accomplishment. Within the comparatively short period in which he was engaged in composition, he produced about 650 songs, ten symphonies, and fifteen string quartets, in addition to many other pieces of chamber music and a great quantity of music for piano, including sonatas and characteristic shorter pieces such as the *Impromptus, Moments musicaux,* marches, and many works for piano duet. He also wrote two operas, some dramatic music, and much sacred music, including six masses. The sum total of his works, over eleven hundred, comprises what is beyond doubt one of the most extraordinary records of musical fertility.

It was Schubert's habit to spend every morning in composition; it is said that he slept with his glasses on so that he might set to work without delay upon arising.[1] His method of composition was the exact opposite of Beethoven's; all of Schubert's works were conceived wholly without effort, and with a spontaneity that is often astounding. Many of his famous masterpieces were dashed off at great speed; as many as six songs were composed in one morning. But hand in hand with this seemingly limitless flow of music there went a lack of self-criticism, a lack of concentration and sustained development, which resulted in prolixity and diffuseness, particularly in the instrumental compositions. What was a priceless virtue in the shorter works, such as the songs and the *impromptus* for piano, became almost a fault in works calling for more careful organization of material and attention to detail.

While his instrumental works, particularly the Unfinished Symphony, the String Quartet in D minor (*Death and the Maiden*), and the String Quintet in C major, Opus 163, show Schubert to be a worthy successor to Beethoven, he is most important in the field of the song (German: *Lied*)—a form which he was the first to bring to the fore. As has been shown to be true in the case of other great creative artists, Schubert was preceded by many lesser composers in this form, notably the composers of *Singspiele*—plays of a popular nature in which dialogue was interspersed with songs, duets, and so forth, which in their simplicity and unaffectedness constituted a reaction to the stiff formalisms of the opera of the period.

The Art-Song

The *art-song,* to use a term that distinguishes the form now being discussed from the *folk song,* is a musical setting of a poem for voice and some accompanying instrument. Some modern composers have used prose texts. The accompanying instrument is almost invariably the piano, sometimes aided by another instrument such as the viola or the clarinet. Songs will occasionally be written for voice and orchestra or they may, in rare instances, be entirely unaccompanied.

Inasmuch as a song is a musician's interpretation of a poem, the form is a combination of the work of two creative artists, the poet and the composer. It is a fusion of two media of communication, rhythmic speech and music, two auditory phenomena that readily

[1] Karl Kobald—*Franz Schubert and His Times,* page 78.

combine to form a vivid and effective means of expression. So strong is this power of combination that inspired musical settings associate themselves indissolubly with their poems and become part of their very being. For example, a knowledge of Schubert's setting of *Der Erlkönig* of Goethe alters one's reading of the poem for all time. As with all vocal forms, the listener's enjoyment of the song in its totality depends in large measure on his knowledge of its text. Most of the world's great songs have been written by German composers, who have employed poems either written in or translated into their own tongue. The translation of these poems into English verse, while feasible, is difficult to bring about without distortion of the subtler shades of meaning of the poem, and resultant destruction of the unity of text and music. *Traduttori—traditori* (Translators are traitors). A study of the German language holds no greater reward than the pleasure to be derived from a knowledge of its extensive wealth of lyric poetry as so happily revealed and interpreted by the great German masters of song.

Considered structurally, songs are usually divided into three types. The first, the *strophic* type, is a song in which each of the various stanzas of the poem has received an identical setting. A *modified strophic* song is one in which most of the stanzas have identical settings, while one or two, because of the demands of their text, have received a different treatment. The third type is always described by the untranslatable German adjective *durchkomponiert* (approximate translation—"composed throughout"). The *durchkomponiert* song follows no rigid formal pattern; its design and plan are dictated entirely by the poem. In its comparative freedom from formal considerations the *durchkomponiert* type offers excellent possibilities for expressive combination of poetry and music, and many of the world's great songs fall into this category.

Schubert's Songs

Schubert was primarily a creator of melodies, tunes capable of expressing all shades of emotion and yet retaining a simplicity and a directness of utterance which frequently recall the naturalness of folk song. The most distinctive feature of Schubert's vocal writing is the manner in which he has reconciled the formal demands of his melodies with the rhetorical implications of his poems. There are hundreds of beautiful melodies in the songs of Schubert; but despite their perfection of outline, there are practically no errors in accentuation. With this lyrical gift there was coupled a wide knowledge of the expressive possibilities of the human voice. All of Schubert's songs are eminently singable.

But Schubert does not always utilize pure melody as a means of setting poetry. Declamation is frequently employed, and in a manner which is thoroughly realistic. Magnificent examples of the dramatic effectiveness with which Schubert introduces declamation are to be found in such songs as *Gretchen am Spinnrade,* and *Der Erlkönig.*

The piano accompaniment of the Schubert songs may either provide a simple rhythmic and harmonic support, create a mood, or describe or portray persons, things, or situations mentioned in the poem. Or, by the use of harmonic coloring, it may throw words or phrases into high relief. It was Schubert who raised the piano accompaniment to a position of importance; and it was he who first endowed it with a measure of self-sufficiency, occasionally laying greater emphasis on it than on the voice. In the creation of delineative piano figures Schubert's genius seems inexhaustible, and the range of subjects for which he found musical representation is enormous. The following examples chosen from among the better-known songs will serve to demonstrate this phase of Schubert's art.

The mood of *Heidenröslein* (Little Hedge Rose), a setting of one of Goethe's lyric poems, is created by this innocent little figure which makes its appearance between the verses:

Ex. 1

The accompaniment of the celebrated *Ständchen* (Serenade) is merely the reproduction of the sounds of a guitar:

Ex. 2

Die Forelle (The Trout) has a piano accompaniment which describes the trout's darting to and fro in the brook:

Ex. 3

Die Post (The Post), from a cycle of twenty-four songs entitled *Die Winterreise* (The Winter's Journey), possesses an introduction that portrays the galloping of the horses drawing the post-coach and reproduces the notes of the postillion's horn:

Ex. 4

The opening measures of *Der Leiermann* (The Hurdy-Gurdy Man), the concluding song of the *Winterreise* cycle, not only reproduce the sounds of the hand-organ, but also suggest the bleakness of winter:

Ex. 5

Beethoven had shown the expressive possibilities of modulation[1] in his larger instrumental works. Schubert, who was well-acquainted with Beethoven's compositions, makes persistent use of modulation as a means of differentiating the various sections of the poem, or of emphasizing emotional crises. In this respect his style is an anticipation of that of Richard Wagner. Vivid contrasts of major and minor are also frequent. That many of Schubert's songs have been called "miniature dramas" is due in large measure to his ability to create continued dramatic interest through utilizing the attention-sustaining potentialities of skilful modulation.

Of the many great Schubert songs, two have been selected for closer examination here as typical illustrations of his art: *Gretchen am Spinnrade* and *Der Erlkönig*.

"GRETCHEN AM SPINNRADE"

The text of *Gretchen am Spinnrade* (Gretchen at the Spinning-Wheel) is an excerpt from Part I of Goethe's *Faust*. The rejuvenated Faust has fallen deeply in love with Gretchen, a simple village maiden. Her bewilderment at being the object of the affections of a man of his type is expressed as she sits alone in her room and spins. Her anxiety finds utterance in the first two lines: *"Meine Ruh' ist hin, Mein Herz ist schwer"* (My peace is gone, My heart is heavy). The Schubert setting of these lines accentuates the four important words, *Ruh', hin, Herz, schwer,* by making them much longer than the others and placing them on the strong beat of the measure; and the word *Herz* is made doubly prominent by elevation in pitch:

Ex. 6

Mei-ne   Ruh'____   ist   hin, ___   mein   Herz __   ist   schwer;

The piano accompaniment, which, with the exception of one momentary halt, continues throughout the song, is based on an undulating figure which portrays the spinning-wheel, and which, by means of tension-creating harmonic alterations typical of Schubert's style, reflects the mental state of Gretchen:

[1] See page 38.

Ex. 7

Gretchen commences to describe her beloved: *"Sein hoher Gang, Sein' edle Gestalt"* (His high bearing, His noble appearance). Her recital of his attributes becomes increasingly ecstatic and culminates in *"Und ach, sein Kuss!"* (And ah, his kiss!). The setting of these four words is an example *par excellence* of Schubert's art. The voice part suddenly breaks into free declamation. *Sein Kuss* is thrown into high relief by a preceding pause, by elevating it in pitch, by suddenly terminating the restless figures of the piano accompaniment, and by prolonging the word *Kuss* and underscoring it with a strikingly dissonant chord:

Ex. 8

From this point on there is a gradual decrease in the intensity of Gretchen's utterance. Schubert has taken the liberty of repeating the first two lines at the conclusion of his setting, with excellent dramatic effect. The facts concerning the composition of the song are almost incredible: Schubert wrote it in October, 1814, in one afternoon; he was then a youth of only seventeen.

"DER ERLKÖNIG"

Der Erlkönig (The Erl King), composed in 1815, is Schubert's most famous song. Its text is also a poem of Goethe, the title of which is the result of an incorrect translation from the Danish. The correct

German word should have been *Elfenkönig* (Elf King). The poem
tells of a father who rides through the night clutching his sick son
to his bosom. The wild gallop is vividly represented by a rain of repeated notes which constitute an accompaniment so energetic and so
taxing that few pianists are capable of playing it adequately:

Ex. 9

With the exception of the first and last verses, which are in the third
person, the poem consists of a series of utterances by three characters
—father, son, and Erl king. A faithful setting of the poem demands,
therefore, that these individuals be clearly differentiated despite the
fact that only one voice is employed. Schubert has solved the difficulty
in masterly fashion by continual change of key, by change in the
tempo of recitation, and by change in the style of vocal writing.
When, for example, the Erl king enticingly invites the child to his
realm, the key changes to the bright B-flat major, and the Erl king
sings this melodic passage:

Ex. 10

The anguished cries of the terror-stricken child are written in a declamatory manner, and are intensified in the piano by chords which
produce piercing dissonances, as, for example, when the E-flat of
Vater impinges against the D of the accompaniment:

Ex. 11

Der Erlkönig is a striking instance of the manner in which Schubert
employs modulation as an intensifying medium. After each successive alluring promise of the Erl king, the child cries to its father.
Each of these cries is made more intense than the preceding one
through being pitched in a higher key. Schubert writes the gripping
last lines—*"In seinen Armen das Kind war tot"* (In his arms the child
was dead)—in pure declamation, with a dramatic pause before the
last two words.

SUGGESTED READINGS

Sir George Grove, the first editor of the *Dictionary of Music and Musicians,*
which bears his name, wrote for it a compendious article on Schubert, which
is of the dimensions of a book. An excellent one-volume treatise on Schubert
and the Vienna of his day is Karl Kobald's *Franz Schubert and His Times*
(Knopf). Another work of the same type is Newman Flower's *Franz Schubert,
the Man and His Circle* (Stokes). The authentic biography is the German
treatise of Otto Eric Deutsch—*Franz Schubert, die Dokumente seines Lebens
und Schaffens* (Müller). The *Musical Quarterly* for October, 1928, is a Schubert
number and contains many valuable articles.

Detailed studies of individual works are to be found in Paul Mies' *Schubert,
der Meister des Liedes* (Hesse), in Willi Kahl's article *Schubert* in *Cobbett's
Cyclopedic Survey of Chamber Music,* and in Volume I of Sir Donald F. Tovey's
Essays in Musical Analysis (Oxford University Press).

Chapter XIV

CARL MARIA VON WEBER

CARL Maria von Weber has often been called the father of German opera. Like other musical paternities, the extent of this fatherhood is somewhat exaggerated, for the German people already possessed two great operas in their own tongue—Mozart's *Die Zauberflöte* and Beethoven's *Fidelio*. But while the language of these works was German, their libretti and the many Italian conventions to be found in them prevented their having popular appeal. The roots of von Weber's art are to be found more in the German *Singspiel*[1] with its emphasis on folk life. In raising this form to a position of dignity, von Weber displaced the empty and shallow Italian opera and brought a truly indigenous German opera into being. Rooted in the people, in their folk-lore and their folk music, the "romantic opera" quickly established itself as a significant art form. In its later perfection at the hands of von Weber's most ardent disciple, Richard Wagner, it became one of the most important manifestations in the history of music.

Born December 18, 1786, at Eutin, near Lübeck, von Weber spent the first years of his life in the atmosphere of the theater. His father, a former soldier, court official, and musician, now turned actor, had organized the several members of his family into a theatrical troupe which wandered through Germany performing in the principal towns. Von Weber received his first musical instruction from his father and an older stepbrother; but as had been the case with both Haydn and Schubert, possession of a fine voice earned him a place in an institution, in this instance, the choirboys' school at Salzburg. Here he re-

[1] See page 193.

ceived thorough training at the hands of Michael Haydn, a younger
brother of the more famous Joseph.   In 1803 he journeyed to Vienna
and placed himself under the tutelage of the celebrated Abbé Vogler.[1]
Vogler was an ardent student of folk music and directed von Weber's
interest to it, an interest that was to have magnificent results.

Von Weber's active musical career commenced when he was nineteen years old; on Vogler's recommendation, he was given the post
of opera conductor in the theater at Breslau.   Operatic conducting
was von Weber's principal activity throughout his lifetime, with the
exception of an interval of six and a half years.   Part of this time was
spent as private secretary in the service of Duke Ludwig of Württem-
berg at his dissolute court at Stuttgart, and the rest in travel and
concert appearances as a piano virtuoso.   From 1813 to 1816 he directed operas in Prague, and from 1817 till his untimely death in 1826
he was Kapellmeister in charge of German opera at Dresden.   As an
operatic conductor, von Weber aroused antagonism in his colleagues
because of his painstaking method of rehearsal and the meticulous
care which he bestowed upon every aspect of an operatic presentation,
including acting, costuming, and stage-setting as well as music.   He
was one of the first orchestral conductors to use a baton.

All of von Weber's great zeal as an operatic conductor was dedicated
to one cause—the furtherance of German opera.   Most of the important opera houses of the period were parts of the musical establishments of various royal houses, and the predominating taste of the
sovereigns who dictated the destinies of these opera houses was
Italian.   Italian musicians were engaged to direct them and Italian
operas were given preference.   The two great German operas already
in existence, *Die Zauberflöte* and *Fidelio,* were performed in-
frequently if at all.   The German language was considered vulgar,
and regular performances in the native tongue were usually given only
in the smaller popular theaters.   The situation which existed at the
Saxon capital, Dresden, during von Weber's nine years of service there
was thoroughly typical of the times.   The King of Saxony had two
Kapellmeisters in his employ, the Italian Morlacchi and the German
von Weber.   All the honors and royal approbation were bestowed
upon the now-forgotten Italian.   Despite the fact that von Weber had

---

[1] The Abt Vogler of Browning's poem.

CARL MARIA VON WEBER

organized and conducted a splendid German opera company, his efforts were not appreciated, and he and the art for which he stood were almost completely ignored by the Royal House. The situation at Berlin paralleled that at Dresden, and in all of his relations with the Prussian king, von Weber, as the representative of German opera, met with a condescension and an apathy that bordered on insult.

Von Weber was catapulted into fame when his opera *Der Freischütz* was given in Berlin on June 18, 1821. The applause at the first performance, which was unattended by the Prussian Court, was tumultuous; so great was the enthusiasm of the audience that the overture and one of the choruses had to be repeated. No other opera in the history of the German theater had ever met with such ready acceptance and with such popular demonstrations of approval. Within eighteen months there were fifty performances of the work in Berlin alone. The fame of the work spread quickly, and it was not long before it was heard not only on all the German stages, but in foreign capitals as well. A performance in English took place in New York as early as 1825. *Der Freischütz* was followed by *Euryanthe,* written for Vienna, and *Oberon,* written for London; but neither of these works, despite many features of merit, achieved the artistic level of their forerunner. The fame of von Weber rests almost entirely on his one masterpiece; of the two later operas only the brilliant overtures are regularly performed today. An earlier work for piano, *Invitation to the Dance,* was salvaged from the fragments of an uncompleted opera and dedicated by von Weber to his wife. An orchestration of the work, frequently heard today, was made by Hector Berlioz in 1841 to be inserted as ballet music in the performances of *Der Freischütz* in Paris. Wholesale mangling of operas was not infrequent at that time, and garbled versions of works often appeared. At earlier Paris performances of *Der Freischütz* various liberties had been taken with the text, and the title of the work had been changed to *Robin des Bois.*

Like Mozart's and Schubert's, von Weber's life was tragically brief. While his music won him tremendous popular acclaim, the indifference of the ruling houses of Germany to one of the finest flowerings of their native art all but broke von Weber's heart. Continued exasperation slowly wore him down; and in a desire to provide for his wife and children he accepted an offer to compose *Oberon* for Eng-land, and to make the long and arduous journey to London to conduct the première of the work.   The financial results of this London ven-ture were disappointing, however, and von Weber's bitter sense of failure served further to undermine his already fragile constitution. He died of consumption in London on June 5, 1826, and was buried there.   Eighteen years later his body was brought back to Germany, largely as a result of the efforts of Richard Wagner.

The Romantic Opera

Typical texts of romantic operas are based on medieval epics, on folk-lore, especially on legends dealing with supernatural manifesta-tions, or on exotic subjects distantly removed in time or place.   But no matter how fantastic the plot or how extreme the various elements of the supernatural or marvelous, the entire action is treated seriously. Hand in hand with this imaginative aspect there goes an effort to achieve realism, particularly in the handling of scenes dealing with folk life.   Local incidents and local customs receive detailed and sym-pathetic treatment from which, however, sentimentality is seldom absent.   In its representation of native folk life and customs the ro-mantic opera serves to awaken nationalistic feelings, and it is inter-esting to note that the two greatest composers of romantic operas, von Weber and Wagner, were both ardent nationalists.

Der Freischütz: the Text

As an example of the text of a romantic opera, the libretto of *Der Freischütz,* with its emphasis on folk customs and its depiction of supernatural phenomena, may be briefly summarized here.   It was written by Friedrich Kind and is based on a tale appearing in Apel and Laun's *Gespensterbuch* (Ghost Book).   The title, *Der Freischütz,* means "the free-shooter," one who shoots with magic bullets.

The action takes place in Bohemia shortly after the end of the Thirty Years' War (ca. 1648).

Act I. A clearing in the forest.

The peasants have assembled for a shooting contest.   Max, a young hunts-man, is unsuccessful in his display of marksmanship.   He aspires to the hand of Agathe, daughter of the chief forester; but in order to become the chief forester's son-in-law, he must demonstrate publicly his skill with the rifle. In desperation, Max falls easy prey to the designing Caspar, a grizzly huntsman in league with the Evil One, Samiel. Max agrees to meet Caspar at midnight in the haunted *Wolf's Glen* to assist in the casting of magic bullets which, thanks to the power of Samiel, never fail to hit their mark.

Act II, Scene 1.   A room in the Chief Forester's house.

Agathe, distressed by various unlucky omens, awaits Max. She prays to Heaven to protect him. Max arrives and is joyfully hailed by Agathe. She tells him of the ominous portents. He refuses to heed her warning and rushes off to the Wolf's Glen.

Scene 2.   The Wolf's Glen.

Caspar converses with the invisible Samiel to whom he has forfeited his life in exchange for magic bullets. He proposes to Samiel that Max be accepted as a substitute. Max arrives on the scene and the two huntsmen proceed to cast the magic bullets. Samiel has allowed them seven. Six will strike their mark; the seventh will go as Samiel directs. During the casting of the bullets all kinds of supernatural manifestations occur in the haunted glen. Wild boars and wheels of fire rush across the stage, a terrible storm arises, dogs howl, a ghost-like hunting party is heard, owls hoot, trees fall down, and so forth.

Act III, Scene 1.   The forest.

The young huntsmen of the vicinity sing lustily of the joys of forest life. Max has already shot away all but one of his quota of magic bullets and now has only one left for the contest.

Scene 2.   The Chief Forester's house.

Agathe, disturbed by bad dreams, utters a fervent prayer that all will go well with Max. The maidens of the village, following local custom, bring Agathe her bridal wreath; but when it is unwrapped it turns out to be a funeral wreath. Greatly perturbed by this additional omen of misfortune, Agathe and the maidens depart for the shooting contest.

Scene 3.   A clearing in the forest.

The populace has assembled for the shooting contest which is to take place in the presence of their Prince. Max takes aim at a pigeon flying overhead and fires. Agathe with a shriek sinks unconscious to the ground, and Caspar, who has been perched in a tree, falls dead. The bullet which Max had fired was the seventh, Samiel's. Samiel had intended it for Agathe; but she was beyond his power, and so he had claimed Caspar as forfeit. General consternation ensues. Agathe is revived. Max confesses that he has used magic bullets. The Prince orders him to be banished; but a kindly and wise old hermit appears and intercedes for him. Max is pardoned and told that after a trial year of service as a forester, he may marry Agathe. There is general rejoicing and thanks to God for the defeat of the forces of evil.

Der Freischütz: the Music

The music that von Weber created for this highly imaginative libretto cloaks it with vividness and credibility. The vocal writing, particularly in the choruses, is distinctly folk-like in character, so that the listener readily imagines that he is hearing villagers singing actual folk songs. All of the melodies of *Der Freischütz,* however, are original; it was von Weber's study of folk music which enabled him successfully to simulate its style. There is no better proof of the inherently folk-like nature of several of the choruses of this opera than the fact that they immediately became very popular and were even sung on the streets by students. So well known are they in Germany today that they may be said actually to have become folk music; and some have found their way, with new texts, into English and American hymnals.

The most striking feature of *Der Freischütz* is the manner in which the orchestra is employed. Von Weber was one of the first operatic composers to utilize fully the dramatic potentialities of many of the orchestral timbres. He himself stated in a letter to a young musician that "the composer must bring out the essential character of his work by means of tone-colors." [1] Colorful use is made of the horns in the numerous scenes dealing with life in the forest. The low tones of the clarinet, coupled with tremolando and pizzicato effects in the lower strings, are used to represent Samiel and the forces of evil. The most original use of the orchestra is to be found in the Wolf's Glen scene. The astonishingly realistic orchestral effects introduced by von Weber in this gruesome episode have become well known through widespread imitation, but for their time they were quite revolutionary. It must be borne in mind that *Der Freischütz* was completed in 1820, and that it antedated Beethoven's Ninth Symphony by three years. In no previous opera had the orchestra played so important a part in the action of the play, and von Weber's vivid demonstration of its dramatic potentialities was an important influence in the development of the orchestral technique of composers such as Hector Berlioz and Richard Wagner.

[1] Julius Kapp—*Carl Maria von Weber,* page 226.

OVERTURE TO "DER FREISCHÜTZ"

The well-known overture to *Der Freischütz,* a dramatic synthesis of the opera, is based on thematic material heard in it. Using the sonata form, von Weber portrays in the overture the place of the action and the conflict of the opposing forces of good and evil. The influence of the dramatic plan of the Beethoven overtures is obvious. In his capacity as opera conductor, von Weber had broken many lances for Beethoven's *Fidelio.*

After a portentous introduction, the use of horns indicates that the action takes place in the forest:

Ex. 1

Tremolos in the strings, the ominous low notes of the clarinet, and the dull thuds of the kettledrums and double basses, pizzicato, are associated in the opera with the Evil One, Samiel. The episode is an outstanding example of von Weber's coloristic use of the orchestra:

Ex. 2

The tempo now becomes fast, and the clarinets, over an agitated accompaniment in the strings, give out another theme associated with the forces of evil which are enveloping Max:

Ex. 3

A tempestuous outburst of the orchestra is drawn from the music accompanying the violent storm which terminates the scene in the Wolf's Glen (Act II):

Ex. 4

The transition to the second group is accompanied by a moving clarinet solo, an instrumental version of Max's cry of despair:

Ex. 5

The second group begins with the celebrated melody which is identified with Max's redeemer, Agathe:

Ex. 6

The development, a dramatic working-out of Examples 3 and 4, is brought to a hushed end by Example 6. Von Weber, always willing to forsake convention for dramatic expediency, does not repeat the exposition literally. The first group, representing the forces of evil, is heard again, but instead of repeating the second group, von Weber first interposes a violent climax in which the Samiel thuds (Example 2) reappear. Three tense pauses are then followed by the repetition of Example 6 in the bright key of C major. The forces of good have been victorious. The close of the overture is drawn from the jubilant finale of the opera.

SUGGESTED READINGS

The best English discussion of von Weber is Philipp Spitta's article in Grove's *Dictionary of Music and Musicians*. A good general discussion of von Weber's life and works is the German treatise of Julius Kapp, *Carl Maria von Weber* (Deutsche Verlags-Anstalt). Informative essays on the three famous overtures are to be found in *Philip Hale's Boston Symphony Programme Notes*, edited by

John N. Burk (Doubleday, Doran).   There is a detailed study of *Der Frei-*
schütz in Ernest Newman's *Stories of the Great Operas* (Garden City Publishing Company).   The literary aspect of von Weber's activity is summed up in
the *Sämtliche Schriften von Carl Maria von Weber* (Breitkopf und Härtel).

Chapter XV

FELIX MENDELSSOHN

THE REPUTATION that Felix Mendelssohn enjoys today rests on a few works, imperishable masterpieces which could not have been written by any other composer. The nature of Mendelssohn's compositions combined with his own personal charm and refinement caused him to be one of the most popular musicians of his day, and made him the object of almost universal praise and adulation. That this uncritical excess of enthusiasm should be followed by a wave of depreciation was to be expected. Today, however, the status of Mendelssohn has attained a fair degree of equilibrium, and the unique, even if circumscribed, nature of his talents is generally conceded.

Felix Mendelssohn, born at Hamburg on February 3, 1809, was the son of a wealthy banker and the grandson of a celebrated philosopher. The family moved to Berlin when he was three years old and he grew up there in an atmosphere of culture and refinement. His education, in which music was not given undue emphasis, was entrusted to numerous private tutors. He appeared as pianist in his tenth year, and two years later he commenced active composition under the tutelage of Carl Zelter. All his youthful works were performed before the gatherings of distinguished men and women who frequented the Mendelssohn household. One of his most celebrated compositions, the overture to Shakespeare's *Midsummer Night's Dream,* was written in 1826, when he was only seventeen years old. In 1829 Mendelssohn revived and directed the St. Matthew Passion of Bach, the first performance of the work since the death of the composer in 1750. He visited England in the same year, and at his appearances as a pianist and as conductor of his own works he laid the foundation for his great popularity in that country. A visit to Scotland led him to compose the *Scotch* Symphony and the overture *Fingal's Cave.* The trip to England was followed by extensive travel on the Continent.

His first important post was that of music director of the Rhine town of Düsseldorf; but after two years he resigned to be conductor of the famous Gewandhaus Orchestra at Leipzig. In 1843 he added to his duties the post of director of the newly established Leipzig Conservatory. Despite all his official obligations, the round of receptions, and his prolific activity in composition, he managed to find time to participate in the affairs of the school. In 1846 he completed his great oratorio *Elijah,* which had its first performance in Birmingham, England, in the same year. So great was the composer's popularity there that four choruses and four arias were encored. But the strain of ceaseless public appearances had undermined his health. The sudden death of his beloved sister Fanny in 1847 was the final blow, and he himself passed away in November of the same year at the age of thirty-eight.

The atmosphere in which Mendelssohn had been brought up, the contacts which the wealth and social position of his family permitted him to make, and his wide travels all helped to make him a cultured, polished gentleman capable of moving in the highest levels of society with ease. He was, for example, a favorite of Queen Victoria and Prince Albert. He was fastidious in every respect, and almost made a fetish of gentility and refinement. He possessed more than the usual accomplishments, for in addition to his musical talents, he was a fluent writer of letters, a fine sketcher, an energetic sportsman. A brilliant conversationalist, he was endowed with much personal charm and was always the center of any gathering.

Mendelssohn's Style

While these personal traits may have made Mendelssohn a thoroughly desirable participant in a soirée, they also left an indelible stamp on his music, which is equally polished, equally refined, and correct almost to a fault. The music of Mendelssohn, like the voice of its creator in the drawing room, is always suave, gracious, and well-mannered. It never becomes intense or boisterous, and anything that might offend the more fastidious is absent from it.

Mendelssohn was the most conservative of the romantic composers.

FELIX MENDELSSOHN

He adhered to classical forms, although he cloaked them with fanciful titles, and all of his works exhibit a perfection of formal outline
which puts them almost in the class of those of Mozart. But the listener often feels that this formal perfection has been achieved a bit
too self-consciously. Mendelssohn's melodies, which he created with
facility, seldom strike a note of intensity or pathos. Many are somewhat saccharine, and possess an almost cloying sentimentality.
Rhythmic and harmonic monotony is often found in his works, particularly in the shorter piano pieces, the *Songs without Words*; yet
their charm cannot be denied.

The most praiseworthy features of Mendelssohn's art are the skilful-
ness of his orchestration and the delicacy of his scherzos. Mendelssohn handled the orchestra in a thoroughly original manner and drew
from it tonal effects which were truly romantic. In his symphonic
works he aimed more for clarity and contrast than sonority or brilliance. The fairy-like quality of a work such as the overture to
A Midsummer Night's Dream remains unrivalled; the colorful scoring of the *Fingal's Cave* overture even elicited praise from Wagner.

The Mendelssohn scherzos are wholly unlike those of any other
composer. They are light-footed, elfin, playfully humorous pieces.
Whether written for piano, string quartet, or orchestra, they possess a
transparency of texture and a lucidity of statement in which Mendelssohn has never been surpassed.

Two works which best typify the unique idiom of Mendelssohn are
the overture and incidental music to *A Midsummer Night's Dream*
and the overture *Fingal's Cave*. Both are representative of the romantic trend towards the use of descriptive titles to indicate the aim
or the content of a composition.

The Concert Overture

The overtures *A Midsummer Night's Dream* and *Fingal's Cave* are
not overtures in the true sense at all, for neither was conceived as a
preliminary to a drama. The former work was designed for the concert hall and was not linked to Shakespeare's play until seventeen
years later. In his use of the term overture Mendelssohn is responsible for a new designation—*concert overture*. Additional confusion
has been created by the practice of calling fantasias on popular mel-

odies, overtures—for example, Brahms' overture *The Academic Festival*, Tchaikovsky's overture *1812*, Rimsky-Korsakoff's overture *The Russian Easter*.

MUSIC FOR SHAKESPEARE'S "A MIDSUMMER NIGHT'S DREAM"

As has been previously stated, the overture to Shakespeare's *Midsummer Night's Dream* was composed in 1826. In 1843 King Frederick William of Prussia commissioned Mendelssohn to write incidental music for the play. Of the twelve numbers which were composed for this purpose, three are played on concert programs in conjunction with the overture—the *Scherzo,* the *Nocturne,* and the *Wedding March.*

Of the content of the overture, Mendelssohn himself has written: [1] "It follows the play closely, however, so that it may perhaps be very proper to indicate the outstanding situations of the drama in order that the audience may have Shakespeare in mind or form an idea of the piece. I think it should be enough to point out that the fairy rulers, Oberon and Titania, appear throughout the play with all their people, now here, now there; and thereafterwards come in, first a Duke Theseus of Athens, who goes hunting in the forest with his bride; then two pairs of lovers, who lose and find one another again; then a troop of rude clumsy journeymen, playing their boorish jokes; and at last the elves again, making fun of everyone—these are the elements from which the play is put together. At the end, after everything has been satisfactorily settled and the principal players have joyfully left the stage, the elves follow them, bless the house and disappear with the dawn. So the play ends and my overture too."

The overture, which is in sonata form, begins with four prolonged wood-wind chords:

Ex. 1

[1] *The Musical Quarterly,* April, 1933, page 184, quoted by Georg Kinsky from v. Hase— Breitkopf und Härtel: *Gedenkschrift und Arbeitsbericht II.*

They are followed by a nimble pianissimo passage for violins divided into three, later four, parts. The mischievous nature of this episode identifies it with the elves:

Ex. 2

·It is rudely interrupted by the fortissimo entrance of the full orchestra with this vigorous tune:

Ex. 3

In the course of a forte statement of Example 1, the bray of the "translated" Bottom is imitated by the tuba, which takes the place of the now obsolete ophicleide for which Mendelssohn scored:

Ex. 4

The second group commences with a theme associated with the young lovers and given out by the clarinet:

Ex. 5

This is immediately followed by another theme of the same type, which, according to Adolph Marx, a friend of the composer, depicts the wanderings of the lovers:

Ex. 6

A boisterous episode which follows is later employed for the "bergo-

mask" dance, which is performed after the presentation of the interlude by "the hard-handed men, that work in Athens here" (Act V):

Ex. 7

The call of hunting horns brings the exposition to a close.

The development, based almost entirely on Example 2, is a masterpiece of orchestral coloring. As the strings continually toy with the
theme, all manner of delicate figures are tossed off by the wood-winds.
A series of loud blares from the horns reminds us that the lovers are
lost in the forest. The transition to the recapitulation is effected by
the chords which were heard at the outset (Example 1). The coda
commences with Example 2, but after a few wood-wind chords gives
way to this beautiful transformation of Example 3, played at a slower
tempo by the violins over sustained wood-wind chords:

Ex. 8

The melody of Example 8 appears at the very end of the incidental
music for the drama, where it is played by the orchestra as Oberon
says:

> , With this field-dew consecrate,
> Every fairy take his gate;
> And each several chamber bless,
> Through this palace, with sweet peace:
> Ever shall in safety rest,
> And the owner of it blest.

The work closes with the same wood-wind chords with which it
opened. Mendelssohn's overture ranks as one of the finest musical
interpretations of Shakespeare among the large number of works inspired by that master's plays.

The celebrated *Scherzo,* entr'acte between Acts I and II, is an
Allegro vivace in sonata form. Wood-winds give out the weightless
first theme:

Ex. 9

The second group begins with a playful subject assigned to all the strings except the double basses, and accompanied by crisp chords in the wood-winds:

Ex. 10

The development devotes itself to delicate manipulation of Example 9. The coda contains a celebrated solo for the flute. The entire movement is a striking example of the delicacy with which Mendelssohn could write for orchestra.

The *Nocturne* serves as an entr'acte between Acts III and IV. The forest and the two pairs of lovers who lie asleep in it are portrayed by a solo horn:

Ex. 11

The festive *Wedding March,* played after Act IV, is one of the least typical and at the same time, needless to say, the most frequently performed of all of Mendelssohn's compositions.

SUGGESTED READINGS

The most recent biography of Mendelssohn is by Schima Kaufman (Crowell). The lengthy article "Mendelssohn" in *Grove's Dictionary of Music and Musicians* is very complete. *The Romantic Composers* of Daniel Gregory Mason (Macmillan) contains an excellent critical study. There are many editions of Mendelssohn's letters.

Chapter XVI

ROBERT SCHUMANN

R OBERT Schumann, one of the great leaders of the Romantic
Movement, was born on June 8, 1810, in Zwickau, a town in
Saxony about forty miles from Leipzig. His father was a bookseller
and publisher, and the boy grew up in an atmosphere of culture. As
a youth Schumann not only played the piano and composed, but also
showed decided literary propensities. An important influence on him
at this time was the extravagantly romantic writer, Jean Paul Richter.
Schumann read his works with avidity, and in his enthusiasm compared Richter to Bach. In 1828 Schumann commenced the study of
law at Leipzig, continuing later at Heidelberg; but his interest in
music outweighed all other considerations, and he finally abandoned
law to make himself a piano virtuoso. Returning to Leipzig in 1830,
he commenced active study under the pedagogue Friedrich Wieck.[1]
Typical romantic impatience caused him to experiment with an ap-
paratus designed to develop strength in the fingers, and thus to accelerate technical mastery. Unfortunately the device was too efficient
and permanently lamed the second finger of his right hand.

The career of a virtuoso being closed to him, Schumann turned to
composition, and for a time was the pupil of a local Kapellmeister,
Heinrich Dorn. His literary tendencies remained strong, however,
and in 1834, when still a young man of twenty-four, he associated himself with a group of Leipzig musicians and writers in the publication of
a critical journal, the *Neue Zeitschrift für Musik*. Shortly after the
magazine was founded, Schumann became its editor and contributed

---

[1] Wieck ran a small circulating library in Leipzig. In 1828 a boy of fifteen, whose enthusiasm for music had been awakened by hearing a Beethoven symphony, decided to become
a musician himself and borrowed a manual of harmony from Wieck's library. His name was
Richard Wagner.

many excellent and discerning articles to it. In his characteristically whimsical manner Schumann made the magazine an organ of expression for an imaginary league, the *Davidsbund* (the League of David, that is, the opponents of Philistinism). He also signed many of his articles with the pseudonyms *Florestan, Eusebius,* or *Raro,* each name typifying a different aspect of his own personality. *Florestan* represented to Schumann the fiery and impetuous part of his nature; *Eusebius,* the gentle and meditative; while the more logical *Raro* strove to reconcile these contrary viewpoints. These pseudonyms were used for musical as well as literary works.

For four years Schumann conducted an ardent courtship of Wieck's daughter and pupil, Clara. Wieck objected to the match because he saw in it the end of the virtuoso career that he had planned for Clara. Schumann finally took the matter before a court of law; Wieck was forced to consent, and the marriage took place in 1840. In his newly found happiness Schumann devoted himself assiduously to composition, and the first year of his marriage was characterized by the writing of a large number of songs. The Schumanns, in their mutual devotion, were an artistic couple comparable to the Brownings. In addition to Clara, an important influence on Schumann during this period at Leipzig was Felix Mendelssohn, who took a lively and sympathetic interest in Schumann's compositions.

For a short time Schumann was on the faculty of the Leipzig Conservatory; but the peculiar nature of his personality prevented his having any success as a teacher. After some years of residence in Dresden (1844–1850) he accepted an invitation to become music director at the Rhine town of Düsseldorf. Temperamentally unfitted for conducting, however, and suffering from mental disturbances, Schumann failed to meet the expectations which his fame as a composer had engendered, and after much unpleasantness, he withdrew in 1853. Shortly before leaving Düsseldorf he was visited by the twenty-year-old and as yet unknown Johannes Brahms. In his enthusiasm for Brahms' compositions, Schumann wrote a prophetic essay entitled *"Neue Bahnen"* (New Paths) for the *Neue Zeitschrift für Musik.* This article, Schumann's last, created much interest. The manner in which his prophecy was fulfilled testifies to Schumann's acumen as a critic.

ROBERT SCHUMANN

Schumann's mental aberrations now became more frequent, and in 1854 he attempted suicide by throwing himself into the Rhine. It was necessary to confine him in an asylum until his death in 1856. His wife, who survived him by forty years, returned to the concert stage. Despite the responsibilities of caring for a large family, she won for herself a reputation as a great artist and interpreter, particularly of her husband's works. Schumann's widow continued her husband's friendship with Brahms and his interest in Brahms' compositions.

Unlike so many of his contemporaries, Schumann was a shy, retiring individual who had great difficulty in expressing himself by means of the spoken word. He was phlegmatic only superficially, however. His literary works are animated and penetrating, and are often enlivened by apt wit. Most of the composers of the period were critically appraised by Schumann in the *Neue Zeitschrift* and many of his criticisms have stood the test of time.

Characteristics of Schumann's Music

The music of Schumann does not contain the excesses to be found in the works of some of his contemporaries. It wholly abjures virtuoso display or sensational programs. Schumann's gifts are observed at their best in his shorter works; the larger compositions often exhibit formal deficiencies which may be attributed in the main to Schumann's zest and exuberance in the handling of his material. Rhythmic novelty, particularly syncopation and cross-accents, are usually found in his works, and their texture is full and rich, occasionally to the point of heaviness. Perhaps the best characterization of Schumann's music was supplied by himself in superscribing his Sonata for Piano in F-sharp minor, Opus 11, *"by Florestan and Eusebius,"* for these two fictitious characters embody the most typical traits of Schumann's music—impetuosity and animation combined with warm lyricism and fanciful reverie. While Schumann's poetic imagination caused him to dispense with many formal conventions, he created no intrinsically new forms. Nor can it be said that his works had a strong influence on any composer other than Brahms. A staunch advocate of the romantic movement, he pointed out its more sensitive aspects when he declared that "romanticism is not a question of figures and forms, but of the composer's being a poet or not."

Schumann's activity as a composer may be divided into several phases. His first important composition, a work for piano, was written in 1830, and until 1840, the year of his marriage, he confined himself entirely to this instrument. Most of his finest works date from this period. The year 1840 is called the "song year," the period having been devoted to the composition of songs. In similar fashion, the year 1841 was devoted to the composition of orchestral works, and the following year to chamber music. Later works of importance were the Second, Third, and Fourth Symphonies, the last a reinstrumentation of a product of the "symphony year," a concerto for piano and one for violoncello. Schumann also made settings of several scenes from Goethe's *Faust,* and of Byron's poem *Manfred.* The overture to the latter ranks as one of his best works. An opera, *Genoveva,* proved unsuccessful.

A thoroughly charming aspect of Schumann's personality was his love for and understanding of children, as is shown in his *Scenes from Childhood* and *Album for the Young,* collections of short descriptive piano pieces. Schumann was not the first composer to write for children; it should not be forgotten that Bach wrote music for the members of his family. Comparison of Schumann's pieces for children with those of his predecessor in this field again indicate the fascination for the picturesque and the legendary so characteristic of the romantic spirit. Bach restricts the musical studies of his offspring to the more formal business of inventions, short preludes and fugues, minuets, sarabandes, and the like. Schumann, on the other hand, who was the product of an entirely different artistic environment, portrays episodes in a child's daily life, and characters from German fairy tales. The titles of many of Schumann's works should not be taken too literally. He writes as follows about the superscriptions of his *Scenes from Childhood*: "The titles came into being afterwards, and are, indeed, nothing more than delicate directions for the rendering and understanding of the music." [1]

Piano Music

Schumann's piano music forms an important part of the repertory of the modern recitalist. In addition to three sonatas and a splendid

[1] Frederick Niecks—*Robert Schumann,* page 186.

set of variations entitled *Symphonic Etudes,* there are numerous sets of shorter pieces appearing under group superscriptions such as *Papillons* (Butterflies), *Novelletten* (Romantic Tales), *Phantasiestücke* (Phantasy Pieces), *Nachtstücke* (Nocturnes), and the ever-popular *Carnaval.* The last-mentioned work, one of the most frequently played of Schumann's piano compositions, may be analyzed in some detail.

"CARNAVAL"

Schumann entitles this work, his Opus 9, composed in 1834–1835, *Carnaval. Scènes mignonnes composées pour le pianoforte sur quatre notes* (Little scenes composed for the piano, based on four notes). As he explained in a letter, the four notes represent the name of the town Asch from which an earlier love, Ernestine von Fricken, had come. The four letters also happen to be the only musical letters in Schumann's name. In the German language they represent four tones: *H* in German corresponds to our B-natural, *As* to our A-flat, while the pronunciation of the letter *S* is the same as *Es* denoting our E-flat. Of the various combinations which are possible, Schumann employs:

AS C H—A-flat, C, B

and

A S C H—A, E-flat, C, B

Schumann was fond of using acrostics of this sort as a basis for musical works. His first important composition is a series of variations on a family name ABEGG, while *The Album for the Young* contains a *Greeting to GADE,* a prominent contemporary.

The *Carnaval* describes a masked ball in a series of sketches in variation form which, with the exception of the opening *Préambule,* are based on a combination of notes derived from ASCH. The sketches bear descriptive titles which, although superimposed after the work was completed, serve as excellent clues to the subject matter. In this musical portrait gallery are to be found Chopin, Paganini, Clara

Wieck (under the affectionate name *Chiarina*), as well as two revealing self-portraits entitled *Florestan* and *Eusebius*. The final variation
depicts the triumphant cause of romanticism. Bearing the bilingual
title *Marche des Davidsbündler contre les Philistins* (March of the
Members of the League of David against the Philistines), this last
piece employs an old and well-known German tune *Der Grossvater
Tanz* (The Grandfather's Dance) to symbolize the reactionary Philistines who are finally put to route by the Davidsbündler wielding
weapons fashioned from ASCH.

This set of variations with its whimsically derived theme is again
an excellent example of the manner in which romantic imagination
altered older forms. Schumann's treatment of the theme is quite fanciful, and the origin of some of the variations is more apparent to the
eye than to the ear. A few examples will demonstrate the manner
in which the various musical derivations of ASCH are employed:

Ex. 1
  (a) No. 2. *Pierrot.*

  (b) No. 4. *Valse noble.*

  (c) No. 10. *Lettres dansantes.*

  (d) No. 11. *Chiarina.*

  (e) No. 14. *Reconnaissance.*

(f)   No. 20.   *Marche des Davidsbündler contre les Philistins.*

The first public performance of the *Carnaval* was given by Liszt, who played ten sketches from the work at his concert in Leipzig on March 30, 1840.

Songs

As a writer of songs Schumann is the direct successor of his greatly admired Schubert.   Like Schubert, Schumann composed his songs with amazing spontaneity; about 150 songs were written in 1840, "the song year."   Many of these songs were inspired by Clara.   Schumann's literary sensitivity is shown by his choice of poems, notably those by Eichendorff and Heine.   The character of the songs ranges from the simple, warm lyricism of *Der Nussbaum* (The Chestnut Tree) to the animated *Die Beiden Grenadiere* (The Two Grenadiers) with its typically romantic introduction of the *Marseillaise*.   Many of the songs possess significant instrumental postludes.

PIANO CONCERTO IN A MINOR

Schumann's Piano Concerto in A minor, Opus 54, completed in 1845, is the direct successor of the piano concertos of Beethoven.   The solo part is not written in a virtuoso style and lacks the brilliancy demanded of concertos by the prevailing taste of the time.   The work, for example, possesses only one cadenza, written by Schumann himself.   This cadenza is not the customary opportunity for the display of technical facility, but rather a poetic interlude for the solo instrument.   Schumann has abandoned the double exposition formerly employed for the concerto, and the piano shares with the orchestra the exposition of the thematic material.   The contrast of impetuous and lyrical moods in this work again shows the hands of its joint authors, *Florestan* and *Eusebius*.

The first movement of the concerto, an *Allegro affettuoso* (lively, with feeling) in sonata form, begins with a brief prefatory gesture

on the part of the piano, after which the wood-wind instruments give
out the beautiful first theme:

Ex. 2

The second group commences not with a new theme, but with a
subject which is largely another version of Example 2:

Ex. 3

The long development begins with an idyllic *Andante espressivo* in
which the piano presents this version of the principal theme:

Ex. 4

Further elaboration leads to the recapitulation, which is largely a
repetition of the exposition and ends with the cadenza. In the lively
coda the principal theme appears in a march-like form:

Ex. 5

The second movement, which Schumann calls an *Intermezzo,* is written in the style of a *romanza,*[1] and is in three-part form. The manner in which Schumann has united piano and orchestra as strands in a common texture is seen to best advantage in this movement. The opening, for example, consists of a dialogue between the piano and the strings:

Ex. 6

The middle section is based on a broad song-like theme played by the 'cellos:

Ex. 7

The Intermezzo proceeds without pause into the last movement, but not before the first movement has been furtively recalled by the wood-winds:

Ex. 8

The last movement, an *Allegro vivace* in sonata form, is an excellent example of the rhythmic originality found so often in Schumann's music. The buoyant first theme is given out by the piano:

Ex. 9

---

[1] See page 151.

The rhythmic complexity of the theme which appears at the beginning of the second group renders it especially attractive:

Ex. 10

The energetic development is followed by a somewhat curtailed recapitulation. The coda, which is quite long, contains some beautiful passage-work for the piano.

Orchestral Music

Schumann composed four symphonies, which, although rich in content, suffer from the composer's inability to handle the larger forms with ease. The best movements of these works are the shorter ones in slow tempi, in which Schumann's essentially lyrical style appears to best advantage. Schumann was one of the few great composers who did not have an adequate grasp of the art of orchestration. The scoring of his symphonies is thick and monotonous, more pianistic than orchestral. The wealth of beautiful music in these works, however, atones for their mechanical defects.

Chamber Music

Schumann's "chamber music year" was 1842, during which he wrote his most important compositions in this category: the three string quartets, Opus 41, and the celebrated Quintet in E-flat major for piano and strings, Opus 44. The latter work was the first combination of these ostensibly incompatible instrumental groups. It has justifiably won a place for itself as one of the world's most popular chamber-music compositions.

SUGGESTED READINGS

The standard biography is the *Robert Schumann* of Frederick Niecks (Dutton). The *Schumann* of Victor Basch (Knopf) can also be recommended.

There is an excellent article on Schumann in Volume I of Sir William Hadow's *Studies in Modern Music* (Macmillan). The chamber music has been discussed and analyzed for *Cobbett's Cyclopedic Survey of Chamber Music* by Richard Aldrich. *Philip Hale's Boston Symphony Programme Notes,* edited by John N. Burk (Doubleday, Doran), includes critical commentaries on the symphonies and the piano concerto.

Chapter XVII

FRÉDÉRIC CHOPIN

FRÉDÉRIC Chopin belongs with the small number of composers who have confined themselves exclusively to one medium of musical expression. With the exception of a few unimportant pieces, all of Chopin's music was written for the piano. The mechanical improvement which the piano had undergone in the early part of the nineteenth century had greatly increased its potentialities, and these were effectively revealed in Chopin's compositions.

Chopin was a Pole. He was born not far from Warsaw on February 22, 1810, and was brought up in that city, receiving a somewhat limited general education. His musical talents manifested themselves when he was quite young, and when he was eight years old he appeared publicly as a pianist. His piano instructor was a local teacher, Adalbert Zwyny, who, when the boy had reached his twelfth birthday, declared he had nothing more to teach him. Studies in composition were undertaken under the guidance of the capable Joseph Elsner. Chopin's Opus 1 was published when he was fifteen years old. It is important to note that Chopin as a boy came in close contact with the folk music of his native country. In 1830 he left Warsaw on a concert tour, in the course of which he appeared in the principal German cities. His destination was Paris, and it was here that he made his home for the rest of his short life.

His reception in Paris was an enthusiastic one, and he quickly became an idol of the salons as well as a teacher whose services were much in demand. He was on friendly terms with many of his fellow-artists in Paris, notably Franz Liszt, with whom he appeared at a concert given for the benefit of Hector Berlioz' fiancée, Henrietta

Smithson.   The number of his public appearances was, however, quite
small.   As opposed to the prevailing tendencies of the day, his pianistic style was of an intimate nature, successful only in a small hall.
From 1837 to 1847 he was intimate with the French writer of romantic novels, George Sand (Mme. Amandine Dudevant).   His uneventful life came to a premature end when he finally succumbed to the
ravages of consumption in 1849.

Chopin and the Piano

Chopin made many important innovations in the art of writing for
the piano. Many of these innovations had their origin in the attempt
to overcome the fundamental limitation of the instrument—its inability to produce sustained tones. The usual solution of this problem
consists of some repetitive figure in which the tones of a chord are
sounded in quick succession and thus give rise to a unified harmonic
impression, much as the quickly repeated images of the motion picture merge into a unified optical sensation. In the discussion of the
F minor Sonata of Beethoven (page 166) the accompanying figures of
Examples 3 and 4 demonstrate the manner in which chords may be
sustained by repetition of their elements. Chopin's method, however,
was to attenuate these chords over a much wider span, producing a
figure of greater clarity and also of greater rhythmic interest. The
following illustration, from the fourth Ballade, is typical of Chopin's
chord spacing:

Ex. 1

None of the chords written in this fashion would possess any effectiveness whatsoever if the piano did not have pedals. The most important of these pedals is the one actuated by the right foot. When
this pedal is depressed, all the dampers are lifted from the strings,

FRÉDÉRIC CHOPIN

some of which are now free to vibrate in sympathy with those strings that have already been struck. The result is that instead of a single tone, many tones are produced, the fusion of all resulting in a rich, full sonority. Intelligent use of the pedal is an indispensable factor in the artistic performance of Chopin's works.

Chopin's Style

Although Chopin's compositions bear only generic titles, they represent some of the most typical products of the romantic school. His style is essentially lyrical, based on an intimate and poetic type of melody of highly original stamp. On occasion these melodies may seem somewhat sentimental and effeminate; but they are just as often vigorous and dramatic. His harmonic language is often bold and original, and many of the chordal progressions to be found in his works anticipate the methods of latter-day composers.[1]

Examination of the list of Chopin's works shows that he wrote almost exclusively in the shorter forms. His two sonatas (Opus 35 in B-flat minor, and Opus 58 in B minor) exhibit formal deficiencies. Each is more a series of four independent pieces than a unified work. The two concertos for piano possess the same formal defects in addition to rather inept orchestration. The shorter pieces, however, are an important part of the piano literature and are played with great frequency.

Before passing to a detailed discussion of these forms, a few of their general characteristics may be pointed out. Two of the more outstanding of these are elegance and refinement. Chopin's sensitive nature shrank from excesses of any kind, yet his music does not lapse into the conventionalities of the equally fastidious Mendelssohn. A third feature of Chopin's art is its variety, even within the limitations of the shorter forms. Of the fifty-one mazurkas, for example, no two are alike. A fourth feature is the manner in which Chopin embellishes his melodies by embroidering them with brilliant festoons of notes containing many delicately implied dissonances. The following excerpt from the first Ballade, Opus 23, in G minor, is a beautiful example of these tonal sprays:

[1] See Example 3, page 236.

Ex. 2

The nineteen *Nocturnes* are Chopin's most popular pieces, since they are easier to play than most of his other compositions. Chopin found the designation *Nocturne* in the works of a contemporary Irish composer, John Field. The nocturne is a short piece in three-part form, pensively lyrical in style, and tinged with a quiet melancholy. The two outer sections are in a slow tempo, and the middle section is somewhat faster. The title indicates a romantic interpretation of the mood of the night.

The four *Impromptus* are also three-part forms. The contrast of tempi is the reverse of that of the nocturnes: the outer sections are lively and the middle sections are slower. The title, indicating a piece composed on the spur of the moment, should not be construed too literally.

The twenty-four *Preludes* (Opus 28) comprise a collection of short poetic pieces in varied moods. These works are not preludes in the older sense of the term, for they are not preliminary movements like the Bach preludes, but rather brief sketches, expressions of momentary fancies. They contain some of Chopin's finest writing for the piano.

The twenty-four *Études* (Opus 10 and Opus 25) are earlier works. Like the Inventions of Bach, they are more than mere exercises, and the artistic inspiration which pervades them overshadows the problems in pianistic technique with which they are ostensibly concerned. Almost all the *Études* are three-part forms and each is constructed on only one motive, whose proper execution constitutes the technical problem. Almost all of Chopin's innovations in piano-writing are contained in these works. The names, such as *Black-Key Étude, Revolutionary Étude, Butterfly Étude,* given to some of them, while not inappropriate, did not originate with Chopin.

The four *Scherzos* have nothing in common with the scherzos of Beethoven other than triple rhythm and rapid tempo. Nor are they humorous pieces. They are vigorous and forceful works, striking a dramatic note. With the exception of the first, which is in three-part form, their formal construction follows no conventional pattern.

In using the term *Ballade* as a title for four extensive pieces, Chopin has indicated that they are narratives in music. They are said to have been inspired by poems of the great Polish poet, Adam Mickiewicz. The four Ballades are extensive pieces worked out on a large scale. In their grandeur of conception and forcefulness of expression they serve as an effective refutation of the common classification of Chopin as a composer of pleasing music for the delectation of the Parisian salons.

The influence which the music of his native country had upon Chopin is shown most clearly by his dance music. The *Waltzes* are idealized versions of a German dance form; but the *Mazurkas* and the *Polonaises* are genuinely Polish. They typify another aspect of the romantic interest in folk life. As has been mentioned before, Chopin while still a boy had manifested a keen interest in the dances of the Polish peasants.

The *Mazurka* is a lively peasant dance, whose name is derived from the Polish region in which it originated, Mazovia. It is lively in tempo and is in triple rhythm, usually with a strong accent on the third beat. In his fifty-one mazurkas Chopin has effectively caught the mood of this dance. While preserving its fundamental rhythmic scheme and employing melodies of a folk-like nature, he has raised it to a high artistic level through originality of melodic elaboration and harmonic treatment. A frequently cited example of the modernity of Chopin's harmony is this progression from the Mazurka in C-sharp minor, Opus 30, No. 4, a far cry indeed from the crude harmonies of a peasant dance:

Ex. 3

The other Polish dance which Chopin has immortalized is the *Polonaise*. This is not a peasant dance like the mazurka, but a stately processional dance of courtly origin. It is in well-accented triple rhythm and moderate tempo. It owes its French name to the fact that a French prince, Henry, Duke of Anjou, reigned as King of Poland for thirteen months. At a great reception, which he held in Cracow in 1574, the assembled Polish nobles passed in ceremonial procession. Through Henry and his followers the stately music which accompanied this procession was brought to Paris; and, as usual, it eventually acquired both the French name and the French characteristics that we have already observed in the suites of Bach. Chopin in his twelve polonaises has restored the original courtly grandeur and pomp of the form. In no other works is he so intensely Polish, so ardently nationalistic.

POLONAISE IN A-FLAT MAJOR, OPUS 53

Chopin's most characteristic Polonaise is the brilliant one in A-flat major, Opus 53, one of his most eloquent compositions. It is in three-part form. The sixteen opening measures serve as a tense preliminary to the majestic first theme:

Ex. 4

The middle section begins with a trumpet-like melody accompanied by a celebrated series of repeated bass figures, the effectiveness of which has made his Polonaise a favorite recital piece:

Ex. 5

The return to the main section is preceded by a wistful interlude from which march rhythms are absent:

Ex. 6

Suggested Readings

The standard biography is the two-volume *Life of Chopin* by Frederick Niecks (H. W. Gray). The *Chopin* of Henri Bidou (Knopf) is a more recent treatise which relates the compositions to the life. James Huneker's *Chopin, The Man and His Music* (Scribner's) is a brilliant study. An excellent essay on Chopin is to be found in the second volume of Sir William Hadow's *Studies in Modern Music* (Macmillan). Detailed technical analyses of almost all of the compositions are included in the exhaustive *Analyse von Chopins Klavierwerken* of Hugo Leichtentritt (Hesse).

Chapter XVIII

HECTOR BERLIOZ

THE LIFE and music of the French composer Hector Berlioz represent one of the most typical manifestations of the romantic movement. An impetuous and intense individual, Berlioz possessed a limitless imagination which, coupled with an apparently inexhaustible supply of energy and enthusiasm, led him to undertake colossal musical ventures and to compose works of which some may be regarded today merely as historical curiosities, museum pieces indicative of the movement under whose influence they were conceived. But like his German predecessor, von Weber, he composed one work which in its revolutionary significance has won for him an undeniable position of importance in the development of the language of music. This work, the name of which might well be the title of a novel based on the composer's own life, is the *Symphonie fantastique* (Fantastic Symphony).

Hector Berlioz, the oldest son of a country doctor, was born in the small town of La Côte Saint-André, near Grenoble on December 11, 1803. As a boy he showed keen interest in music; but his early musical training was confined to a few flute and guitar lessons, plus an almost negligible amount of theoretical instruction. An amateur's proficiency in the playing of the two above-mentioned instruments represented the sum total of Berlioz' ability as an instrumental performer during his entire lifetime. When Berlioz was eighteen his father sent him off to Paris to study medicine; but the opera house proved more attractive than the dissecting room, and medical studies were soon abandoned in favor of music. The ambitious youth set to work at composing with great zeal despite his lack of technical equipment, and when he was twenty-one years old he ventured to present a Mass of his own composition with an orchestra of 150 players. Eventually he was enrolled as a pupil in the Paris Con servatoire, but he found formal instruction irksome. He learned in strumentation by following operatic performances from score, and so well did he come to know the repertory of the opera house that mistakes in playing or "improvements" in the score would cause this tall, red-headed individual to rise from his seat in the midst of a performance and in a loud voice question the rectitude of the proceedings.

In 1827 he fell madly in love with Henrietta Smithson, an Irish actress whose performances in the plays of Shakespeare had made her the idol of Paris. The tortures of this "interminable and inexhaustible passion" drove Berlioz to write his great masterwork, the *Fantastic Symphony,* which was first performed on December 5, 1830. In 1833 he finally married Henrietta, whose fame as an actress had, in the interim, dwindled to the vanishing point. Their marriage turned out unhappily, however, and after ten stormy years they separated.

Berlioz presented many concerts composed of his own works in Paris. But to his chagrin, no lasting public acclaim ensued, and his compositions, almost invariably calling for musical forces of gigantic dimensions, were regarded more as ephemeral novelties than as art works. He also held the position of critic on the important *Journal des débats,* and the writing of *feuilletons* occupied much of his time.

But if Paris denied Berlioz the recognition for which he longed, other European cities, particularly those of Germany, gave him a full measure of acclaim. He was particularly triumphant in the concerts he directed at St. Petersburg and Moscow, and notable performances of his works were given at Weimar by Liszt. Despite all the reports sent back to Paris, however, the Parisian public failed to become enthusiastic about either Berlioz or his music. The continued postponement and eventual failure of his opera *Les Troyens* (The Trojans) was the last rebuff in his unsuccessful efforts to win recognition in his own land. He died in 1869, a bitter and disappointed man.

No brief summary of the life of Berlioz does full justice to the hectic career of this extraordinary individual. He was continually and ardently enamored, and even when he was an old man in his sixties, his romantic nature impelled him to attempt to rekindle the

HECTOR BERLIOZ

ashes of a childhood love. His unbounded imagination permeated his
life as well as his compositions, and his *Mémoires* are an exaggerated
and none-too-reliable account of the outstanding incidents of his
career. In characteristic fashion, Berlioz omitted no lurid detail
from them, and even considered it necessary to include an account of
the exhumation of Henrietta's corpse. In some respects his memoirs
are more interesting today than his music. In fact, although the Parisian public did not appreciate Berlioz as a composer, it did hold a good
opinion of his literary abilities. His *feuilletons* appeared in collected
form, and one series, *Les Soirées de l'orchestre* (Evenings in the Orchestra), ran through two editions within his lifetime.

The principal works of Berlioz are the *Fantastic Symphony,* the
"dramatic" symphony *Romeo and Juliet,* the symphony *Harold in
Italy*; the "dramatic legend" *The Damnation of Faust,* the two unsuccessful operas *Benvenuto Cellini* and *The Trojans,* and two gigantic
choral works, a *Requiem* and a *Te Deum.* Of these only the following may be heard today with some degree of regularity: the
Fantastic Symphony, the *Queen Mab* scherzo from the *Romeo and
Juliet* symphony, three orchestral excerpts from *The Damnation of
Faust*; the overture to the opera *Benvenuto Cellini,* and the concert
overture *The Roman Carnival,* originally the introduction to the
opera's second act.

The importance of Berlioz is in no manner commensurate with
the amount of his music heard today. With rare exceptions, almost
every contemporary composer and not a few successors were indebted
to him. His ideas and methods, even if somewhat unsuccessful in
their realization at his own hands, were such as to command attention. It was necessary, however, for composers of greater talent, such
as Liszt, Wagner, and Strauss, to bring them to fruition.

Berlioz and Program Music

The avowed aim of Berlioz was to write descriptive music, that is,
program music. He attempted to portray in his compositions not
only such easily recognizable aural images as the sounds of nature,
but also the flow of moods and feelings. This was, in truth, an introduction into music of the "stream-of-consciousness" technique of
the modern psychological novel. But in his desire to achieve realism

in the portrayal of mental states Berlioz sacrificed formal considerations. His larger works, therefore, despite their obvious sincerity of purpose, tend to become vague and diffuse, and while moments of great beauty and effectiveness are frequent, lack of organization militates against the success of the whole. The melodic abilities of Berlioz were also of an inferior order. Furthermore, his choice of subjects for musical portrayal was questionable. One of the movements of the *Fantastic Symphony,* for instance, describes decapitation by the guillotine, and the finale of *Harold in Italy* depicts a drunken orgy of murderous brigands. But his procedures were absolutely novel at the time, and they served as the principal impetus for the widespread development of program music during the nineteenth century.

Orchestration

Parallel with Berlioz' development of this programmatic concept of the function of music went an intense study of the delineative possibilities of the orchestra. His famous manual of instrumentation, originally a series of *feuilletons,* is an imaginatively written compendium in which every orchestral instrument is painstakingly discussed and its timbre and expressive potentialities clearly set forth. It was revised and brought up to date by Richard Strauss in 1905, and is still a basic work. Berlioz' mastery of instrumentation was universally conceded during his lifetime, and it is in this sphere that his influence has been greatest. All of his scores abound in passages in which the orchestral instruments, both as entities and as groups, are handled with the greatest originality and effectiveness. The same fertility of orchestral imagination that created the heaven-storming sonorities of the *Rakoczy March* from the *Damnation of Faust* also brought forth the delicate *Dance of the Sylphs* from the same work, as well as a masterpiece of orchestral gossamer, the *Queen Mab* scherzo from the *Romeo and Juliet* symphony. This scherzo may well be regarded as Berlioz' greatest triumph in instrumentation.

Musical Symbolism

Another important innovation was brought about by the dramatic plan of his works. In the *Fantastic Symphony* and in *Harold in Italy,* a musical phrase is definitely associated with the personage on whom the work is based, and recurs throughout its various movements. This musical symbolism was later adopted and brought to perfection by Wagner.

THE FANTASTIC SYMPHONY

This threefold significance of Berlioz is well illustrated by his *Fantastic Symphony,* a work which cannot be understood without examination of the circumstances which caused it to be written. Berlioz, after falling violently in love with Henrietta Smithson, set himself to chronicle the tortures of his soul in an autobiographical symphony. While he was so engaged, rumors, which later proved to be false, reached his ears about certain scandalous actions of Henrietta in London. His anger at what he considered his betrayal brought forth a desire for revenge. This found musical utterance in the last movement of the work, in which the former object of his passion is portrayed as a courtesan unworthy of his love. This description of Henrietta was even printed in a newspaper, but was later deleted from the program notes. At the first performance of the work a printed version of its program was given to every member of the audience. As an excellent example of the new trends in musical thought, it merits reproduction in its entirety.

PROGRAM OF THE SYMPHONY

A young musician, of a sickly sensitivity and an ardent imagination, poisons himself with opium in a fit of lovesick despondency. The dose of narcotic, too weak to kill, plunges him into a heavy sleep accompanied by strange visions, in the course of which his emotions, his feelings, his memories, translate themselves in his sick brain into musical thoughts and images. The beloved one herself has become for him a melody, like a fixed idea which he finds and hears everywhere.

Part I
Reveries, Passions.

He first recalls the discomfort of the soul, the emptiness of passions, the fits of melancholy, the causeless joys which he experienced before having seen the one whom he loves; then the volcanic love which she suddenly inspired in him, his delirious anguish, his jealous rage, his returns to tenderness, his religious consolation.

Part II
A Ball.

He finds his beloved again at a ball in the midst of the excitement of a brilliant fête.

Part III
Scene in the Fields.

One summer evening in the country, he hears two shepherds piping away in turn at their herdsman's tune. This pastoral duet, the setting of the scene, the light murmur of the trees gently stirred by the wind, some grounds for hope which he had recently imagined, all conspire to bring back to his heart an unaccustomed calm; but she appears again, he suffers anguish of heart, agitated by sorrowful presentiments: were she to deceive him. . . One of the shepherds takes up the simple melody, the other does not reply. The sun goes down. . . Distant rumbling of thunder. . . Solitude. . . Silence. . .

Part IV
March to the Scaffold.

He dreams that he has killed the one he loves, that he is condemned to death, and led to the scaffold. The procession moves ahead to the tones of a march now somber and wild, now brilliant and solemn, in which the dull thud of heavy steps follows without transition upon a most clamorous uproar. In the end, the fixed idea reappears for an instant like the last thought of love interrupted by the fatal stroke.

Part V
Dream of a Witches' Sabbath.

He sees himself at a witches' sabbath in the midst of a troop of terrible shadows, of sorcerers, of monsters of all kinds reunited for his funeral. Strange noises, groans, bursts of laughter, distant cries to which other cries seem to answer. The beloved melody again reappears; but it has lost its noble and modest character; it is no more than a dance tune, ignoble, trivial and grotesque; it is she who comes to the witches' sabbath . . . roars of joy at her arrival. . . . She participates in the diabolical orgy. . . . Funereal tolling, burlesque parody of the *Dies Irae*. Witches' dance. The witches' dance and the *Dies Irae* together.

H. *Berlioz*

It should be observed that the composition has five movements and that the plan of the classical symphony has been wholly abandoned. The design of the work is now determined by extra-musical considerations—the details of the program.

The musical phrase which reappears throughout the symphony is associated with "the beloved one," hence its designation by Berlioz as an *idée fixe* (fixed idea). It is important, however, to notice that the *idée fixe* undergoes transformation from movement to movement, and does not appear merely as an arbitrary and invariable symbol.

In the first movement, *Reveries, Passions*, the *idée fixe* appears as:

Ex. 1

The second movement describes a ball. The orchestra plays an
animated waltz whose strains are interrupted by this version of the
idée fixe:

Ex. 2

In the third movement, *Scene in the Fields,* the reappearance of
"the beloved one" in the thoughts of the artist is again portrayed by
the *idée fixe*:

Ex. 3

A short fragment of the *idée fixe* is heard in the fourth movement,
the *March to the Scaffold,* just before the loud chord describing the
fall of the knife. It is not until the last movement, the *Dream of a
Witches' Sabbath,* that the *idée fixe* is radically transformed. Berlioz
changes the melody to "a dance tune, ignoble, trivial and grotesque"
and makes it doubly vulgar by assigning it to the E-flat clarinet, a
high-pitched instrument which imparts a shrewish quality to the
music:

Ex. 4

The last movement also contains one of Berlioz' most imaginative
strokes, the introduction by the tubas of a melody based on the tradi-

tional chant for the dead, the *Dies Irae* (Day of Wrath), a part of the
Requiem Mass of the Catholic Church. In its original form the
chant is:

Ex. 5

Di - es i - rae, di - es il - la,   Sol-vet   sae - clum   in fa-vil - la,

Berlioz not only introduces the *Dies Irae* literally, but later proceeds
to parody it in these incisive phrases:

Ex. 6

Berlioz' use of this chant was followed by Franz Liszt in his *Toten-
tanz*, Camille Saint-Saëns in the *Danse macabre*, and Ernest Schelling
in *A Victory Ball*.

SUGGESTED READINGS

The most detailed biography of Berlioz is the three-volume work of Adolph
Boschot, *L'Histoire d'un romantique* (Plon-Nourrit). A condensed version of
this has appeared as *Une Vie romantique*. It is unfortunate that neither of these
works has been translated, for there is no adequate biography in English. The
Memoirs of Hector Berlioz (Knopf) have been edited by Ernest Newman. A
recent defense of Berlioz against his numerous critics, and a scholarly clarification of the many misconceptions concerning his art are to be found in the *Berlioz*
of Tom S. Wotton (Oxford University Press). There is a valuable article by
Julien Tiersot, "The Berlioz of the Fantastic Symphony," in *The Musical Quarterly*
for July, 1933. Other important articles are to be found in Sir William Hadow's
Studies in Modern Music (Macmillan) and Arthur Locke's *Music and the Romantic
Movement in France* (Dutton). For details of Berlioz' contributions to orchestration see *The History of Orchestration* by Adam Carse (Dutton).

Chapter XIX

FRANZ LISZT

THE LONG and brilliant career of Franz Liszt spans one of the most glamorous periods in the history of music. He was born on October 22, 1811, at a time when Beethoven was occupied with the composition of his Seventh Symphony. The whole romantic movement unfolded itself during his lifetime, and he not only lived to see the triumph of Wagner, but survived him by three years. His playing as a boy was heard by Beethoven, and as an old man by individuals who are still living today.

Liszt's birthplace was the town of Raiding, then in Hungary. When only ten years old he was taken to Vienna by his father and placed under the tutelage of Carl Czerny, the composer of the dull but efficient piano studies known to every pupil today. Not long afterwards he appeared before the Viennese public as a pianist, arousing great enthusiasm. Beethoven was present at a concert given by Liszt on April 13, 1823, and at the end of the performance is said to have rushed forward and kissed the phenomenal child on the forehead. Beethoven was stone-deaf at the time and must have appreciated the visual rather than the aural aspects of Liszt's playing.

Father and son now removed to Paris where efforts to gain admittance to the Conservatoire were unsuccessful, as the boy was not of French birth. With the exception of occasional concert tours, Liszt spent the next eleven years of his life in the French capital and grew up under French influences. The total amount of musical instruction, instrumental as well as theoretical, that he received during his entire lifetime consisted merely of his year of piano study under Czerny and some exercises in composition in Vienna and Paris. His Parisian appearances soon brought him much fame, and he became a familiar figure in the salons of the city. Here he came in contact

FRANZ LISZT

with other artists of a strongly romantic nature—Hugo, de Musset, Balzac, Dumas, Heine, and Delacroix. He was also on terms of close artistic friendship with Chopin, and with Berlioz, whose ideas awakened a particularly sympathetic response. The playing of the virtuoso violinist Paganini inspired him to perfect a comparable pianistic facility. Liszt also met and fell in love with the Countess d'Agoult, a brilliant figure of the Parisian salons, who wrote extensively under the pen name Daniel Stern. In 1835 the pair removed to Switzerland, and in the five years in which they lived together, three children were born to them. The second child, Cosima, later became the wife of Richard Wagner.

After his separation from the Countess, Liszt commenced a series of concert tours. During the years 1840–1847 he appeared in every city of importance in Europe. Every concert was a triumphal event. So great was Liszt's fame that the passport which he carried bore the following as a description of him—"Celebritate sua sat notus" [1] (Sufficiently known through his fame). During his travels in Russia, he became friendly with the Princess Carolyne Sayne-Wittgenstein, a wealthy and cultured noblewoman. She fled from Russia in 1848, met Liszt in Austria, and went with him to Weimar, where Liszt, having abandoned his concert tours, had become Kapellmeister. The Princess, who was exceedingly devout, possessed a strong personality which greatly influenced Liszt's development as a composer. Intricacies of ecclesiastical law prevented their marriage.

During his thirteen years as Kapellmeister at Weimar (1848–1861) Liszt, despite poor facilities and official indifference, devoted himself whole-heartedly to the performance of contemporary operatic and symphonic music. Such were his efforts that Weimar became a Mecca for composers, and had the ruling house seen fit to support his assiduity with commensurate financial backing, the glories of the days of Goethe and Schiller would assuredly have been revived. Despite the obstacles put in his path, Liszt performed valiant deeds for his fellow musicians. Of the forty-three operas which he presented at Weimar, no less than twenty-four were by contemporary composers, notably Berlioz and Wagner. Of these operas the most important was Wagner's *Lohengrin,* which had its première in 1850.

[1] Raabe—*Liszts Leben,* page 55.

Many of Liszt's own orchestral works were also given their first performances here, but he did not lavish as much attention upon them
as he did on the works of other composers. Amidst all these labors
he still found time for teaching and for participation in the varied
social activities of the court and of his own home, the *Altenburg,* over
which the Princess presided.

Of all the composers that Liszt befriended during his lifetime,
Richard Wagner stands out as the one who received the most understanding and encouragement. Liszt, who was an ardent admirer of
the latter's operas, conducted three of them at Weimar, presented
extracts from them at symphonic concerts, and transcribed excerpts
from them for piano solo. A firm believer in Wagner's genius and
its ultimate destiny, Liszt encouraged all of his efforts and even gave
him financial assistance. But as was true of many of Liszt's bene-
factions, the relationship was rather one-sided. Although Liszt had
been of incalculable assistance to him, Wagner never conducted a
single one of Liszt's numerous orchestral works.

Discontentment with the reception of his efforts at Weimar caused
Liszt finally to resign his Kapellmeistership in 1861. He went to
Rome, where he studied theology, and in 1865 was admitted to a
monastic order. Although he took clerical garb largely to gratify the
Princess, Liszt had possessed strong religious feelings from early man-
hood. During his stay in Rome he frequently played before the Pope,
Pius IX. But his clerical obligations did not exclude secular activity,
and he appeared in various European capitals as conductor of his own
works and occasionally as soloist. Most of the compositions of this
period were sacred choral works. During the summers Liszt, who
despite his age possessed unusual vitality, returned to Weimar to devote himself to the pupils who came from all over the world to receive instruction from him. His interest in Wagner continued, and
he was an honored guest at the opening of the theater at Bayreuth in
1876. Liszt died at Bayreuth on July 31, 1886. Although he was
seventy-five years old, he had appeared publicly as a pianist only
twelve days before his death.

The personality of Franz Liszt is not easy to describe. By means
of selected evidence it can be proven that he was essentially a poseur
possessed of a wonderful mechanical dexterity, or, with equal facility,

that he was one of the world's most sincere artists. He himself seems to have been conscious of this double nature. It is for some of his proclivities as an instrumental virtuoso that one can find the most fault with Liszt. During his concert tours he pandered to public taste in a way that seems quite objectionable today; the note of sensationalism was seldom absent from either his concert manner or the programs he presented.

But while Liszt was a master showman, he was not motivated by a desire for mere pecuniary gain. Huge as the receipts from his concerts were, he gave the greater part of them to local charities. Other worthy causes also received his help. He was a prime mover in the formation of societies for the publication of the music of Bach, Handel, and Mozart, and he gave a substantial sum of money for the erection of a Beethoven monument at Bonn. In all his relationships with other musicians he was kind and sympathetic. Busy as his life was, he found time for extensive teaching. Only talented pupils were accepted by him, and they received their instruction absolutely free. Liszt lacked many of the weaknesses usually associated with virtuosi. Fêted everywhere, received by almost every crowned head in Europe, the recipient of many honors, medals, and decorations, the most celebrated performer of his time, he was essentially a modest individual, particularly with regard to his own works, and his mode of life was unusually simple and unpretentious.

Although Liszt received little formal schooling, he was a man of wide culture whose personality was just as dominating in the salon as it was in the concert hall. He read avidly, and in addition came in contact with the best minds of his day. His wide travels also left a strong impress upon him. Although he took an active interest in Hungary and its music, he never mastered the Hungarian tongue. All of his numerous prose works were written in French, and in many respects the art of Liszt stands closer to French culture than to German or Hungarian.

In discussing the musical importance of Liszt, one again finds a diversity as confusing as it is impressive. He was not only a pianist, but also a writer of six volumes of prose and eight volumes of letters, a teacher, a conductor, and a composer of almost seven hundred works.

Piano Music

Franz Liszt was the greatest pianist the world has ever known. Under his hands the sonorities and variety of timbres to be obtained from the piano were so augmented that an entire evening's performance on the instrument could be given in a large hall. He did away with the custom of performing publicly only with orchestra, and he may thus be credited with being the originator of the piano recital. It is interesting to note that when Liszt commenced to appear as a solo performer his seeming audacity met with considerable censure, particularly from those musicians who envied his ability to fill the hall completely while saving the usual expenses for orchestra. Unfortunately, all of Liszt's pianistic accomplishments are buried with him. The phonograph was invented only nine years before his death, and no attempt was made to record his playing on what was then but a primitive instrument. Contemporary opinions were unanimous in stating that Liszt made the piano sound like an entire orchestra.

It is nevertheless possible to obtain a fairly close approximation of Liszt's technical procedures by examining the music which he wrote for his recitals. His works abound with rapid passages in tenths as well as octaves, simultaneous use of several registers of the piano calling for great surety in leaping, adroit crossing of the hands, trills, tremolos, elaborate arpeggios, repeated notes, and brilliant ornamental cadenzas utilizing the higher octaves of the piano. Every finger of both hands is kept continually occupied. The two staves usually employed for piano writing often proved insufficient, causing Liszt to introduce a third. His playing was based largely on free play of the arms, and by introducing a higher chair than had been customary, he found it possible to apply their full weight. The achievement of mere volume, however, was not Liszt's sole aim. There are many passages in his piano works that for delicacy and sheer beauty of tone-color have never been excelled.

Over two hundred diverse works of various composers were arranged by Liszt for piano solo. These arrangements, in which much freedom of treatment is to be found, he called *transcriptions,* a term which he was the first to employ. Many of the transcriptions were written merely to serve as vehicles for the display of Liszt's technique;

they are still used by many modern virtuosi for similar purposes. An examination of the list of compositions transcribed by Liszt for piano, all of which he performed, will illustrate not only his talents as a pianist, but also his ability to obtain orchestral sonorities from the instrument. Among the works so treated are the nine symphonies of Beethoven, the *Symphonie fantastique* of Berlioz, and even the overture to Wagner's *Tannhäuser*. The more artistic transcriptions are those of the organ fugues of Bach and the songs of Schubert. Liszt's performance of these works played an important part in making their composers known to the public.

The nature of Liszt's original compositions is such as to make generalization difficult. It is invariably necessary to bear in mind his one great weakness—deference to public taste; he was often called a "slave of the public." Some of his works are somewhat banal, while others lack the essential note of sincerity. On the other hand, not a few of his efforts are the result of a genuine artistic impulse. Although Liszt was well acquainted with the compositions of the great masters, his own works were apparently uninfluenced by them and employed no conventional forms. The majority are programmatic in character. The programmatic indications, however, are generally of a poetic nature, and Liszt makes no attempt at detailed treatment. The following titles used for piano works are typical: *Waldesrauschen* (Forest Murmurs), *Au bord d'une source* (At the Spring), *Après une lecture de Dante* (After Reading Dante), *Consolations*. The harmonic procedures of Liszt constitute one of his most original contributions to the language of music. Wagner himself admitted his indebtedness to Liszt in this regard.

In the original compositions for piano one finds again a curious mixture of shallow sentimentality, empty pretense, and indulgence in virtuoso display, combined with true poetic feeling and an excellent facility in using the instrument as a means of delineating moods and situations. Many of the shorter pieces possess definite charm. The nineteen Hungarian Rhapsodies, based on Hungarian melodies, bespeak Liszt's later interest in the music of his native land.

PIANO SONATA IN B MINOR

The monumental Sonata in B minor written in 1852–1853 and dedicated to Schumann is Liszt's greatest original composition for the piano. It is not a sonata in the customary sense, for none of its three movements is cast in the conventional sonata form. These three movements, prefaced by a brief introduction, are welded to one another in a manner that makes the sonata one large musical unit. Liszt has labeled them *Allegro energico, Andante sostenuto, Allegro energico.* The work has no program. Its formal construction is based on a method of thematic development which Liszt himself called "transformation of themes," that is, the use of one or more themes as the basis for an entire composition, no matter how many movements it may possess. In these movements the themes appear in a variety of transformations. The technical procedure, therefore, is rooted in the older variation form, now utilized in a more poetic, if less organized, manner. While Liszt's use of this formal device had been anticipated by Berlioz in the *idée fixe* of his *Symphonie fantastique,* he employed it so extensively and so imaginatively in all his larger works that it has been almost universally adopted in some form or other by subsequent composers.

The sonata, whose playing-time is thirty-three minutes, is based on four themes. The first theme, a descending scale figure, appears in the slow introduction:

Ex. 1

The first movement proper commences with the second theme, a forceful subject given out in octaves:

Ex. 2

This is followed at once by the third theme, an emphatic repeated-note motive:

Ex. 3

After a long development of these three motives, the fourth theme, a somewhat pompous *Grandioso,* makes its appearance:

Ex. 4

Of the numerous transformations, which all of these four themes undergo in the course of the three movements, the most important is the following variant of Example 3, augmented and transformed into a treble melody:

Ex. 5

Works for Piano and Orchestra

Of the nine works for piano and orchestra, the Concerto in E-flat major is the most important. Its first performance at a Court concert in Weimar (February 1855) must have been a thrilling occasion, for the composer himself was the soloist, and Berlioz was the conductor. Although the piano part is written in Liszt's best virtuoso style, the orchestra is not used merely as a background but is assigned a role equal in importance to that of the solo instrument. The form of this work, which differs materially from the conventional design of the concerto, is analogous to that of the B minor Sonata. The concerto is a long single movement, divisible, however, into four sections in contrasted tempi. Of the many transformations to which the four themes of the work are subjected, one of the most striking is the change made in a theme which appears at the opening of the second section as:

Ex. 6

At the beginning of the last section, an *Allegro marziale,* this becomes a vigorous march:

Ex. 7

The Symphonic Poems

With the abandonment of his virtuoso career and the commencement of his activity at Weimar, Liszt directed his energies to composition in the larger forms, particularly for orchestra. The principal fruit of this activity was a series of twelve symphonic poems, the term *symphonic poem* being Liszt's own creation. Although the symphonic poem cannot be said to have a definite form, certain attributes are almost invariable. The principal characteristic of the symphonic

poem is its attempt at orchestral representation of some poetic con
cept in a work which, no matter what its length or changes of tempo
may be, is performed as a single movement. The form which thi
movement may take is based on the same method of thematic trans
formation employed in Liszt's Sonata in B minor and his Piano Con
certo in E-flat major; but the nature of these transformations is deter
mined by the poetic concept which the work seeks to embody. The
symphonic poem is, therefore, a species of program music, the pro
gram of which may consist of a poem affixed to the score, or merely of
a suggestive title. Each and every symphonic poem, while abjuring
any rigid form, possesses its own definite musical logic, which for
many listeners is sufficient in itself. But while the symphonic poem
exhibits the same principles of balance and thematic development that
have been observed in its predecessor, the classical symphony, its for
mal plan is dictated by the poetic idea. The development of the
symphonic poem is one of the important phenomena of the romantic
movement.

"LES PRÉLUDES"

Of the twelve symphonic poems of Liszt, only two seem to have re
mained in the symphonic repertory—*Tasso,* written for the centennial
of Goethe's birth, and *Les Préludes.* The latter work derives its title
from one of the *Méditations poétiques* of the French poet Alphonse
Lamartine, paraphrased by Liszt and printed as a preface in the score.
Lamartine's poem, which portrays man's life as but a series of preludes
to the final song of death, contrasts the ephemeral joys of pastoral ex
istence with the dangers of war. The orchestral composition which
Liszt entitled *Les Préludes* was originally, however, the overture to an
uncompleted choral work. This overture was revised at a later date,
supplied with an extract from Lamartine, and published as a sym
phonic poem. Inasmuch as the music preceded the poem, the listener
is under no compulsion to approve of the fitness of Liszt's choice of
poetic preface. Examination will show that *Les Préludes* is a well-
constructed work which in its musical sufficiency stands in no need of
explanation in terms of the now faded sentiments of Lamartine.

Les Préludes consists of four well-contrasted sections prefaced by a
short introduction and merged into a single movement. The entire

work is based on two themes, which are subjected to numerous melodic, harmonic, and rhythmic transformations. The first theme, a
short motive of three notes, makes its appearance in the introduction
as part of a broad passage for strings:

Ex. 8

In the *Andante maestoso,* which follows, this theme appears in these
variants:

Ex. 9
(a)

and

(b)

The second theme is a suave cantabile melody assigned on its first
appearance to the violas and horns:

Ex. 10

This first section, in its presentation of these two themes contrasted in
mood and tonality, functions as an exposition, the content of which
is developed in the three succeeding sections.

The stormy section, which follows, begins with another variant of
the first theme, which, after a somewhat unconvincing chromatic succession, assumes this form:

Ex. 11

This portion of the work is rather bombastic and illustrates that aspect of Liszt's art with which critics have found the most fault.

The third section, the finest of the entire composition, is a beautiful *Allegretto pastorale,* whose mood is established by a series of colorful passages in the wind instruments, beginning with this horn call:

Ex. 12

The cantabile second theme (Example 10) reappears in the pastoral section in combination with a motive derived from the horn call:

Ex. 13

The last section, an *Allegro marziale animato,* is based on a series of variants of the two basic themes, both of which have now taken on a martial character. Two typical transformations are:

Ex. 14

(a)

and

(b)

The work is brought to an impressive if somewhat noisy close with a repetition of the variant of the first theme quoted in Example 9(a).

Two fine orchestral works of Liszt are based on the character Faust. The first, entitled *Mephisto Waltz* (The Dance in the Village Tavern), is based on an episode in the *Faust* of the Hungarian poet Lenau. The impressive *Faust Symphony,* based on Goethe's play, is considered by many to be Liszt's finest orchestral composition. Liszt's interest in Goethe's work had been awakened by the settings of portions of it by Berlioz, to whom the symphony was later dedicated.

The Influence of Liszt

No discussion of Liszt is complete without mention of his relationships with contemporary composers. All of Liszt's manifold obligations did not prevent him from finding time to receive other composers, play over their compositions, and give them sympathetic advice and encouragement. The long list of individuals so befriended is, of course, headed by the name of Richard Wagner, and includes Brahms, Saint-Saëns, and Franck. Many of these composers were young men who were attempting to create national musical literatures in their own lands, and they found in Liszt, who had pointed the way with his Hungarian Rhapsodies, an inspiring counselor. Among the nationalistically minded composers so influenced were the Russians, Balakireff, Borodin, and Rimsky-Korsakoff; the Bohemian, Smetana; the Norwegian, Grieg; and the Spaniard, Albéniz.

There is no more convincing proof of the importance of Liszt in the history of music than the firm manner in which his various innovations have taken root. The symphonic poem, in particular, has found universal acceptance as an art form. Such works as the symphonic poems of Saint-Saëns and Strauss, *The Sorcerer's Apprentice* of Dukas, and *The Afternoon of a Faun* of Debussy, as well as many of the instrumental works of César Franck, trace their ancestry back to the symphonic poems of Liszt.

SUGGESTED READINGS

There is no adequate detailed biography of Liszt in the English language. The best work in this field, the *Liszt: Leben und Schaffen* of Peter Raabe (Cotta), has not yet been translated. The finest work in English is the brilliantly written *Franz Liszt* of James Gibbons Huneker (Scribners). This book contains a valuable collection of impressions of Liszt by his contemporaries. Arthur Her vey's *Franz Liszt and His Music* (Lane) is a serviceable treatise. The article on Liszt by Cecil Gray in the second volume of *The Heritage of Music* (Oxford University Press) is a vigorous refutation of the adverse criticisms of Liszt's music. *Music Study in Germany* by Amy Fay (Macmillan) and *My Memories of Liszt* by Alexander Siloti (Simpson) are illuminating accounts written by individuals who studied under Liszt at Weimar. The romantic aspects of Liszt's art are treated by Arthur Locke in *Music and the Romantic Movement in France* (Dutton). *The Musical Quarterly* for July 1936 is a Liszt issue and contains many valuable articles.

Chapter XX

ITALIAN OPERA OF THE
EARLY NINETEENTH CENTURY

EVER since the opening of the first opera house in Italy in 1637, operatic performances have played an important part in Italian life. Creative musical activity in Italy during the latter half of the eighteenth century and the entire nineteenth century was confined almost exclusively to the writing of operatic music. Well-patronized theaters existed in most of the larger cities and towns, and a vast quantity of music was written for performances on their stages. The predilection which the Italian people have shown for the opera in preference to any other type of music has existed to this day.

Italian opera, with but few exceptions, has always placed its emphasis more on. fine vocalism and ingratiating melody than on dramatic propriety. It has not been so much a play enhanced by music as a form of musical entertainment, in which accomplished singers have delighted their audiences with beautiful melodies expertly delivered in a language rich in mellifluous vowels, and consequently well adapted to song and to vocal display. For this reason the Italian opera has always enjoyed great popularity everywhere. This popularity has often been excessive and has frequently served to impede public recognition of other types of operatic compositions of a less colorful nature. The harsh manner in which German composers such as von Weber spoke of the Italian opera was more a reaction to what they considered an unjust discrimination than a true aesthetic judgment. The comment which Beethoven made about one of the most famous Italians explains why German composers found the competition difficult: "Rossini is a talented and melodious composer; his music suits the frivolous and sensuous spirit of the times; and his productivity is so great that he needs only as many weeks as the Germans need years to write an opera." [1]

Rossini

Of the many composers who were busily fulfilling the requirements of the Italian opera theaters during the early part of the nineteenth century, one met the popular demand for effective vocal writing and tuneful melody with such perfection that his fame spread far beyond the borders of his native land. His name was Gioacchino Rossini, and he was born in February 1792, in the small Adriatic seaport of Pisaro. He wrote his first opera when he was eighteen years old, and before his twenty-second birthday had several successes to his credit. His greatest opera, *Il Barbiere di Siviglia* (The Barber of Seville), was composed in 1816 within the space of two weeks.

Rossini's fame grew with each new opera. In 1822 he journeyed to Vienna where every performance of his works was a great personal triumph. While in Vienna he called on Beethoven who spoke of *The Barber of Seville* with the highest praise. In the following year he went to London and was again the object of much adulation. So great was his importance in the operatic world that the French government appointed him to a high-salaried post. His activity in Paris culminated with the presentation of *William Tell* in 1829, after which Rossini, although only thirty-seven years old, abandoned operatic composition entirely, an act of renunciation which has never been completely explained. From 1829 until his death in 1868 he lived in retirement, first in Italy and for the last thirteen years of his life in Paris, where his residence was the center of many brilliant musical gatherings. The only significant composition to be written during these thirty-nine years of retirement was a choral work, the *Stabat Mater*. Of the thirty-eight operas which Rossini composed, only two, *The Barber of Seville* and *William Tell,* survive.

Rossini was regarded, during his lifetime, as a daring innovator; but to show the origin of this reputation would necessitate an extended examination of the Italian operas written before his day. It is important to note, however, that *The Barber of Seville* is the oldest Italian opera to hold a firm place in the repertoire. Rossini elimi-

---

[1] Thayer-Krehbiel—*The Life of Ludwig van Beethoven*, Vol. III, page 77.

GIOACCHINO ROSSINI

nated the time-honored prerogative of the virtuoso singer to elaborate at will upon the music which the composer had written. He brought about this change not by dispensing with showy passages entirely, but by writing them out in a specific manner and demanding that the singers adhere to them literally. His skill in writing for the voice is evident everywhere in his works. He was the first composer to give a bass voice a prominent role in a serious opera. He also made excellent use of the chorus, and shares with Mozart the distinction of being one of the world's great composers of spirited operatic ensembles. Rossini abbreviated the long and tedious recitatives that had encumbered the older Italian opera, and made them more musical by having their accompaniments played by the orchestra. In the realm of orchestration he far excelled any of the contemporary Italian composers. He possessed a decided gift for orchestral color, many excellent examples of which are to be found in his fine overtures, notably that to *William Tell*.

Rossini was, above all, a facile melodist. His melodies, though rarely as expressive as those of Mozart or Schubert, are bright and spirited, and possess a freshness and a spontaneity that are somewhat unique. They are almost always set forth in a purely homophonic style. To Rossini's discredit may be mentioned his frequent lapses of taste, particularly the incessant use of well-worn clichés such as the celebrated Rossini *crescendo*. This device, one of the composer's most persistent mannerisms, consisted of the repetition of a short phrase over an obvious accompaniment, commencing pianissimo and working up to a fortissimo in a somewhat mechanical manner.

Opera Buffa

Rossini's masterpiece *The Barber of Seville* is a perfect example of *opera buffa* (comic opera), a type of opera in which Rossini's talents showed themselves at their best. The opera buffa had developed from the comic interludes which had appeared in the previous century between the acts of an *opera seria* (serious opera). In many respects the opera buffa was unrestricted by the conventions which hindered the development of opera seria. The number of characters was not rigidly fixed; low male voices might be utilized; the libretto did not have to be historical or legendary, but might deal with events in the lives of the common people; emphasis was placed on effective characterization, tuneful arias, and vivacious ensembles; the action moved speedily. In short, the opera buffa was not only excellent music, it was also excellent theater. The first successful opera buffa was *La serva padrona* (The Maid as Mistress) composed by Giovanni Pergolesi in 1733. This charming little work has had many performances in America.

The text of *The Barber of Seville* was adopted from the celebrated comedy of the same name by the French dramatist Beaumarchais, whose *Marriage of Figaro* had been set by Mozart. The action, dealing with the contest between the young Count Almaviva and the dour Dr. Bartolo for the hand of the latter's ward, Rosina, is replete with intrigue, skilfully manipulated by the town factotum, the barber Figaro. Rossini's sparkling music characterizes the various parties to the intrigue and at the same time provides all of the singers with excellent opportunity to display their vocal technique. Rossini himself was quite a wit, and the many farcical situations afforded by the plot elicited a fitting musical response from him.

The famous overture to *The Barber of Seville* had done service for two other operas before Rossini decided to attach it to the work with which it is now associated. It first saw the light of day as the introduction to an opera, *Aureliano in Palmyra,* which dealt with an adventure of the Roman Emperor, Aurelian, in the Syrian desert. This work was unsuccessful, but its overture was salvaged and attached to *Elisabetta,* an opera based on an episode in the life of Queen Elizabeth of England. Rossini actually wrote an overture employing Spanish themes for *The Barber of Seville,* but this was lost, and since he was either too occupied or too indifferent to write another overture, he borrowed the one from *Elisabetta.* This incident not only is typical of the manner in which Rossini continually re-used material from his older works, but it also indicates what dramatic significance Italian composers of this era attached to the overture. Inconstant as its dramatic affiliations may have been, however, the overture to *The Barber of Seville* is thoroughly representative of Rossini's art.

Grand opéra

William Tell stands apart from Rossini's other operas. It was written to a French text and in the tradition of the French opera, and laid the foundation for the French *grand opéra* of the nineteenth century.   The *grand opéra* was based on an historical text, made effective use of large crowd scenes, and emphasized extravagantly staged spectacles, the delineation of local color, and the intense portrayal of emotions.   It differed from the German romantic opera largely in the character of its subjects, which were factual rather than fictitious. The greatest exponent of *grand opéra* was the German composer Jakob Meyerbeer, a foreigner who, like Rossini and Gluck before him, dominated operatic activity in Paris over a long period.[1]

Before taking leave of Rossini it should be emphasized that his artistic activity came to an end in 1829, and that he should be grouped chronologically as a contemporary of von Weber and Schubert.

Bellini and Donizetti

The successors of Rossini in the sphere of Italian opera were Vincenzo Bellini (1801–1835) and Gaetano Donizetti (1797–1848). Bellini's contributions to the modern repertoire are *La Sonnambula* (The Somnambulist) and *Norma*.   Bellini's style, in contradistinction to that displayed by Rossini, was thoroughly lyrical.   His melodies possess a poetic character and a certain elegiac quality which awakened a particularly strong response in Chopin, in many of whose works there are persistent echoes of Bellini's music.

Donizetti, like Rossini, composed operas with incredible speed; within sixteen years he wrote no less than sixty-six dramatic works. Of this imposing list only one opera has survived—*Lucia di Lammermoor,* written in 1835.   The celebrated "Mad Scene" in the third act of this opera is a great *tour de force* for a coloratura soprano.   Donizetti, like Bellini, was primarily a creator of beautiful if slightly obvious melodies.   Both composers lacked Rossini's command of the orchestra, and the orchestral writing in their works ranges from a thin guitar-like type of accompaniment to noisy, blatant use of the brass instruments; but of true orchestral coloring there are only slight traces.

It has often been customary to compare the works of the Italian operatic composers with those of Richard Wagner.   Wagner's adherents, in their zeal for his works, adopted a belittling attitude towards

---

[1] Jean Baptiste Lully (1639–1687), director of *Les Petits-Violons* of Louis XIV and the first great writer of French opera, was also an Italian.

the Italian opera. Wagner himself, however, spoke of both Rossini and Bellini in terms of high praise, and had the greatest respect for their works, many of which he conducted. He also wrote a long article on Rossini in which he spoke of him as "the first truly great and reverable man I had as yet encountered in the art-world." [1]

Suggested Readings

The *Rossini* of Francis Toye (Knopf) is a lively study of the composer and his age. Discussions of *The Barber of Seville* and *William Tell* are to be found in Ernest Newman's *Stories of the Great Operas* (Garden City Publishing Company). Gustav Kobbé's *The Complete Opera Book* (Putnam) includes synopses of the libretti of the principal operas of Bellini and Donizetti.

[1] *Richard Wagner's Prose Works,* translated by Wm. Ashton Ellis, Vol. IV, page 271.

Chapter XXI

RICHARD WAGNER

THE LIFE of Richard Wagner was a continuous and undaunted struggle for the attainment of one objective: a fusion of dramatic poetry and music into an artistic whole—the music-drama. Wagner's convictions on the application of music to the drama amounted almost to an obsession. This monomania drove him relentlessly forward to the composition of gigantic operatic works which, judged by the standards of the period, possessed no possibilities whatever of being performed. Wagner's works, literary as well as musical, stirred up a hornet's nest of discussion and engendered violent displays of partisanship. No other composer was so enthusiastically praised or so bitterly condemned during his lifetime. In the face of all this, Wagner not only completed a great series of music-dramas, but also built a theater to be devoted exclusively to their production. Grandiose as Wagner's conceptions were, all were successfully realized on the operatic stages of Europe during his lifetime. The music-dramas are now the very foundation of the operatic repertory, and excerpts from them are among the works most frequently performed at orchestral concerts.

Wilhelm Richard Wagner, born at Leipzig on May 22, 1813, was the ninth child of Friedrich Wagner, a clerk in the local police court. Wagner's father had shown some dramatic inclinations, and a brother and two sisters were actively engaged on the stage during his youth. The father died not long after Wagner's birth, and in the same year the widow married Ludwig Geyer, an artistically-minded individual, gifted not only as an actor but also as a painter and a dramatist. Wagner's youth was spent in Dresden, where he conceived an intense admiration for the local Kapellmeister, Carl Maria von Weber, and his works. He had as yet not demonstrated any strong musical bent; as a student his interests were predominantly literary, and before his

RICHARD WAGNER

fifteenth birthday he had made some translations from Homer and
had written a tragedy, modeled largely after Shakespeare. Piano
studies were pursued with much indifference. Wagner, like Berlioz,
was not an instrumental virtuoso; nevertheless, he possessed in later
years a pianistic ability adequate for the performance of extracts from
his own works in the privacy of his home.

In 1827 the family, which had again been left fatherless, returned
to Leipzig. Wagner's conversion to music dates from the following
year, when he heard a Beethoven symphony, the Seventh, for the first
time. He at once borrowed a textbook of harmony from a local
lending library,[1] neglected school, and devoted himself avidly to rather
amateurish efforts at composition. An eccentric "Concert-Overture,"
played in 1830 at a concert given in the Leipzig Theater, was his
first composition to be given a public performance. In 1831 he enrolled as a *studiosus musicae* at the University of Leipzig and for
some time gave himself over to the excesses in which students of
the time were prone to indulge. But his stay at the university was
soon terminated in favor of his all-absorbing interest in music.

Wagner now placed himself under the tutelage of an able theorist,
Christian Theodor Weinlig, who as Cantor of St. Thomas' Church
occupied the position which had been held by Johann Sebastian Bach
in the previous century. Wagner was subjected to a severe contrapuntal discipline by Weinlig, who at the end of six months dismissed him with the remark that he had nothing more to impart to
him. The compositions of this period of Wagner's life were almost
entirely instrumental works of a not particularly promising nature.

Wagner's active musical career commenced in 1833 when he became chorus master at the opera theater at Würzburg. Subsequently
he directed operatic performances at Magdeburg and at Königsberg,
where in 1836 he married the actress Minna Planer. In the following
year Wagner and his wife journeyed to the distant city of Riga (then
in Russia), where he became Kapellmeister at the German Theater.
Here he composed the first two acts of his first important opera,
Rienzi, whose libretto he had adapted from the novel of Bulwer-
Lytton. But Wagner was forced to flee from Riga because of the
huge burden of debt which his extravagances had incurred. This un-

---

[1] See page 219, footnote.

fortunate habit of continually accumulating debts that he could not possibly ever repay persisted throughout his lifetime.

The harassed Kapellmeister and his wife took passage on a small sailing vessel bound for London; but the boat was blown far off its course by storms, and the voyage which normally consumed eight days lasted for three and one half weeks. Episodes on this journey later found their way into *Der Fliegende Holländer* (The Flying Dutchman). The pair stayed in London for only a brief period and then headed directly for Paris, where Wagner hoped to make a name for himself in what was then the center of the operatic world. He was unsuccessful in his plans, however, and for two and one half years he earned a miserable living by journalistic hack writing and such lowly musical tasks as arranging operatic tunes for cornet and piano. While in Paris he completed *Rienzi* and *Der Fliegende Holländer*. *Rienzi* was accepted for performance by the Dresden opera in 1841, and the composer returned to Germany to supervise its production (October 20, 1842). The work was a great success, and in the following year Wagner was appointed to the comparatively well-paid post of Kapellmeister at Dresden. Here he gave fine performances of the operas of Mozart and Gluck. In 1846 he conducted what was to all intents and purposes a "revival" of the Ninth Symphony of Beethoven, the result of which was to restore to an important place in the repertory what had been a neglected and undervalued work. The operas *Tannhäuser* and *Lohengrin* were composed at Dresden, the former being performed in 1845. Wagner, despite the fact that he was a Royal Kapellmeister, had taken an important part in the political agitation then current in Dresden, and when the popular unrest broke out in street riots, a warrant was issued for his arrest. He fled in 1849, taking refuge for a few days with Liszt at Weimar and eventually making his way over the border into Switzerland.

For the next eleven years Wagner was an exile from his native land. He settled in Zurich where his principal activity for the first few years was the writing of his great theoretical treatise *Oper und Drama* (Opera and Drama) completed in 1851, and the composition of the dramatic poem *Der Ring des Nibelungen* (The Ring of the Nibelungen), which was to be the libretto for the cycle of four operas of the same name. The poem was finished and privately printed in

1852. The musical setting of it was begun in 1853, after a period of six years in which Wagner had written only a very small amount of music, and during which his style had undergone a complete meta-morphosis. *Das Rheingold,* the first opera of the *Ring* cycle, was finished in 1854 and *Die Walküre,* the second, in 1856.

About this time Wagner became intimate with Mathilde Wesen-donk, the wife of a wealthy Swiss merchant. In 1857 he was forced to cease work on *Siegfried* because of straitened finances. He now turned to the composition of what he naïvely believed would be a "simple" opera, easy to perform and consequently financially remuner-ative. The "simple" opera turned out to be one of his most difficult works—*Tristan und Isolde,* finished in 1859 and not performed until 1865. *Tristan und Isolde* was in many respects the direct result of his hopeless love for Mathilde Wesendonk. His relationship with Frau Wesendonk served to accelerate what had been going on for years—his drifting away from his wife Minna. They separated in 1861 after twenty-five years of a union in which neither had found happi-ness. *Tristan und Isolde* was followed by the great comic opera, *Die Meistersinger von Nürnberg* (The Mastersingers of Nuremberg), which was commenced in 1861 but was not completed until 1867. In the interim he had, in 1861, revised and added a scene to *Tann-häuser* for a performance of the work in Paris. After six months of heart-breaking rehearsals, the revised opera was finally given three presentations at which the fashionable members of the Jockey Club, incensed because Wagner had not written a second-act ballet, created so much disturbance that the work was withdrawn. His enforced exile from Germany was terminated in 1860 when he received a partial amnesty which excluded him from Saxony only. This restriction was removed two years later.

The long series of disappointments which had been Wagner's fate since his flight from Dresden came to an end when Ludwig II, the young King of Bavaria, became interested in him after hearing a performance of *Lohengrin.* In 1864 he dispatched a messenger to find Wagner and bring him to Munich. Ludwig now took him under his protection, and for a long time supplied him with funds. Cabals were formed against Wagner in Munich, and as the result of much criticism of the King's partiality to him, he withdrew to Switzerland. But the King's interest, both financial and artistic, served to sustain him for many years.

From the year 1864 dates also the beginning of Wagner's relationship with the daughter of Franz Liszt, Cosima Liszt von Bülow, then the wife of the celebrated pianist-conductor Hans von Bülow. In 1866 Cosima left von Bülow to live with Wagner at Triebschen on Lake Lucerne. They were married in July, 1870. Three children had already been born to them, the youngest a son, Siegfried. Wagner's conduct with Cosima for a long time estranged him from his father-in-law and best friend, Liszt, and also caused an abatement of the King's interest in him. In his new-found happiness Wagner completed *Die Meistersinger von Nürnberg* and turned again to the long-neglected *Siegfried*. It was not until 1874 that the composition of the music for *Der Ring des Nibelungen* was brought to an end with the completion of *Götterdämmerung* (The Twilight of the Gods).

From the commencement of his labors on *Der Ring des Nibelungen* Wagner had been convinced that it could not be mounted in any of the theaters of Europe. At first he planned to erect a theater for the performance of the Ring operas in Zurich; at another time he mentioned locating it on the banks of the Rhine. The contact with King Ludwig resulted in the drawing up of plans for a festival theater to be erected in Munich, but these were abandoned when the popular opposition to Wagner's presence at the Bavarian Court caused his withdrawal to Switzerland. In 1871 Wagner decided to build his own theater at Bayreuth, a small Bavarian town centrally located in Germany, yet far enough away from a city and in the heart of a beautiful countryside. To raise the necessary funds, Wagner Societies were established in the principal cities of Germany and even in London and New York. The cornerstone of the *Festspielhaus* was laid in 1872 on Wagner's fifty-ninth birthday, and the event was celebrated by a magnificent performance of Beethoven's Ninth Symphony with Wagner conducting. After herculean labors on the part of all concerned, the theater was opened to the public on August 13, 1876, and *Der Ring des Nibelungen* was performed on four nights (August 13, 14, 16, 17) before a distinguished audience. While the first festival was an unqualified artistic success, the financial results were disappointing, and the season ended with a large deficit.

A desire to wipe out this deficit was responsible for Wagner's journey to London in the following year. Here he directed eight concerts comprising extracts from his operas. His works met with an enthusiastic response, but the expenses were large and the profits small. Shortly after his return to the Continent Wagner finished the poem of his last opera *Parsifal*. This work was completed in January, 1882, and Bayreuth reopened its doors for the première in July of the same year. At the same time an excellent travelling company under the impresario Angelo Neumann was busy performing *Der Ring des Nibelungen* in the principal German cities. Audiences flocked to the presentations, and Wagner's name was on every tongue. The composer's success was now complete, but the exertions attendant upon the mounting of *Parsifal* at Bayreuth had seriously undermined his health. He died in Venice in February, 1883, and was buried in the garden of his villa *Wahnfried* in Bayreuth.

It is doubtful that the personality of any other artist rivalled in complexity that of Richard Wagner, yet probably no other artist has so completely revealed himself. Wagner left no stone unturned in the expression of his ideas. Not only did he write the text and the music for thirteen operas, but he also penned ten volumes of prose, including wordy essays on many non-musical topics, and approximately six thousand letters. At social gatherings it was always Wagner who monopolized the conversation. Unlike Liszt, he was not particularly interested in the music of other composers, and he continually imposed upon such of his friends as were willing to put up with his demands. In short, he rode roughshod over everyone without feeling any qualms of conscience. But this cannot be attributed to vanity or conceit. It was, rather, the result of a limitless faith in himself and in his ideas, which would brook no opposition. This faith, which did not disdain to sacrifice the careers of others for the attainment of its own selfish purposes, also brought Wagner to create gigantic masterworks at a time when his cause seemed almost hopeless. Even when he was a young man he was convinced that he would become a person of importance. In 1835, when he was only twenty-two years old and still a fledgling operatic conductor, he commenced to keep careful notes for his autobiography.

The Fates were kind to Wagner and granted him a long life; he

lied a few months before his seventieth birthday. Yet he was never
n perfect health, and suffered from various stomach disorders and
painful facial eruptions. The life and the works of Wagner constitute
a phenomenon so unusual and so provocative that more books have
been written about him than about almost any other creative artist.
He was, beyond doubt, one of the most important characters of the
nineteenth century and one whose influence made itself felt in many
non-musical fields.

The Earlier Operas

The operas of Wagner that are regularly performed today may be
divided into two groups: (1) the earlier works—*Der Fliegende Holländer, Tannhäuser,* and *Lohengrin,* and (2) the works of his maturity—
the four *Ring* operas: *Das Rheingold, Die Walküre, Siegfried,* and
*Götterdämmerung; Tristan und Isolde, Die Meistersinger von Nürn-
berg,* and *Parsifal.* The three earlier operas are, when compared to
the works of contemporary composers, masterpieces whose sole fault
is that they are overshadowed by Wagner's later creations. In
Tannhäuser and *Lohengrin* Wagner broke with the convention of
dividing an opera into a series of "numbers"—set pieces such as arias
and duets—and the unfolding of the drama is therefore continuous.
The vocal writing of the earlier operas is essentially lyrical, and the
orchestra frequently plays a subordinate role. Pageantry and procession are still employed in a manner which contributes little to the
drama, but nevertheless justifies the interpolation of effective music;
for example, the entrance of the guests in the second act of *Tannhäuser.* These earlier works are, as the composer himself called them,
"romantic operas" in the accepted sense of the word; but as regards
the nature of the text, effectiveness of characterization, and treatment
of the orchestra they are worthy forerunners of the music-dramas.

THE MUSIC-DRAMAS

Our analysis of the works of Wagner will be restricted to the second
group, the music-dramas. In the sense that Wagner's methods
struck a decisive blow at the abuses which prevailed in the opera
house at the time, he may be called a reformer. But on closer observa-
tion it becomes apparent that whatever Wagner's contributions may

have been, they were merely incidental to the reassertion of tha
concept of the application of music to the drama which had guidec
the Florentine progenitors of the opera. It will be recalled that the
earliest opera writers wrote works in which music was utilized only
as a means for heightening the effectiveness of dramatic poetry. The
situation which prevailed during the first half of the nineteenth century, despite the reforms of Gluck and the innovations of von Weber,
is beautifully summed up by Wagner in his treatise *Opera and Drama.*
He writes that the error in the art-genre of opera had been "that a
means of expression (music) has been made the object, and the object
of expression (the drama) has been made the means." The music-
dramas of Wagner restored music to its initial role as an aid in the
accomplishment of a dramatic purpose.

The Texts

Wagner's first departure from accepted convention was his choice of
text. With the exception of *Die Meistersinger von Nürnberg* the subjects of both the romantic operas and the music-dramas are derived
from mythology or folk legend. The reason why Wagner went to
mythology for his texts is stated by him in *Opera and Drama*: "The
incomparable thing about the mythos is that it is true for all time, and
its content, how close soever its compression, is inexhaustible throughout
the ages. The only task of the poet was to expound it." [1] Wagner
has in every instance treated his materials with the greatest freedom,
and some of his libretti, especially *Der Ring des Nibelungen* and
Tristan und Isolde, occupy an important place in the long list of
works inspired by folk legend or medieval epic. *Der Ring des Nibelungen* is one of the most significant of the ten or more Nibelungen
plays turned out by German dramatists during the nineteenth century.
Of these, three antedate Wagner's setting. The myths were recast
by Wagner into dramas whose plots are somewhat confused, and
sometimes, as in *Der Ring des Nibelungen,* contradictory. Wagner's
claim to distinction as a dramatist rests largely upon his ability to
create characters and portray emotions; his attempts at allegorical
philosophizing are long-winded and often unconvincing. But he has

---

[1] *Richard Wagner's Prose Works* (translated by W. A. Ellis), Vol. II, page 191.

created individuals such as *Brünnhilde, Isolde, Wotan, Tristan,* and *Hans Sachs,* whose names alone are common coin; and *Tristan und Isolde* has even been given as a play, without the music. Furthermore, it was these texts and these alone which brought forth the music.

With the exception of the early *Faust Overture* and the *Siegfried Idyll,* the latter written for Cosima's birthday, all of Wagner's purely instrumental works are of an inferior order. Of the three marches which he composed, the *Huldigungsmarsch* (March of Homage) written to honor King Ludwig, the *Kaisersmarsch* celebrating the German victory at the close of the Franco-Prussian war, and the *Centennial March* written by commission for the Philadelphia Exposition in 1876, not one can be compared with the march from the second act of *Tannhäuser.*

The Wagner operas are frequently deficient in stage action; in a work like *Tristan und Isolde* action is almost entirely lacking. The listener will, therefore, find it difficult to realize what is transpiring unless he has familiarized himself with the text in advance. This prior study should never be undertaken with the aid of any versified translation. The poetry of Wagner is complex even in the language in which it was written. Recourse is had to alliterative verse in *Der Ring des Nibelungen* and parts of *Tristan und Isolde.* Most translations make the text even more confused and serve to cast Wagner and opera in general into disrepute. Prose translations are available and should be freely used—before the performance. An intimate knowledge of the text is the *sine qua non* for the enjoyment of a Wagner opera.

The manner in which Wagner combined his dramatic poetry with music to produce the music-drama had been anticipated by Bach in his cantatas and by Schubert in his songs. The problem, simply stated, was to associate music with speech in two ways—first by cloaking the speech with music, second by writing instrumental music to be performed simultaneously with the vocal music, the two in combination producing an artistic result which is incomparably greater than the sum of its parts. We shall now proceed to examine the constituent parts of the music-drama, but in so doing it must not be forgotten that they are always coexistent and have little meaning apart from one another.

The Voice

For Wagner, the singer was simply a vocalist to whom was entrusted the task of delivering words in a style which may be described as melodious declamation, a fusion of speech and song. The manner in which the poetry is set has as its aim the augmentation of the accents and cadences of speech and is indifferent to the metrical scheme of the poetry itself. Music becomes, therefore, a medium for illumination of the text by means of which words, or important parts of words, can be brought out in high relief. The vocal writing is not melodious in the usual sense, for it does not consist of a series of clear-cut, easily recognizable tunes capable of ready extraction, but is a part of what Wagner called "endless melody." This melody is not broken up into arias or choruses, but flows along in uninterrupted association with the poetry, the illumination of which is its sole aim. At certain emotional climaxes, such as "Wotan's Farewell" (*Die Walküre*), the voice part may become pure song. But at no time can any of the music entrusted to the singer be regarded as having any existence apart from the text which it cloaks.

The Orchestra

Associated with the voice in the creation of the "endless melody" is a large orchestra, which, according to Wagner's demands, must not be visible to the audience. The orchestra of the music-dramas differs from all previous operatic orchestras in that its role is not subordinate to that of the stage action, but parallels it throughout. The orchestra is neither accompanist nor commentator, but rather a dramatic protagonist which expresses itself concurrently with another medium of communication—the spoken word raised to the level of musical speech. It is on the complete fusion in the mind of the listener of three simultaneously operating factors—action, the spoken word, and music—that the Wagnerian music-drama depends for the attainment of its objective. In his *Opera and Drama* Wagner has enumerated some of the potentialities of the orchestra.[1] He points out that the orchestra has a faculty of speech that is unique in its ability to utter the unspeakable; that is, the orchestra can express those ideas or

---

[1] *Richard Wagner's Prose Works* (translated by W. A. Ellis), Vol. II, page 316.

emotions for whose communication the spoken word is inadequate. The orchestra can, furthermore, ally itself with gesture; it can recall past situations and past emotions; it can express foreboding or, on occasion, predict what is to come. The orchestra is in reality an organ of expression whose potentialities are limitless. Wagner has employed it to impart verisimilitude to the stage action; to give a distinctive color to each scene; to vivify the words as given out by the singer; to recall past events; to prophesy future events; to tell the audience what characters on the stage themselves do not know; to establish the mood of either an entire opera or an opening scene by means of an instrumental prelude; to deliver a moving commentary. All of these functions are performed by means of a continuous flow of music which is coexistent with the stage action. As commentator, interpreter, and prophet, the orchestra may be compared with the chorus of the Greek drama.

Wagner's concept of the role of the orchestra demanded that that body of instruments be enlarged. The greatest augmentation of the orchestral forces was called for in the *Ring* operas. Here Wagner demanded four instruments each of the flute, the oboe, and the clarinet groups; that is, three flutes and a piccolo, three oboes and an English horn, three clarinets and a bass clarinet. The horn quartet was doubled, a bass trumpet was added to the trumpet group, and a contra-bass trombone to the trombones; Wagner also specified that new instruments, now called "Wagner-tubas" (though in reality modified horns), be played on occasion by the second horn quartet. He meticulously stated the required number of string instruments, though in this respect he had been anticipated by Berlioz in the *Symphonie fantastique*. Wagner turned the genius of each and every orchestral instrument to his own dramatic purpose, and for each he opened up new avenues of expression and revealed hitherto hidden possibilities of execution. Many devices which were at first deemed impracticable have now become the common property of all orchestral composers. But Wagner's art of orchestration did not emphasize single instruments so much as instruments in combination. The richness and fullness of any Wagner chord, no matter how softly it may be played, can be attributed to his ability to create subtle mixtures of tone-colors in which no particular timbre predominates and a perfect balance is

achieved.   There is no better demonstration of Wagner's contribution
to the vocabulary of orchestral language than a comparison of the sonority of one of his orchestral chords with one from a symphony of Haydn,
Mozart, or Beethoven.

The Wagner orchestra pours forth what appears to be "endless
melody." Closer examination will show, however, that this endless
melody is comprised of very short phrases deftly interwoven in
a tapestry-like manner which entirely obliterates the junction points.
The apparent jointlessness of a Wagner score is due to the composer's
mastery of modulation and his ability to fuse successive orchestral
colors. He himself wrote in a letter to Mathilde Wesendonk:[1] "It
now seems to me that the finest and most profound feature of my
art is the art of transition, for its entire texture consists of such
transitions."

The Leading-Motive (Leitmotiv)

The orchestral language is made specific through repetition of certain phrases which have identified themselves with some aspect of the
drama as enacted on the stage, a person, a thing, a phenomenon of
nature, or some abstract concept. These phrases have been called
leading-motives, and are short, striking, easily recognizable themes.
They make their appearance in the orchestra at some salient moment,
or on some occasions appear as vehicles for the text. In any case
their associations are vivid. It is of the utmost importance to realize
that the leading-motives are not labels which bob up mechanically
whenever the persons, things, or ideas associated with them appear or
are mentioned. The motives are subjected to a system of variation that
casts a strong light on the transformations which their associated
persons, things, or ideas have undergone. The variations may be of
all conceivable types—melodic, harmonic, rhythmic, or instrumental.

A few examples will illustrate the dramatic potency of this variation
technique. The following theme appears for the first time in Das
Rheingold as the light of dawning day illumines the abode of the
gods, Walhall:

---

[1] Richard Wagner an Mathilde Wesendonk, Tagebuchblätter und Briefe, page 189.

Ex. 1

It thus definitely associates itself with *Walhall* and, by transference, with Wotan, its lord. In the succeeding opera, *Die Walküre,* Wotan foresees the tragic end of the gods, and this is expressed by the orchestra in an intense variant of Example 1:

Ex. 2

The following buoyant horn call is associated with the young Siegfried, the child of the forest:

Ex. 3

In *Götterdämmerung* Siegfried has reached man's estate and has become the husband of the Valkyrie maiden—Brünnhilde. Before he appears on the stage, this transformation of the motive associated with him indicates how he himself has been transformed:

Ex. 4

And after Siegfried is slain, the long orchestral interlude [1] which serve
as his eulogy concludes with:

Ex. 5

Wagner was not the first operatic composer to make use of recurring
phrases as unifying dramatic elements. The procedure may be ob
served as far back as the works of Monteverdi; and it had also been
anticipated in instrumental music in such works as the *Symphonie
fantastique* with its *idée fixe,* and in the symphonic poems of Liszt
No other composer, however, has approached Wagner in his ability
to use the leading-motive as a plastic factor in the development of a
drama.

For purposes of identification the leading-motives were supplied with
names, not by Wagner, but by writers of didactic commentaries on the
music-dramas. It must be borne in mind, however, that many of the
leading-motives are associated with dramatic situations of a complex
emotional hue, and that as a result the names assigned to them are merely
suggestive. The use of these names is not objectionable provided the
listener realizes that they are only arbitrary labels representing a third
person's summaries in word-speech of the dramatic functions of the
motives. To "translate" the sounds of these motives as they are given
out by the orchestra is tantamount to defeating Wagner's purpose in
employing them.

Chromaticism, the use of semitonal progressions within the frame-
work of the diatonic scale, was carried to new extremes by Wagner,
particularly in *Tristan und Isolde* and *Parsifal.* The following excerpt
from the Prelude to Act III of the former work sums up the chromatic
idiom, both harmonic and melodic, which pervades these operas. The
melody includes every note of the chromatic scale from C to C with
the exception of B-natural, and the bass descends in half-steps:

Ex. 6

This procedure serves in large measure to obliterate our feeling for a definite tonality. In many respects Wagner's style, with its breaking down of older concepts of the function of the scale and the chord, is prophetic of twentieth-century procedures. It is only fair, however, to point out that the works of Liszt were important influences on Wagner's harmonic vocabulary, as Wagner himself acknowledged.

The Preludes

Wagner seems never to have made up his mind about the function of the overture, despite the preachments to be found in an essay on the overture, which he wrote in 1841. No less than three different types of preliminary pieces are to be found in his works. Up to and including *Tannhäuser* they bear the designation *Overture,* afterwards they are called *Vorspiel* (Prelude). In none of these introductions does Wagner adhere to the sonata form, which had been employed by his great predecessors Beethoven and von Weber. The first type of prelude is found in the four *Ring* operas wherein the orchestral preliminary is simply an introduction to the first scene. Examples of the second type are the preludes to *Lohengrin, Tristan und Isolde,* and *Parsifal.* In these Wagner has confined himself to symbolizing in music the basic concept of the entire opera. The third type shows a close affiliation with the dramatic overture of Wagner's predecessors in that it is a condensation of the entire opera. In this category are the overtures to *Der Fliegende Holländer,* and *Tannhäuser,* and the prelude to *Die Meistersinger von Nürnberg.* A notable feature of almost all the operas is the presence in each of a beautiful and significant third-act prelude, not at all like the old *entr'acte* music, but rather an important instrumental introduction, an overture to the act.

Because of their vividness of portrayal, their richness of orchestration, and their wealth of beautiful melody, the Wagner overtures and preludes have acquired an existence apart from the operas which they were intended to preface and are now among the most frequently performed orchestral works. While they are dominated throughout by a dramatic purpose, their formal structure, although following no conventional pattern, is such as to make them intelligible concert pieces.

Like that of Bach and Beethoven, the art of Wagner does not permit satisfactory illustration by means of selected examples. Each of his works has a markedly individual character, and it would be difficult to state which opera is the most typical. One of the music-dramas, however, *Die Meistersinger von Nürnberg,* is beautifully condensed in its Prelude, one of Wagner's finest. A study of this composition will therefore serve as an excellent introduction to Wagner's art.

PRELUDE TO "DIE MEISTERSINGER VON NÜRNBERG"

The action of *Die Meistersinger* takes place in the Bavarian city of Nuremberg during the sixteenth century. The *Meistersinger* were tradesmen and artisans banded together in a powerful guild, whose aim was to foster the creation of songs. The high artistic purpose of the *Meistersinger* was thwarted by their belief that works of art could be created according to an elaborate set of rules, mastery of which was a prerequisite to membership in their order. The leader of the guild was the liberal-minded cobbler-poet, Hans Sachs. The essential conflict of the opera is the struggle between the conservative spirit in art, as typified by the *Meistersinger* and carried to an extreme by the ridiculous town clerk Sixtus Beckmesser, and the progressive youthful spirit which is impatient with outworn canons, and desires to create its art according to its own lights. The symbol of this viewpoint is a young knight, Walther von Stolzing, who comes into conflict with the pedantic regulations of the *Meistersinger* when he aspires to win the hand of Eva Pogner, daughter of a goldsmith who is a member of the guild. At a contest of song held on the meadow outside of Nuremberg, Walther triumphs over Beckmesser, his opponent in love as well as in art. The opera closes with a magnificent address by Hans Sachs, in which he reconciles the old and the new and points out the debt of the new to the old.

The prelude to the opera may be divided into three sections, the third of which refers back to the first in a manner which, although quite free, creates the impression of a three-part form. The work commences with the resplendent theme of the *Meistersinger*, the earnest, dignified custodians of art:

Ex. 7

This is considerably extended by the full orchestra, and finally gives way to a rapturous wood-wind melody identified with young Walther's love for Eva:

Ex. 8

A brilliant scale passage in the violins then serves to introduce another theme of the *Meistersinger*, a march-like fanfare adapted by Wagner from an actual *Meistersinger* melody encountered by him in an old tome which treated of their customs:

Ex. 9

This leads to one of Wagner's richest orchestral passages, based on a

theme which reappears at the close of the opera as Hans Sachs delivers
his praise of German art:

Ex. 10

An agitated interlude, describing young Walther's perturbations of
heart, is followed by the middle section. This commences with a
theme that is associated with Walther, and also becomes part of the
Prize Song heard in Act III:

Ex. 11

The course of this beautiful melody is interrupted by an impetuous
phrase derived from a song sung by Walther in Act I, and symbolic
of his impatience:

Ex. 12

After a sudden change of instrumentation Wagner depicts the ridiculous Beckmesser as he makes himself a laughing stock before the
assembled populace of Nuremberg. The music is a parody of the
Meistersinger motive quoted in Example 7 and is given out with
carping incisiveness by the wood-winds:

Ex. 13

The conclusion of the prelude is practically identical with the close
of the opera, in which Hans Sachs reconciles the old and the new.

Wagner effects a reconciliation of these opposing viewpoints by contrapuntal combination of their musical symbols:

Ex. 14

The prelude concludes with a triumphant pronouncement of the *Meistersinger* motive (Example 7), followed by jubilant fanfares in the trumpets. The concert version of the prelude brings it to a full close; in the opera itself there are no terminating chords and the music leads directly into the first scene.

SUGGESTED READINGS

Ernest Newman's *The Life of Richard Wagner* (Knopf), of which two volumes, dealing with his career as far as the year 1860, have already been published, is the most authoritative English treatment of a comprehensive and difficult subject. The standard German biography is the "authorized" six-volume work of Carl Glasenapp (Breitkopf und Härtel). A part of Glasenapp's treatise has been translated into English by William Ashton Ellis and published as *The Life of Richard Wagner* (Kegan Paul, Trench, Trübner). The last three volumes of Ellis' biography represent original work and not a translation; but they go only as far as the year 1859.

Wagner's autobiography *My Life* (Dodd, Mead) is a valuable work which, however, must be read with the greatest circumspection. It extends only to the year 1864. *Richard Wagner: A Critical Biography* by G. A. Hight (Arrowsmith) is an accurate treatise which contains synopses and critical discussions of the operas as well as fine accounts of their legendary backgrounds.

Ernest Newman's *Wagner as Man and Artist* (Knopf) is an important study. *Fact and Fiction about Wagner* (Knopf), by the same author, dispels some popular misconceptions. *The Women in Wagner's Life* by Julius Kapp (Knopf) treats a significant phase of Wagner's career.

There are many collections of Wagner's letters. The best selection is that of Wilhelm Altmann—*The Letters of Richard Wagner* (Dutton). *Richard Wagner's Prose Works* (Kegan Paul, Trench, Trübner) is an English translation by William Ashton Ellis of all the important essays.

The best introduction to the texts and the music of the operas is to be found in Ernest Newman's *Stories of the Great Operas* (Garden City Publishing Co.), in which most of the leading-motives are given. Gertrude Hall has made translations of the texts of the operas into English prose in *The Wagnerian Romances* (Knopf).

Chapter XXII

ITALIAN OPERA OF THE
LATE NINETEENTH CENTURY

A T THE same time that Wagner was formulating new operatic standards with his music-dramas, an Italian contemporary, Giuseppe Verdi, was content to follow in the footsteps of Rossini, Bellini, and Donizetti. But while adhering in the main to the basic traditions of Italian opera, Verdi won for himself a position as Wagner's most formidable rival in the sphere of dramatic music.

Giuseppe Verdi

Giuseppe Verdi was born in the Parmesan hamlet of Le Roncole on October 10, 1813, the son of a poor innkeeper. He was thus only a few months younger than Wagner. He received his first instruction in music from a local organist and displayed so much talent that when he was eighteen years old fellow-townsmen provided him with funds for study in Milan. The conservatory in that city refused to admit him, however, and he therefore became the pupil in composition and orchestration of an excellent teacher, Vincenzo Lavigna. Verdi's earliest opera, which showed strong influences of Bellini, was performed in 1839, but his first great success was scored with *Nabucco,* which had its première in 1842. This was also the year in which the opera *Rienzi* brought Wagner his first taste of fame. The chronicle of Verdi's life after the triumph of *Nabucco* is largely a record of his operas.

The successive stages of Verdi's evolution as a creative artist may be divided into three periods. All of the operas of the first period (1839–1850) have now disappeared from the repertoire. The second period (1851–1867) includes some of Verdi's most popular works—*Rigoletto* (1851), *Il Trovatore* (1853), and *La Traviata* (1853). In

the last period (1871–1892) are found his three great masterpieces—
Aïda (1871), *Otello* (1887), and *Falstaff* (1893). Verdi wrote twenty-
six operas in all, about twice as many as Wagner. The success which
most of his works achieved brought him a considerable income; but
despite the wealth which he accumulated, he always remained a simple
peasant at heart.

Verdi and Nationalism

It was not until 1871 that the various Italian states were unified to
form what is now the kingdom of Italy; during the period in which
most of the operas of Verdi were written, political disturbances aiming
at the overthrow of the Austrian domination were rife throughout
the peninsula. The libretti of some of Verdi's operas contained scenes
dealing with oppression, and operatic audiences of the day were
prone to see in them representations of their own subjection to a
foreign yoke. As a consequence, patriotic demonstrations in the theater were frequent occurrences. In addition, the letters of Verdi's
name were the same as the initial letters of the Sardinian king, whom
the Italian nationalists wished to see as King of Italy. Audiences
could therefore defy the Austrian authorities by shouting *"Viva Verdi"*
at the end of a performance, as a disguise for *Vittorio Emmanuele, Re
d'Italia.* Verdi himself was an ardent patriot; but his nationalistic
tendencies, as far as his music was concerned, consisted of a devotion
to an Italian style of operatic composition to the rigid exclusion of
German influences. His brand of nationalism was, like Wagner's,
more intuitive than purposeful.

Libretti

The libretti of most of Verdi's operas were of a romantic nature,
although the type of romanticism displayed by them differed in large
measure from that of the German opera with its predilection for folk-
lore. Verdi leaned towards lurid, melodramatic plots from which
sanguinary elements were seldom absent. *Rigoletto,* which concludes
with the murder of the jester's daughter, is typical. The three operas
of Verdi's last period are couched in a more restrained idiom; the
libretti of *Otello* and *Falstaff* were adapted from Shakespeare by a
fellow-composer, Arrigo Boito.

GIUSEPPE VERDI

Style

The most striking feature of Verdi's operatic style is his power of portraying a dramatic situation in eloquent vocal melody. The popularity of Verdi is attributable to the vigorous, forceful nature of the broad tunes which abound in his operas—virile melodies which, despite their adaptability to the hand-organ, possess a highly dramatic flavor. Verdi's sole aim was truthfulness of dramatic presentation; none of his operas was written to serve as a medium for the display of vocal pyrotechnics. Like all Italian opera composers, he had a consummate knowledge of the expressive powers of the human voice; and it is from the dramatic potency of straightforward melody rendered by an accomplished vocalist that the effectiveness of his operas derives.

In Verdi's last three operas, *Aïda, Otello,* and *Falstaff,* the orchestra assumed a role of importance, and the traditional division into set pieces was abandoned in favor of a continuous flow of music. But the human voice still remained the dominant factor. The analogy between these later developments in Verdi's style and some of the innovations of Wagner at once brought forth the comment that Verdi had fallen under Wagnerian influences—an accusation which he bitterly resented. The idiom of the last operas, while in a limited sense analogous to that of Wagner, was the result not of any external influence, but rather of Verdi's natural evolution as a composer.

The Manzoni Requiem

The death in 1873 of the Italian poet and novelist Alessandro Manzoni affected Verdi so deeply that he composed a Requiem Mass in his memory. The text of the Requiem Mass is rich in dramatic suggestion, and Verdi responded to it with the same instinct for dramatic representation that characterized his operas. The charge has been made that the idiom of the Requiem is too theatrical. There are, to be sure, episodes in the Requiem which recall the style of Verdi's operatic music, but the sincerity and depth of conviction which pervade the work as a whole cannot be questioned.

Verismo

Two operas that appeared in Italy at the close of the nineteenth century are now the Siamese twins of the operatic repertoire—Mascagni's *Cavalleria rusticana* (Rustic Chivalry), first performed in 1890, and Leoncavallo's *I Pagliacci* (The Clowns), which appeared two years later. These operas set the fashion for *verismo,* a type of operatic realism. The texts of these works, based on events in the lives of the common people, are compact and terse; emotional climaxes are frequent, and the bloody dénouements are swift.

From the musical standpoint the most important feature of these operas is the close association of text and music. The orchestra plays a comparatively important role, and the manner of writing for it suggests the influence of Wagner; but as is customary in Italian opera, the voice remains supreme. The music of these works is, however, not of a consistently high order, and the effectiveness of many of the melodic ideas is negated by overinflation. It must be conceded, however, that an opera like *I Pagliacci* is a remarkably effective integration of drama and music. Neither Mascagni nor Leoncavallo ever succeeded in fulfilling the promise of these two operas, and the numerous dramatic works which followed them have failed to win a firm place in the operatic repertory.

Puccini

The successor to Verdi was Giacomo Puccini (1858–1924), a composer of exceptional attainments. Puccini's style, although far from eclectic, was a fusion of three important features of nineteenth-century opera: the expressive melody of Verdi, the dramatic potency of *verismo,* and the illuminative commentary of the Wagner orchestra. Puccini's masterworks are *La Bohème* (1896), *Tosca* (1900), and *Madama Butterfly* (1904); he wrote a fine one-act comic opera *Gianni Schicchi* (1918).

In addition to his melodic gifts and his fine sense of the theater, Puccini possessed an excellent grasp of orchestral values. The orchestra plays an important part in all of his works, but as is customary in Italian opera, it refrains from encroaching on the domain of the voice. Puccini's orchestration is colorful, if none too original, and the many picturesque scenes which occur in his operas owe their effectiveness as much to the orchestra as to the scene painter. Puccini also made use of the leading-motive, although in a somewhat limited fashion.

Suggested Readings

The best works in this field are: *Giuseppe Verdi, His Life and Works,* by Francis Toye (Knopf), and *Puccini: The Man, His Life, His Work,* by Richard Specht (Knopf). The principal operas of Verdi and Puccini are described by Ernest Newman in *Stories of the Great Operas* (Garden City Publishing Company). Synopses of *Cavalleria rusticana* and *I Pagliacci* are to be found in Kobbé's *The Complete Opera Book* (Putnam).

Chapter XXIII \

JOHANNES BRAHMS

THE OPENING of the festival theater at Bayreuth in 1876 was a great triumph for Wagner, the creator of music-dramas. But Wagner, the theorist, went down to defeat when the First Symphony of Johannes Brahms was performed at Karlsruhe less than three months after Bayreuth had opened its doors. Strange as his words may sound today, Wagner had confidently declared that the expressive possibilities of absolute music had been exhausted in the symphonies of Beethoven; he maintained that Beethoven himself had shown in his Ninth Symphony that instrumental music would have to find its salvation in an alliance with poetry. The compositions of Brahms have demonstrated the error of Wagner's dictum.

Johannes Brahms, born in Hamburg on May 7, 1833, was the son of a musician who played the double bass in the orchestra of the town theater. The father taught his son to play the violin, the 'cello, and the horn, and as a child, Brahms helped augment the family income by playing at dances. When he was seven years old he commenced the study of the piano under a local teacher, Otto Cossel, and made such rapid progress that by the time he was ten, Cossel prevailed upon the learned theorist and somewhat successful composer Eduard Marxsen to accept the boy as his pupil. Marxsen's teaching was an important influence on the development of Brahms. A well-schooled musician, he focussed the attention of his pupil on the works of Bach and Beethoven. It is interesting to note that at Brahms' first appearance as a recitalist (September, 1848) he performed a fugue of Bach. Up to his twentieth year he led a somewhat desultory life in Hamburg. Although it was necessary for him to give lessons, play at dances, make arrangements, and do other musical hack-work, he found time not only for serious study of the technical aspects of composition, but also for the writing of some piano works.

The arrival in Hamburg of a Hungarian violinist, Eduard Reményi, was an important factor in Brahms' career. Reményi, who was impressed by Brahms' ability as an accompanist, suggested that they embark on a concert tour together. The pair left Hamburg in April, 1853, and in the course of their travels played at Hanover, where Reményi's compatriot and former fellow-student, Joseph Joachim, was concertmaster of the Royal Orchestra. Joachim quickly perceived the unusual nature of Brahms' talents and directed him to what was then the Mecca for all young musicians—the Altenburg, Liszt's residence at Weimar. Brahms stayed in Weimar for six weeks. Liszt was enthusiastic over his compositions and looked on him as a new adherent of his group. Brahms, however, found himself unattracted by all that Weimar represented.

Another artistic contact for which Joachim was also directly responsible proved more fruitful. On September 30, 1853, Brahms called on Schumann, who was then music director at the Rhine town of Düsseldorf. Schumann was so impressed with Brahms and with his compositions that he wrote the celebrated article *Neue Bahnen* (New Paths) for the *Neue Zeitschrift für Musik,* the important musical magazine whose editor he had once been. The essay, which hailed the twenty-year-old Brahms as a composer from whom the world might some day expect great choral and orchestral works, had two important results—it served to make Brahms' name known in all the musical circles of Europe, and it placed on his shoulders the responsibility for fulfilling Schumann's prophecy. The enthusiastic Schumann also wrote to the publishers Breitkopf and Härtel and persuaded them to undertake the publication of Brahms' compositions. From that time until Schumann's death three years later, Brahms was in intimate contact with him.

Through the intercession of two pupils of Clara Schumann, Brahms was given a post at the small court of Lippe-Detmold in 1857. His duties were light, and he had ample time for composition and for frequent journeys to Hamburg, where he conducted a small chorus of women's voices. In 1859 he appeared as soloist at Leipzig in his monumental Piano Concerto in D minor, his first composition of

JOHANNES BRAHMS

symphonic dimensions. This somewhat austere work was roundly condemned by all except, interestingly enough, the adherents of Liszt.

Brahms resigned his post at Lippe-Detmold in 1860 and spent two years in Hamburg, where he hoped to receive the position of director of the Philharmonic Society. His name again figured in the public press when he, Joachim, and two other musicians drew up an indiscreet declaration in which they deplored and condemned the artistic tenets of Liszt and his disciples. From that time on Brahms was *persona non grata* with the Weimar group.

Inasmuch as Hamburg did not see fit to honor its native son with a post, Brahms, like his predecessor Beethoven, turned towards Vienna. He appeared in the musical capital as pianist and composer in November, 1862, and established enough of a reputation to warrant his being made conductor of a choral organization, the *Singakademie;* but he resigned his post after presenting four programs on which the works of older masters, particularly Bach, held an important place. Vienna remained Brahms' residence, but after resigning the conductorship of the *Singakademie* he travelled extensively.

In 1868 his great choral work, *Ein Deutsches Requiem* (A German Requiem) was sung in Bremen. The performance was an unqualified success, and the numerous repetitions in all the larger German towns served to bring the composer's name to the attention of the world at large. The Requiem was followed by other important choral works, *Rinaldo,* the *Liebeslieder* (Love Songs), the *Alto Rhapsody,* the *Schicksalslied* (Song of Destiny), and the *Triumphlied* (Song of Triumph). The last named, composed in commemoration of the German victory in the Franco-Prussian War, was received with excesses of enthusiasm wherever it was performed. In 1872 Brahms was reinstalled as a choral director at Vienna. For three years he was director of the *Singverein,* the chorus of the *Gesellschaft der Musikfreunde* (Society of the Friends of Music). This was the last of the three small posts which Brahms held during his lifetime. None can be said to have been very important, nor did they contribute much to what was largely an uneventful life.

The last two decades of Brahms' life were free from any official entanglements, but his work was frequently interrupted by arduous concert tours on which he appeared as performer and conductor. As yet he was known as a composer only of piano, chamber, and choral

music. Brahms, with characteristic reserve, had withheld his First
Symphony until 1876, at which time he was already forty-three years
old. The Second Symphony followed in the next year. Within the
next ten years he had added to the list of his symphonic works two
more symphonies, a violin concerto, a second piano concerto (in B-flat
major), and a concerto for violin and violoncello. In 1879 the University of Breslau conferred upon him a doctor's degree, *honoris causa,*
in acknowledgement of his being, as the diploma said "the foremost
living German master of the art of strict composition." As a gesture
of appreciation Brahms composed the *Academic Festival* Overture,
based on student songs, and conducted it in the Great Hall of the university. The University of Cambridge had given him an honorary
Doctor of Music degree in 1877. Brahms died at the height of his
fame on April 3, 1897, and was buried close to Beethoven and Schubert.
The prophecy which Schumann had made forty-four years before had
been fulfilled.

The long list of distinguished men and women who enjoyed the
friendship of Brahms is headed by Clara Schumann, the widow of
his great benefactor. Brahms was extremely devoted to her and sent
many of his compositions to her for criticism before publishing them.

The personality of Brahms resembled that of Beethoven in that it
was concealed from the world by a rough exterior. To strangers he
seemed crude and almost ill-mannered. Among friends he was
thoroughly charming, genial, and witty, usually quite exuberant, and
fond of jokes. He never married and had the typical old bachelor's
fondness for children. They, in turn, were attracted to the stubby
little man with the beard, who almost invariably had some candy in
his pocket for them. Brahms was essentially modest; he hated pub-
licity and any sort of public function. He was particularly reserved
about his own works, and his estimate of himself as a composer extended almost to self-depreciation. Although he was widely read and
as his letters attest, possessed no slight literary facility, Brahms' only
literary effort was the unfortunate manifesto signed in 1860.

Brahms and Wagner.

Richard Wagner, his theories, and his music-dramas had been revolutionary enough to engender much opposition on the part of those
individuals who chose to remain faithful to the older music. Unfor-

tunately for Brahms, the anti-Wagnerites selected him as their symbol of musical rectitude. The Wagner faction retaliated with much venom, and Wagner himself was not above writing slanderous statements about his younger contemporary. While Brahms may have had his private opinions, he never indulged in any public defamation of Wagner. It may be remarked, parenthetically, that he had an excellent knowledge of the music-dramas and admired much in them. But he could not evince any enthusiasm for them as entities.

No traces of the celebrated squabble remain today. With the passing of time it has become clear that Wagner and Brahms operated in spheres which were remote from each other and wholly unantagonistic. The controversy between them was really a battle between the heirs of Beethoven, each with definite ideas as to how the magnificent heritage should be utilized. Wagner elected to put the orchestral language of Beethoven to new uses; Brahms, on the other hand, was content to follow unquestioningly in Beethoven's footsteps.

Brahms' Position in the History of Music

The position of Brahms in the history of music is somewhat unique, for according to the style of his works his rightful place is directly after Beethoven and Schumann. It would be no exaggeration to say that he wrote as if von Weber, Berlioz, Liszt, and Wagner had never existed. The implications of this statement are clear when one recalls that Brahms was no less than twenty years younger than Wagner. One looks in vain in the list of his works for piano pieces with fanciful titles, for program symphonies, or for symphonic poems. In the sphere of instrumental music he restricted himself to the forms of Bach and Beethoven—the variation, the sonata and its allied forms, the symphony, the string quartet, the concerto; and his concept of these forms, as opposed to those of such of his contemporaries as employed them, remained truly classical and wholly unaffected by the formal innovations of Liszt. It is therefore with a considerable degree of accuracy that Brahms is often called a neo-classicist.

Brahms also shows his kinship with Bach and Beethoven in his predilection for, and mastery of, the variation form. There are two splendid sets of variations for the piano that are frequently performed, the *Variations and Fugue on a Theme of Handel* (Opus 24), and the

twenty-eight *Variations on a Theme of Paganini* (Opus 35).   For orchestra he has written a set of *Variations on a Theme of Haydn* (Opus
56a).   Brahms' crowning achievement as a writer of variations is the
last movement of his Fourth Symphony.   Here he has reverted to so
old a form as the passacaglia [1] and has written thirty-two variations
on this theme:

Ex. 1

But the neo-classicism of Brahms was not the equivalent of an
empty eclecticism.   Although he used the forms of masters who preceded him by approximately half a century, he treated them in a
highly personal manner, and the characteristics of his style are well
marked.

Characteristics of Brahms' Music

The music of Brahms reveals a degree of concentration comparable
to that already encountered in the works of Beethoven.   In the sphere
of absolute music Brahms must be acknowledged one of the greatest
masters of the art of development.   This mastery was the joint product of a fertile imagination and a rich technical equipment.   The
writing of a new work was for Brahms, as for Beethoven, a prolonged
act of labor.   He, too, subjected his works to severe self-criticism.   It
is said that he composed and destroyed over twenty string quartets
before publishing one work in this difficult form.   As a consequence
of this attitude, the formal design of his works exhibits a perfection
which is not to be found in the works of his more impetuous, though
not one whit more romantic, predecessors.   Brahms' attitude toward
composition is perhaps best summed up in a statement made to a
friend, George Henschel, who later became conductor of the Boston
Symphony Orchestra: "One ought never to forget that by actually per-
fecting *one* piece one gains and learns more than by commencing or
half-finishing a dozen.   Let it rest, let it rest, and keep going back
to it and working at it over and over again, until it is completed as a

[1] See page 76.

finished work of art, until there is not a note too much or too little, not a bar you could improve upon. Whether it is *beautiful* also, is an entirely different matter, but perfect it *must* be." [1]

Most of Brahms' finest themes are lyrical in character, and bear a strong resemblance to folk-song. It is often his custom to commence a first movement with a song-like theme rather than with an incisive dramatic one. These cantabile subjects are usually of considerable breadth. During the course of an extended movement they are frequently subjected to elaborate polyphonic treatment. As a harmonist Brahms again reverted to the idiom of his forebears and totally abjured the sensuous chromaticism and frequent modulation of the Liszt-Wagner school. One of the most attractive features of his style is his rhythmic originality. In this respect he was far ahead of Wagner. Syncopations, cross-accents, combinations of rhythms, and irregular groupings of phrases abound in his music.

Beauty of thematic material, conciseness of development, and perfection of form were much more weighty considerations with Brahms than questions of tone-color. His reactionary spirit is again shown in his indifference to the new coloristic potentialities of both the piano and the orchestra, which had been demonstrated by Chopin and Liszt on one hand, and by Berlioz and Wagner on the other. Brahms' writing for both piano and orchestra is thick and muddy. In his writing for the former he meticulously avoids virtuosity for its own sake, and such difficulties as arise are only incidental to the music itself. His orchestration is stolid and sonorous, lacking variety and brilliance. In characteristic fashion Brahms made no use of the new instruments that had recently found a place in the orchestra, or of the mechanical improvements that had given older instruments like the brasses greater melodic freedom.

Piano Music

Brahms' compositions for the piano occupy an important place in the repertoire of contemporary recitalists. That the public was late in granting them the recognition which is their due can be attributed largely to the fact that none of the piano pieces is "brilliant" in the usual sense. As has been pointed out previously Brahms ignored

[1] George Henschel—*Personal Recollections of Johannes Brahms*, page 39.

contemporary trends, and all his works are totally lacking in technical bravura. Brahms apparently aimed at fullness rather than brilliancy in his piano writing, but the frequent doublings and progressions in thirds and sixths, particularly in the lower register of the instrument, often make for thickness and turgidity. Almost all of the piano works exhibit the rich polyphonic texture and the rhythmic complexity so characteristic of his style.

Of the three piano sonatas the Third, in F minor (Opus 5), is considered the finest. The numerous shorter pieces bear titles such as *Capriccio, Intermezzo, Rhapsody, Ballade.* These indications cannot be construed literally; nor does Brahms' use of them approximate that of other composers. They are subjective character-pieces filled with romantic fantasy which expresses itself without the aid of any external program. The great works in variation form have already been mentioned.

Like all great composers, Brahms had his lighter moments. His predilection for Bach and Beethoven did not prevent his possessing an unbounded enthusiasm for the waltzes and operettas of his Viennese contemporary Johann Strauss, composer of the celebrated *Beautiful Blue Danube.* Brahms' own essays in the dance form so closely identified with the city of his adoption have also become very popular. They comprise the sixteen Waltzes for Piano, four hands, (Opus 39); and the *Liebeslieder* (Love Songs) for Piano, four hands, and Vocal Quartet, (Opus 52, Opus 65). The four sets of Hungarian Dances, also for piano duet, include some of Brahms' most popular compositions. Brahms' interest in the folk music of Hungary had probably been aroused by his contact with Reményi. The Hungarian Dances are artistic arrangements of traditional gypsy tunes whose original spirit has been effectively reproduced.

Songs

As a song writer Brahms also held aloof from contemporary practices of combining poetry and music; in his choice of poems and in his setting of them he was predominantly lyrical rather than dramatic. His vocal writing does not aim to bring out the details of the poem by subtleties of declamation, but endeavors instead to portray its underlying mood by cloaking it with beautiful melody. Many of these melodies possess a simplicity which recalls folk song. Of the two hundred Brahms songs the greater part are in strophic form. The piano accompaniments are full and rich, but again do not aim to subject the poem to detailed treatment. The majority of the songs are love songs, a type thoroughly congenial to Brahms' essentially lyrical temperament. The *Vier ernste Gesänge* (Four Serious Songs), Opus 121, occupy a special place in the list of Brahms' compositions. Written in the last year of his life, they constitute an intimate personal document revealing his attitude towards the death which he knew was not far away.

Chamber Music

Of all the romantic composers only Schubert, Mendelssohn, and Schumann had ventured to write chamber music. The more ardent spirits of the movement were too concerned with the piano, the orchestra, and the theater. The nature of chamber music is such as to require mastery of form and power of sustained development. Fanciful programs are seldom used; nor can coloristic facility be used as a cloak for paucity of invention. Of all the successors of Beethoven, Brahms was the only one who possessed the wherewithal to write chamber music works worthy of a place beside those of his great forerunner. Brahms' output in the field of chamber music comprises twenty-four works, including three string quartets (Opus 51, No. 1 in C minor, Opus 51, No. 2 in A minor, and Opus 67 in B-flat major); a great piano quintet (Opus 34 in F minor), and three celebrated sonatas for violin and piano (Opus 78 in G major, Opus 100 in A major, and Opus 108 in D minor).

FIRST MOVEMENT OF THE STRING QUARTET
IN A MINOR, OPUS 51, NO. 2

The first movement of the String Quartet in A minor, Opus 51, No. 2 affords a fine example of Brahms' chamber-music style. The movement is in sonata form and opens as do so many of Brahms' first movements with a cantabile theme:

Ex. 2

The second group begins with one of Brahms' most beautiful melodies, given out by the pair of violins:

Ex. 3

This melody is repeated by the second violin and viola, and after some elaboration gives way to a theme which brings the exposition to a close:

Ex. 4

The development is a concise working out of the first three measures of the first theme (Example 2) and the closing theme (Example 4). Its texture is thoroughly polyphonic, and in many instances the two themes appear in combination. The recapitulation presents no points of departure. The coda, however, is a vigorous development of the first three measures of the first theme.

The Piano Quintet in F minor, Opus 34, Brahms' only composition for this particular combination of instruments, is one of his most famous chamber-music works. Its present form is the result of two recastings; Brahms originally conceived the work as a string quartet with two 'cellos, and later arranged it as a sonata for two pianos before giving it its final form. The first movement, in sonata form, commences with a subject of typical breadth:

Ex. 5

Orchestral Music

As has been stated previously, the first of the four Brahms symphonies did not appear until 1876. Widespread popular acceptance of these works was delayed because of the partisan struggle then prevailing. Brahms' own adherents caused the pro-Wagner faction further irritation by calling the First Symphony the "Tenth." Hans von Bülow found himself moved to excesses of enthusiasm and called public attention to the fact that the names of three great German composers began with B by coining the slogan "Bach, Beethoven, Brahms."

The four symphonies are in many respects the culmination of Brahms' career as a composer of instrumental music. Each is a masterpiece, each is typical Brahms throughout, yet each has its own decided individuality and presents its own special problems. The Third, in F major, completed in 1883, is probably the easiest to grasp since it is the shortest, the most colorful, and the most cheerful of the four.

SYMPHONY NO. 3, IN F MAJOR

The first movement of the Third Symphony, an *Allegro con brio,* opens vigorously with a three-note theme, *a,* which pervades the entire movement and furthermore recurs in the last. As this theme terminates, another vigorous theme, *b,* is announced by the violins over *a* as a bass:

Ex. 6

The second group is in the key of A major and employs a new rhythm, $\frac{9}{4}$. The clarinet gives out this song-like theme in which a small group of notes is continually altered:

Ex. 7

The $\frac{6}{4}$ rhythm in which the movement began is restored as the oboe recalls theme *a* of Example 6, and after a few measures of pleasant dialogue in the wood-winds in which theme *a* is again heard the exposition concludes with a series of syncopated chords. In the development, which is somewhat short, Example 7 is changed into a forceful $\frac{6}{4}$ rhythm and assigned to the violas, 'cellos, and bassoons. Theme *a* again appears, first as a beautiful horn solo:

Ex. 8

It then proceeds to work its way upward from the bass and after considerable dramatic suspense finally serves to usher in the recapitulation. The coda subjects theme *b* to extensive development of a forceful character. The movement closes with peaceful reminiscences of themes *a* and *b*, quotations of the former in the wood-winds being followed by the descent of the latter in the violins.

The second movement, an *Andante*, begins with a simple folk-like subject announced by clarinets and bassoons. Cadences which give the effect of echoes are sounded between the phrases by the lower strings:

Ex. 9

This melody is repeated with figuration, and after a subdued transitional passage is followed by another folk-like subject entrusted to the clarinet and the bassoon:

Ex. 10

The distinctive feature of this theme is the two repeated notes with which it begins. Brahms makes much of this two-note motive during

the course of this movement, and it reappears in the fourth movement. The exposition of the thematic material of the movement
concludes with a series of announcements of this motive in various
registers of the orchestra.

A short development, in which the first theme is subjected to ornamental variation and is presented in various keys, is followed by an
abbreviated recapitulation. A beautiful feature of the movement is
the broad, expansive coda. This begins with a new subject whose
origin can be traced back to the first theme (Example 9):

Ex. 11

Solemn chords in which the trombones play an important part
bring the movement to a quiet end.

None of the third movements of the Brahms symphonies is a
scherzo. They are of a graceful, lyrical character, short and unpretentious, except that of the Fourth Symphony. The third movement
of the Third Symphony is a simple three-part form. The theme of
the first section, of typical length, is sung by the 'cellos and begins
as follows:

Ex. 12

Repetitions of this are heard in the violins and later in the wood-
winds. The middle section, in A-flat major, begins with a lilting
phrase in the wood-winds:

Ex. 13

The repetition of the first section, while containing the same material, is scored in an entirely different fashion. The opening 'cello
passage, for example, is now entrusted to a solo horn.

The last movement, *an Allegro,* is fiery and impetuous and abounds in vivid contrasts. It begins in subdued fashion with:

Ex. 14

The course of this subject is interrupted by a chorale-like passage which recalls the second theme of the second movement (Example 10):

Ex. 15

A vigorous tutti leads to the second group which begins with a boisterous theme played by the 'cellos and the first horn:

Ex. 16

Several other themes appear in the exposition. The protracted development is based on Examples 14 and 15 and is subtly joined to the recapitulation. The coda begins with a wistful statement of Example 14 played by muted violas:

Ex. 17

The solemn tones of Example 15 are now chanted by the woodwinds, and the entire symphony is brought to a romantic close with a quotation of the opening theme of the first movement, *b* of Example 6.

Other important orchestral works of Brahms are the *Variations on a Theme of Haydn,* the *Tragic Overture,* and the *Academic Festival Overture.*

The Concertos

The neo-classic outlook of Brahms is again shown by his four concertos, two for piano (D minor and B-flat major), one for violin, and a double concerto for violin and violoncello. In all these works Brahms has restored the double exposition which Mendelssohn and Schumann had discarded, and the violin concerto permits the soloist to interpolate his own cadenzas. The B-flat major piano concerto occupies an unusual place in the literature inasmuch as it has four movements and no cadenzas whatsoever. The concertos, like those of Beethoven, are not vehicles for virtuoso display. All are works of great dignity, whose thematic content and masterly development place them on an equal footing with the four symphonies.

VIOLIN CONCERTO IN D MAJOR, OPUS 77

The Violin Concerto in D major, Opus 77, was dedicated to and first performed by the composer's friend Joseph Joachim. Joachim served in an advisory capacity during the composition of the work and assisted in various technical details.

The first movement commences with a cantabile theme sung by bassoons, horns, and lower strings:

Ex. 18

The second group includes a lyrical subject of much charm:

Ex. 19

The second movement is based on a simple folk-like theme given out by the oboe:

Ex. 20

The last movement is an animated *Allegro giocoso,* whose first theme, announced by the soloist, reflects Brahms' interest in Hungarian music:

Ex. 21

Choral Music

Of Brahms' numerous compositions for chorus and orchestra the most important is the *Deutsches Requiem* (German Requiem). The Requiem is not music for the ritual of any church. Its text, in the German language, is composed of seven Biblical excerpts selected by Brahms himself. The initial idea for a work of this type was Schumann's. Brahms, as Schumann's disciple, apparently honored his memory by bringing the plan to fruition. Brahms' mother died in 1865, and what is now the fifth movement was added in her memory to the already completed work.

SUGGESTED READINGS

The best single volume on Brahms, the man and his music, is the *Brahms* of Walter Niemann (Knopf). Dr. Karl Geiringer's *Brahms, His Life and Work* (Houghton Mifflin) is a valuable study based upon hitherto inaccessible material. Robert Haven Schauffler's *The Unknown Brahms* (Dodd, Mead) contains interesting biographical data. The most detailed biography is the eight-volume German work *Johannes Brahms* by Max Kalbeck (Deutsche Brahms-Gesellschaft). *The Musical Quarterly* for April, 1933, includes many valuable essays.
    Analyses of the major works are to be found in Edwin Evans' *A Handbook to the Chamber and Orchestral Music of Johannes Brahms* (Reeves), Max Friedlaender—*Brahms' Lieder* (Oxford University Press), Daniel Gregory Mason —*The Chamber Music of Brahms* (Macmillan), and the article *Brahms* written for *Cobbetts' Cyclopedic Survey of Chamber Music* by Sir Donald F. Tovey.
    Two sets of Brahms' letters are available in English: *The Herzogenberg Correspondence* (Dutton) and *The Letters of Clara Schumann and Johannes Brahms* (Longmans, Green).

Chapter XXIV

NATIONALISM IN MUSIC

NATIONALISM in music is not a new manifestation. Compos-ers, like other creative artists, have at all times been conditioned by their racial heritage, by the temperament, customs, and charac-teristic idioms of expression of the ethnic groups from which they have sprung. But these national traits are never pure and undefiled; the works of Bach, for example, show a strong admixture of Italian and French elements. The symphony reached its highest develop-ment at the hands of German masters, but its origin is to be traced to Italy. Corresponding influences are to be found in other spheres. Despite these borrowings from other cultures, composers have im-printed a definitely national stamp on their works. With regard to operatic compositions language itself is not the decisive factor. The Mozart opera *Le Nozze di Figaro,* with an Italian libretto and written in accordance with the prevalent Italian operatic traditions, is a truly German art work. Regional characteristics may also be observed within the confines of one racial group. Brahms' North German origin is reflected in much of his music, Schubert is typically Viennese. Nor were earlier composers oblivious of folk song and folk dance. There are, for example, strong echoes of peasant tunes in the sym-phonies and string quartets of Haydn.

The nationalism of the nineteenth century differs from these earlier efforts, however, in being intensely self-conscious. Its first great ex-ponent was Carl Maria von Weber. The self-consciousness of von Weber's work was a natural reaction to the domination of Italian opera in the German theaters. Similarly, the rise of nationalism in the non-German countries was either a protest against the domina-tion of German composers, a reaction to the political oppression of minorities, or the result of military defeat. These protests took the form of a self-imposed resistance to an art that was not indigenous to the soil on which it was conceived. This act of abnegation was the result not of a stiff-necked pride, but rather of a realization that blind imitation leads only to sterility and that great art must find its roots in its own soil. Whether a composer uses themes actually taken from folk song or not is unimportant. The music of most great composers, however, is written in their national musical language, the idioms of which have found simplest expression in their country's folk songs. These features become most apparent when they have their origin in countries whose modes of expression are most removed from our own. Thus the works of Slavonic composers, Russian or Bohemian, sound more nationalistic to Anglo-Saxon ears than do the symphonies of Brahms, which are, in a sense, equally nationalistic.

Precisely as many romantic works have now become classics, many compositions conceived in an intensely self-conscious nationalistic spirit have carried their message far beyond their local borders. An obvious example is Richard Wagner's *Die Meistersinger von Nürnberg*.

Nationalism because of its exclusiveness contains the ferment of its own decay. The nineteenth-century movements as movements of discovery or of liberation from foreign domination were essentially progressive inasmuch as they brought to light a great store of hitherto hidden or neglected folk music and served to establish national musical literatures. But the great danger of nationalism is that it may become chauvinistic or lend itself to extra-artistic purposes. Robert Briffault has said: "That the artist or the writer should deal with what he knows is common prudence in the interest of his art; that he should feel under the obligation of conforming to a nationalistic prescription on the ground that it is national . . . or be enslaved by a tradition because it is national, is not to the interest of what he shall produce." [1]

Bohemian Nationalism

Before the World War, part of what is now Czechoslovakia was known as Bohemia, and was included in the Austro-Hungarian Em-

[1] "The Nationalist Craze in Culture," *Current History,* August, 1933.

pire. The Bohemians were subjected to much oppression at the hands of their Austrian masters, and like all oppressed minorities they jealously guarded their own customs and language and exhibited a strong self-consciousness as an ethnic group. The interest in Czech music *per se* followed closely on the revival of the Bohemian language and was contemporaneous with the development of a Bohemian literature, all in the face of Austrian attempts to establish German as the sole official language. The two outstanding Czech composers, Smetana and Dvořák, were both zealous patriots, the former's nationalistic activities even making it seem advisable for him to leave Bohemia for a period of years.

Bedřich Smetana

The individual who first brought to light the artistic potentialities of the great store of Czechish music was Bedřich Smetana (1824–1884). As a young man he came under the influence of Franz Liszt, and some of his first works were symphonic poems. Smetana's great masterpiece is the opera *The Bartered Bride,* produced in Prague in 1866. The work is the great folk opera of Czechoslovakia and has been performed in the National Theater at Prague more than one thousand three hundred times. In its nationalistic implications, its wealth of folk melody, and its emphasis on folk life *The Bartered Bride* stands beside von Weber's *Der Freischütz*. The plot of the opera is based on the life of the Czech peasants. One of the most distinctive features of the score is the series of intriguing folk dances, which in their catchy melodies and intricate rhythms stem directly from Czechish peasant dances, notably the *polka*. The brilliant overture is based on the finale of the second act, the scene in which the bride is ostensibly sold.

Smetana's love for his homeland was also expressed in a series of six symphonic poems entitled *My Country*. Of these the second, *The Moldau* (Vltava), is frequently performed. The Moldau is the river which flows past Prague. Smetana's symphonic poem describes its rise from two springs, and various occurrences on its banks, including a peasants' wedding for the description of which the orchestra strikes up a typical Bohemian polka:

Ex. 1

Antonin Dvořák

Antonin Dvořák (1841–1904) is known to American audiences by a work which expresses not the spirit of the Bohemian folk but rather the "state of soul of an uncultured Czech in America" [1]—the symphony *From the New World*. Dvořák, like his compatriot Smetana, was an ardent nationalist. During the four years (1892–1895) which he spent in this country as director of the National Conservatory of Music in New York, he tried to develop a nationalistic outlook in his American pupils. The New World Symphony reflects his own impressions of certain aspects of American folk music. Whether he employed actual Negro spirituals is still a matter for debate. Dvořák may be likened to Schubert, for he had an inexhaustible store of melody which he expressed with great spontaneity. Of his long list of compositions only a few are heard in America today. Of these the most typical is the set of colorful *Slavonic Dances*.

NORWEGIAN NATIONALISM

Edvard Grieg

The fate that has overtaken the works of the Norwegian composer Edvard Grieg (1843–1907) shows that nationalistic feeling alone is not sufficient for the creation of lasting art works. The charm of Norwegian folk music was first brought to the attention of the world through Grieg's numerous piano pieces, incidental music for Ibsen's *Peer Gynt,* works for string orchestra, sonatas for violin and piano, and above all the concerto for piano. Grieg was at his ease only in the shorter forms. He was incapable of any sustained thematic development, and the charm of many of his melodies pales through mechanical repetition, the obviousness of which is not concealed by a sentimentalized chromatic harmonization. Mannered as Grieg's works are, they contain much beautiful music, even if not of the most exalted type.

[1] *Philip Hale's Boston Symphony Programme Notes,* page 133.

The third of his sonatas for piano and violin has for its second movement a *Romanza*[1] which is one of Grieg's most effective creations. Its two themes are characteristically Norwegian. The cadence in the seventh and eighth measures of the first exhibits Grieg's most pronounced melodic mannerism, a sequence of three notes consisting of tonic, leading-tone, dominant:

Ex. 2

The middle section is based on a lively dance tune:

Ex. 3

SUGGESTED READINGS

There is little material on Smetana in English with the exception of the article in *Grove's Dictionary*. Both Grieg and Dvořák are discussed in Daniel Gregory Mason's *From Grieg to Brahms*. The popularity which Grieg enjoyed at the beginning of the twentieth century caused many books to be written about him. Of these the best is Henry T. Finck's *Edvard Grieg* (John Lane). The standard work is the German treatise *Edvard Grieg* by Schjelderup and Niemann (Peters).

[1] See page 151.

Chapter XXV.

RUSSIAN NATIONALISM

NATIONALISM as an artistic creed has borne its finest fruit in
Russia, thanks to the existence of two rich sources upon which
it has been able to draw for its materials—the great wealth of Russian
folk song and the music of the old Russian Church.

The extent of the Russian state and the number of racial groups
included within its borders, plus the inherent musicality of these
groups, are responsible for the fact that the country is so rich in folk
music. This music has always been assiduously cultivated by the
common people. It has also been the object of careful study on the
part of professional musicians, and there is hardly a Russian composer
whose style, consciously or unconsciously, has not been influenced by it.

To Western ears the most striking characteristic of Russian folk
music is its use of modal scales,[1] the preservation of which can be
attributed to the centuries of isolation from Western influences.
Scales like our conventional major and minor are also used, but with
a curious fluctuation between them, producing a somewhat uncertain
tonality. A definite Oriental influence may be observed in the florid
passages executed upon one syllable. Rhythmic irregularity is another pronounced characteristic. The emotional extremes to which
the national temperament is prone are also continually reflected in its
folk music, with a resultant expressiveness which has earned for it a
widespread appreciation outside of its native land.

The Russian Church, one of the branches of the Orthodox Eastern
Church (the Greek Catholic Church), unlike the Roman Catholic
Church, had kept its liturgical music free from secular influences for
several centuries. The modal characteristics of this music, traceable

[1] See pages 35–36.

to its Byzantine origin, had therefore remained pure and undefiled and, because of the role of the church in the life of the people, had exercised considerable influence on the folk music.

During the reign of Catherine the Great (1762–1796) an earnest attempt was made to plant the art and culture of Western Europe on Russian soil. Music was not neglected, but the emphasis fell principally on Italian opera, many composers of which were brought to St. Petersburg. The string quartets of Haydn and Mozart were frequently played by the private ensembles of the nobility. It will be recalled that Beethoven had dedicated his Opus 59 quartets to the Russian ambassador to Vienna, Count Rasoumovsky. Another Russian nobleman, Prince Galitzin, commissioned three of Beethoven's last quartets.

Glinka and Dargomijsky

The composer who overthrew the Western-European domination of Russian music and established a truly national school was Michael Glinka (1803–1857). Although his operas *A Life for the Czar* (1836) and *Russlan and Ludmilla* (1842) had not been the first dramatic works to use Russian folk melodies, they were the first to breathe a truly Russian spirit. *A Life for the Czar,* like *Der Freischütz,* laid the foundation for a distinctly national school of opera. The brilliantly orchestrated overture to *Russlan and Ludmilla* is a frequently performed concert piece. It contains a striking usage of the whole-tone scale. Glinka's successor was Alexander Dargomijsky (1813–1869), the composer of the opera *The Stone Guest,* the libretto of which was a poem by Pushkin, based on the Don Juan story utilized by Mozart in his *Don Giovanni.*

THE RUSSIAN FIVE

During the 1860's a group of five young men living in St. Petersburg took upon itself the task of building a national school of composition on the foundations laid by Glinka. This coterie, known as "The Russian Five," consisted of Mily Balakireff (1837–1910), César Cui (1835–1918), Nicholas Rimsky-Korsakoff (1844–1908), Alexander Borodin (1834–1887), and Modeste Moussorgsky (1839–1881). With the exception of Balakireff, all were initially amateurs. Although bent upon creating truly Russian compositions, they did not escape the influence of the new forces then making themselves felt in Western music—the works of Berlioz and Liszt; most of Wagner's, however, they bitterly condemned. The group, as an entity, broke up about 1875.

Balakireff

Balakireff was the rather tyrannical leader of the group. He had come by his role of mentor in a natural fashion, for he was the only member of the band who at the time possessed a reasonable amount of technical proficiency. The other members of the group subjected themselves to his guidance, and even though his methods were not of the best, he served as an unfailing source of inspiration to his disciples. His work in stimulating the artistic growth of his fellow-composers is his chief claim to fame, for the number of his compositions is small and performance of them infrequent. The best known is *Islamey,* a piano piece reflecting the Orientalism of the times.

Cui

Cui was an officer of artillery, who in addition to being a composer was also a regular contributor of articles on music to the leading journals of Russia and France. Of his numerous compositions, including several operas, the only one likely to be heard today is a little piece entitled *Orientale.* His importance in the development of a Russian national school rests entirely on his work in popularizing its objectives through his journalistic activities.

Rimsky-Korsakoff

Rimsky-Korsakoff had been trained for the career of officer in the Imperial Russian Navy. As a midshipman on a Russian clipper he visited the United States in 1863–1864. While still in the navy he composed a symphony, a symphonic poem, and an opera. In 1873 he was made inspector of naval bands, a civilian post. The demands of this position laid the foundation for his intimate knowledge of wind instruments. Through long years of self-imposed discipline he finally mastered all of the technical factors which enter into the art of composition, so that he eventually became the best equipped of all of the members of "The Five" and supplanted Balakireff as its mentor. His kind and sympathetic nature made him an excellent teacher, and the list of musicians who received instruction from him during his lifelong professorship at the St. Petersburg Conservatory includes the composers Liadoff, Glazounoff, Stravinsky, Prokofieff, and Respighi.

The music of Rimsky-Korsakoff is one of the finest examples of the fusion of a wide knowledge of national music and a thorough command of the technique of composition. He was primarily a composer of operas, of which all except one are based on either national history or national legend. But the works by which he is best known in America are three purely orchestral compositions composed within a short time of one another. These are the *Capriccio Espagnol* (Spanish Caprice) (1887), the symphonic suite *Scheherazade* (1888), and the overture *The Russian Easter* (1888).

Most Russian composers have shown a singular skill in handling the orchestra, but of all of them Rimsky-Korsakoff is the most outstanding in this regard. His scores abound in original and effective orchestral passages vividly colored and sharply contrasted. As opposed to the German composers, Rimsky-Korsakoff strove to achieve brilliancy rather than sonority. As an innovator in the art of orchestration he ranks with his French forebear Berlioz and, like him, has also written a valuable textbook on the subject. His melodies are gracefully conceived and always possess a certain charm, but they are more pleasing than moving. All are pervaded by either Russian or Oriental elements.

OVERTURE, "THE RUSSIAN EASTER"

The Russian Easter overture is not only an example of Rimsky-Korsakoff's skill as an orchestrator, but is also an instance of direct usage of national music—in this case that of the Russian Church, on several of whose canticles, as the composer relates in his autobiography, the work is based. He writes: "This legendary and heathen side of the holiday, this transition from the gloomy and mysterious evening of Passion Saturday to the unbridled pagan-religious merry-making on the morn of Easter Sunday, is what I was eager to reproduce in my Overture." [1] The work is dedicated "to the memory of Mous-

---

[1] Rimsky-Korsakoff—*My Musical Life*, page 249.

NICHOLAS RIMSKY-KORSAKOFF

sorgsky and Borodin." The opening *Lento mistico* presents in dark colors a theme derived from the hymn *Let God Arise*:

Ex. 1

After a short cadenza for the violin, a solo 'cello, delicately accompanied by flutes and harp, intones the hymn *An Angel Wailed*:

Ex. 2

The two hymns are heard alternately, and there are beautiful solo passages for flute, violin, 'cello, and clarinet. The tempo now changes to an *Allegro* and the hymn *Let Them also that Hate Him Flee Before Him* is heard in the violins:

Ex. 3

This is followed by a joyous dance-like motive which appears frequently throughout the overture:

Ex. 4

The excitement subsides and a beautifully scored theme derived from the hymn *Christ is Risen* is introduced:

Ex. 5

After development of Examples 4 and 5 a pontifical recitative for trombone is introduced, apparently in imitation of the chant of the priest. The rest of the overture consists of a series of brilliant episodes based on the themes already quoted, but there is more of vivid change of orchestral timbres than of thematic development. The work comes to a close with a grandiose pronouncement of *Christ is Risen* (Example 5) which is solemnly intoned by the bass instruments amidst fanfares of trumpets and the peal of bells, the sound of which, according to the composer, is an "invariable feature of ancient Russian life." [1]

Some of Rimsky-Korsakoff's colleagues either possessed a knowledge of the orchestra inadequate for the scoring of their works or else died before completing them. Rimsky-Korsakoff, feeling deeply his obligation to his friends and to the music of his native land, devoted much time to revising or completing their works. Among these acts of kindness may be mentioned the completion and revision of Dargomijsky's *The Stone Guest,* the revision of Borodin's Symphony in B minor as well as the completion and orchestration of parts of his opera *Prince Igor* (with the assistance of his pupil Glazounoff), and notably the revision of almost all of Moussorgsky's works, including his masterpiece, the opera *Boris Godounoff.* Despite his kindliness Rimsky-Korsakoff was somewhat pedantic in his treatment of Moussorgsky's great opera, and his "corrections" of what he deemed to be Moussorgsky's "harmonic incoherence" [2] now seem presumptuous to many individuals. But, as Carl Van Vechten has pointed out in his introduction to Rimsky-Korsakoff's autobiography, "it must be remembered that Rimsky-Korsakoff meant it all for the best, that he did no more for his dead friend than he was constantly doing for himself, and that he made it possible for Moussorgsky's music-drama to be performed not only in Russia but also out of it."

Borodin

Borodin crowded a tremendous amount of activity into his lifetime. He was a physician, professor of organic chemistry at the St. Petersburg Academy of Military Medicine, a prime mover in the formation

---

[1] Op. cit., page 281.
[2] Op. cit., page 280.

of a medical college for women and a member of its staff, a writer of several learned treatises on chemical subjects, as well as a musical dilettante who played the piano and 'cello fairly well and composed the opera *Prince Igor,* two symphonies, two string quartets, a few short pieces, and some songs.

With the exception of the descriptive piece *On the Steppes of Central Asia,* all of Borodin's instrumental music is written in the traditional Western European form—the sonata. In this respect he differs from his colleagues, most of whose instrumental music shows the influence of Berlioz and Liszt. Keenly nationalistic, he possessed a facile melodic gift enabling him to create many beautiful melodies which, while thoroughly original, are imbued with the spirit of folk music. His works possess buoyancy and freshness; their form is at all times devoid of complications, and their orchestration is colorful without being sensational. Borodin's Second Symphony, in B minor, is probably the finest purely instrumental work produced by any member of "The Five." It was completed in 1876, the same year in which Brahms finished his First Symphony. The work is in four independent movements, the form of which is as thoroughly classical as that of the contemporary symphony of Brahms—in lucidity and clarity, probably more classical.

The first movement of the symphony may be briefly investigated here. It begins with a forceful unison statement of the principal theme, a stalking subject which makes a vivid impression:

Ex. 6

The second group, in the related key of D major, begins with a lyrical subject whose rhythmic interest is characteristic of most of Borodin's music:

Ex. 7

The development lays especial emphasis on Example 6, which now appears in various contrasting registers of the orchestra and in new rhythmic patterns. The recapitulation, which in true Beethoven manner is the climax of the development, begins with an emphatic statement in augmentation[1] of Example 6, given out by the full orchestra, fortissimo. The coda is a brilliantly scored further elaboration of the same theme. The movement ends with another fortissimo statement of this theme now augmented to four times its original length.

Moussorgsky

When Moussorgsky first joined Balakireff's group he was an ensign of the guards in the Russian army. The son of prosperous parents, he had been brought up on the land and had early in life acquired an interest in the life of the Russian peasants. As a student at the Military Academy he received some desultory piano instruction, and through the friendly interest of a priest, Father Krupsky, became acquainted with the music of the Church. This was the sum total of his musical equipment when he met Balakireff at the home of Dargomijsky and was inducted into his circle. For a short time he was Balakireff's pupil; but Balakireff lacked the ability to impart knowledge systematically, and Moussorgsky learned practically nothing from him. This lack of formal instruction accounts for both the strength and the weakness of Moussorgsky's style. He resigned from the army in 1859; but with the liberation of the serfs in 1861 his income dwindled, and by 1863 he found it necessary to accept a clerkship in the Russian civil service. The last eighteen years of his life were thus spent at routine tasks. But despite the stultifying nature of his governmental post, he managed to find time for composition. His premature death was brought on largely by the failure of his contemporaries to recognize his unique genius. His works were quickly forgotten after his decease. Moussorgsky's biographer, von Riesemann, has pointed out that the revival of interest in his music was the result of the untiring activity, during the early part of the twentieth century, of a French singer, Madame Olenine d'Alheim. The list of Moussorgsky's works that are performed today includes two operas *Boris Godounoff* and *Khovanstchina,* an orches-

---

[1] See pages 70–71.

tral work *A Night on Bald Mountain,* a series of piano pieces *Pictures at an Exhibition,* and numerous songs.

Moussorgsky's sole aim in his masterpiece, the "musical folk-drama" *Boris Godounoff,* was accuracy of delineation, and every other consideration was sacrificed to the attainment of this one end. Unfortunately his technical equipment was defective, so that crudities and ineptitudes are not lacking. Seldom has so high-minded an artist been so poorly prepared for his chosen task. Moussorgsky was like Wagner in that his musical gift demanded the spoken word as its quickening agent. And again like Wagner, dramatic truth was the sole criterion by which he judged the artistic rectitude of any procedure But the manner in which he achieved this dramatic truth differs vastly from the gigantic Wagnerian system with its elaborate texts, its complex of *Leitmotivs,* its huge orchestra. The style of Moussorgsky is so simple and so direct, so lacking in formal device, that he has been called a "realist," though the designation is difficult to define.

To Western ears the most obvious feature of Moussorgsky's music is its strongly modal character. Inasmuch as he had received practically no formal training, he evolved an harmonic language which, in its freedom from the restraint of established convention, was thoroughly original and in many respects prophetic. The use of a modal idiom in itself produced new chordal sequences; but in addition Moussorgsky did not hesitate to write any chordal progression as long as it served his dramatic purpose. The entire instrumental prelude to the Coronation Scene in *Boris Godounoff,* for example, is constructed on only two chords, effectively juxtaposed:

Ex. 8

His modulations are usually abrupt but never capricious. At no time did Moussorgsky strive for novelty or consciously aim to be different. The weak feature of his works is their orchestration, and it is in this respect, more than in any other, that the Rimsky-Korsakoff revisions have proved valuable.

Boris Godounoff was presented for the first time in 1874. It was well received by the populace, but the professional critics were rather harsh and condemned the work for its "amateurishness." It was not until early in the twentieth century that its true artistic significance was realized. The work is now the great Russian national opera, the Russian analogue of *Der Freischütz* and *The Bartered Bride*.

Moussorgsky adapted his libretto from the Russian poet Pushkin's historical drama of the same name. It is a somewhat loosely constructed series of scenes based on the usurpation of the Russian throne by Boris Godounoff in 1598. The principal dramatic protagonist, however, is the Russian people, effectively represented in several moving choral episodes.

The voice parts of *Boris* are written in a melodious recitative which is not interrupted to allow interpolations of arias or ensembles except where dramatically justified. Moussorgsky has made use of several themes derived from folk songs. One of the best known of these, employed as a hymn of praise during the Coronation Scene, had been utilized by Beethoven in the third movement of his second Rasoumovsky quartet (Opus 59, No. 2). Moussorgsky's version is:

Ex. 9

Rimsky-Korsakoff also introduced it in his opera *The Czar's Bride*.

One of Moussorgsky's friends was the architect Victor Hartmann. Hartmann died prematurely, and a showing of his watercolors and drawings was later held to honor his memory. Moussorgsky has left a record of his visit to this exhibition in a series of ten piano pieces entitled *Pictures at an Exhibition*. The most interesting feature of this set of pieces is the appearance of four short interludes entitled *Promenades,* a series of whimsical self portraits of the composer as he wanders from picture to picture. The *Promenades* are based on a theme of characteristic rhythmic interest:

Ex. 10

A brilliant orchestration of these colorful pieces, made in 1923 by the French composer Maurice Ravel, has become popular on concert programs and has helped to disseminate Moussorgsky's art.

Tchaikovsky

Peter Ilitch Tchaikovsky (1840–1893) was among the first Russian composers to win widespread recognition. He conducted his works in the major cities of Europe, was given an honorary doctor's degree by the University of Cambridge, and was invited to America to conduct his compositions at the opening of Carnegie Hall in 1891. His popularity in America dated back to 1875 when his Piano Concerto in B-flat minor was given its world première by Hans von Bülow in Boston. The reason for this ready acceptance of Tchaikovsky's works is due to the fact that they were conceived along the lines of Western European music and yet possessed certain sensational elements attributable to the composer's native temperament. Tchaikovsky was not an ardent musical patriot, nor did he have a very high regard for "The Five" and their theories. Yet like all artists his language was that of his native land, and despite obvious Western influences his music, even if not the product of a self-conscious nationalism, is as typically Russian as that of his more zealous contemporaries. The differences between his works and those of "The Five" are to be explained in terms of personality rather than in degrees of nationalistic sentiment. It should not be overlooked that Borodin, whose works won the wholehearted approval of his colleagues, was as much influenced by Western European music as was Tchaikovsky.

Like his fellow Russian composers Tchaikovsky did not initially plan a professional musical career for himself. It was not until his twenty-first year that he began any serious study; and it was not until his twenty-third year that he gave up a clerkship in the Ministry of Justice to devote himself entirely to music. He was freed from financial care by the interest which a wealthy widow, Nadejda von

PETER ILITCH TCHAIKOVSKY

Meck, took in him. For thirteen years she gave him an annual allowance, but stipulated that they were never to meet; and accordingly their sole contact was through correspondence. Tchaikovsky was thus enabled to devote himself to composition unhindered, and the list of his works is a long one. Among the more frequently performed compositions are the Fourth, Fifth, and Sixth Symphonies, the last of which is entitled *Pathétique* by the composer, the overture-fantasia *Romeo and Juliet,* the Piano Concerto in B-flat minor, the Violin Concerto, the suite from the ballet *The Nutcracker,* and a few chamber music works. Two noisy orchestral pieces, the *Marche Slav* and the overture *1812* were written to order for patriotic celebrations. Two of his eight operas, *Eugen Onégin* and *Pique Dame,* have been performed at the Metropolitan Opera House, but although still given in European theaters they have gone into eclipse in this country.

The instrumental works of Tchaikovsky are unrestrained expressions of his own emotions. But these are emotions of a peculiar kind; for Tchaikovsky, despite his successes as a composer, was a morbidly sensitive individual subject to recurrent periods of depression. This despondency was freely expressed in his music, usually intruding into his gayest movements. The degree to which Tchaikovsky revealed his woes amounts in some cases to a form of self-pity. This morbidity reaches its high point in his last work, the *Pathétique* Symphony, the concluding movement of which is an *Adagio lamentoso.* But to stress the melancholy of Tchaikovsky is to place a false emphasis on one aspect of his art. Of all the Russian composers he stands out as the foremost master of symphonic form. Each of his last three symphonies is constructed with the greatest skill and with absolute mastery of the intricacies of the larger forms. A distinctive feature of the Fourth and Fifth Symphonies is the use of a recurring "motto-theme." But Tchaikovsky has not followed the conventional models slavishly; the third movement of the Fifth Symphony, for example, is a beautiful waltz, and the third movement of the Sixth Symphony is a brilliant march. Tchaikovsky's melodies are usually of a broad, sweeping character. They are rarely modal and usually lack the folk-like qualities of those of "The Five"; but actual folk tunes are occasionally utilized, as in the last movement of the Fourth Symphony. His orchestration is particularly colorful and owes its effectiveness to the habitual employment of the orchestral instruments in sharply contrasted independent groups. Each melodic line therefore stands out with the greatest clarity. A characteristic of Tchaikovsky's style, which has caused occasional adverse criticism, is his predilection for sensational climaxes, usually reached via an ascending series of sequential passages stretched out over a long pedal.[1]

SYMPHONY NO. 4, IN F MINOR

As a typical example of Tchaikovsky's music, his Symphony No. 4, in F minor, Opus 36, has been chosen for examination here. It was completed in 1878 and dedicated "To My Best Friend" (Mme. von Meck). In a long letter to Mme. von Meck the composer has given his own interpretation of the meaning of the work.[2]

The first movement begins with an incisive repeated-note motive for horns and bassoons:

Ex. 11

In his explanatory program Tchaikovsky has called this motive "the kernel of the entire symphony. This is Fate, that inevitable force which checks our aspirations toward happiness ere they reach their goal." The connection between this opening and that of the Fifth Symphony of Beethoven is obvious and is admitted by Tchaikovsky himself. In a letter to a fellow musician he writes that his work is "in reality, a reflection of Beethoven's Fifth Symphony; I have not copied its musical contents, only borrowed the central idea." [3] The main section of the movement, a *Moderato con anima* is in the conventional sonata form. The melancholy principal subject is given out by the violins and the 'cellos, playing in octaves:

Ex. 12

---

[1] See page 47.
[2] Modeste Tchaikovsky—*The Life and Letters of Peter Ilitch Tchaikovsky,* page 275.
[3] Op. cit., page 294.

Repetitions of this theme are followed by a characteristic ascent to a climax. The second group begins with a whimsical clarinet solo:

Ex. 13

Upon repetition of this theme in the flute and oboe, an undulating *cantabile* melody in the 'cellos is combined with it:

Ex. 14

The exposition is brought to a thrilling conclusion as all the strings except the double basses play this broad theme:

Ex. 15

The beginning of the development is heralded by the return of the motto-theme (Example 11) in the trumpets. There is an intense working-out of Example 12 interrupted three times by vigorous pronouncements of the motto-theme by the trumpets. The recapitulation is considerably abridged. The coda introduces two transformations of a motive found in the third measure of Example 11. The first of these is a quiet wood-wind melody:

Ex. 16

and the second a lively string figure:

Ex. 17

The second movement is a simple three-part form, the first theme of which is sung by a solo oboe:

Ex. 18

The middle section is based on a march-like theme, stiffly announced by clarinets and bassoons:

Ex. 19

The return of the first section is a fine instance of Tchaikovsky's skill in orchestration. The theme is played by the first violins while various wood-wind instruments alternate at adorning it with piquant arabesques.

The third movement, marked *Scherzo,* is in the usual three-part form. It is the finest example of the manner in which Tchaikovsky continually divides his orchestra into contrasting groups—in this instance strings, pizzicato throughout the movement, wood-winds, and brass. At no time do these groups lose their independence. The Scherzo itself is given to the strings alone, the Trio to the wood-winds and the brasses. All these groups indulge in sharp retorts in the coda.

The last movement, according to the composer, depicts a popular festival and is an expression of "simple, vigorous, primitive joy." It is a wild, orgiastic movement with many climaxes ably punctuated by the percussion instruments. A Russian folk tune serves as its principal thematic element:

Ex. 20

The motto-theme makes a dramatic entrance in the midst of the tumult, but is quickly forgotten.

SUGGESTED READINGS

The following are the standard works on the composers discussed in this chapter:

N. Rimsky-Korsakoff—*My Musical Life* (Knopf).

Gerald Abraham—*Borodin, The Composer and His Music* (William Reeves).

Oscar von Riesemann—*Moussorgsky* (Knopf).

Catherine Drinker Bowen and Barbara von Meck—*"Beloved Friend": The Story of Tchaikovsky and Nadejda von Meck* (Random House).

Modeste Tchaikovsky—*The Life and Letters of Peter Ilitch Tchaikovsky* (Lane).

M. D. Calvocoressi and Gerald Abraham—*Masters of Russian Music* (Knopf).

Several valuable articles on nineteenth-century Russian music have appeared in *The Musical Quarterly*. Among these may be mentioned:

Edgar Istel—"Rimsky-Korsakoff, The Oriental Wizard" (July 1929).

Victor Belaiev—"Olenin's Reminiscences of Balakireff" (January 1930).

M. D. Calvocoressi—"Moussorgsky's Musical Style" (October 1932).

Chapter XXVI

FRENCH NATIONALISM

BEFORE the Franco-Prussian War (1870–1871) French composers could win appreciation in their homeland only if they confined themselves to the production of operas; and these operas had to follow a tradition which had been established by foreign composers. Since 1831 the favorite operatic composer had been a German, Jakob Meyerbeer. Instrumental music was neglected. It will be recalled that works of Berlioz had been treated with indifference by his fellow-countrymen during his lifetime.

The disastrous results of the Franco-Prussian War served to rally French composers to their own artistic defense. Capitalizing on patriotic sentiment, they formed an organization, the *Société Nationale de Musique* (National Music Society), whose professed aim was "to aid the production and the popularization of all serious musical works, whether published or unpublished, of French composers." [1] The formation of the Society was responsible for the growth of a French school of great importance, a school which definitely marked the end of German hegemony in the sphere of music. Through the existence of this organization worth-while works of native composers were assured a hearing. The long list of important compositions, including many now universally known, which had their first performance at the Society's concerts indicates the significant rôle that the organization played. The necessarily limited scope of the activities of the Society was also responsible for the diversion of emphasis from operatic to instrumental music and, consequently, for the creation of a national literature of chamber and symphonic music. Of the many composers

[1] Romain Rolland—*Musicians of Today*, page 268.

who were active in the affairs of the Society during its early years, the names of two are well known today, Camille Saint-Saëns and César Franck. Saint-Saëns resigned in 1886. Franck was the president until his death in 1890, although he had refused the title.

The French nationalistic movement differed from those taking place around it in that it was not at all preoccupied with folk music. Nor was its purpose a purely chauvinistic one having as its goal the exclusion of German music from French concert halls. Its aim was purely the establishment of a French school of instrumental composition as proof that German composers held no monopoly in this sphere. But like their fellow nationalists in other lands, these French composers could not entirely escape the influence of the innovations in form made by Liszt nor the new harmonic language and orchestral texture of Wagner. These influences were so strong and the adoption of them so fruitful that these French composers may be considered the outstanding successors of Liszt and Wagner; for the majority of German composers who attempted to follow in Wagner's footsteps were uninspired imitators. Curiously enough the influence of Berlioz was negligible, although the Franco-Prussian War helped bring about the final awakening of popular interest in his music as well. Most of the French composers of the last quarter of the nineteenth century were of essentially classical temperament, and the romantic excesses of their predecessor failed to arouse any desire for emulation on their part.

Saint-Saëns

Camille Saint-Saëns (1835–1921) was the French Mendelssohn. He possessed limitless technical facility, and yet had very little of importance to say. Despite the flawless structure, the brilliant orchestration, and the well-turned melodies to be found in his works, they fail to impress one as being the outcome of any earnest convictions. The influence of Liszt is clearly shown in Saint-Saëns' four symphonic poems, of which the *Danse macabre* is the best known. His opera *Samson et Delila* was produced at Weimar in 1877, thanks to Liszt's endeavors in the composer's behalf. Like Mendelssohn, Saint-Saëns was deeply interested in the music of the older masters and did much to popularize the music of Bach in France.

Franck

César Franck (1822–1890), the father of the French school, was a Belgian by birth; but he spent the greater part of his life in Paris and was to all intents and purposes a Frenchman. The life of Franck may be likened to that of Bach, for he also was an obscure church organist who received little recognition during his lifetime. If it had not been for the Société Nationale, it is doubtful if much of his music would ever have been performed at all. Such works as were given a public hearing were indifferently received, and it was not until the last year of his life that he was accorded any expression of public approval. From 1860 until his death Franck was the organist of the church of Ste.-Clotilde in Paris. He was not only a great virtuoso, but also a master of improvisation. Liszt heard him improvise at Ste.-Clotilde in 1866 and in his enthusiasm compared Franck to Bach. In addition to his church post Franck later held the position of professor of organ at the Paris Conservatoire.

Despite his duties at Ste.-Clotilde and the Conservatoire, the drudgery of private instrumental instruction, and his ceaseless creative labors, he found time to be an inspiring teacher of composition. With the exception of Liszt no other great composer has possessed the humanity and the disinterestedness of Franck towards his pupils, and it is therefore not to be wondered at that they worshiped him as "le père Franck." It was through these pupils as well as by his own compositions that Franck laid the foundation for the French school. Among the better known of this band of disciples were Henri Duparc, composer of some fine songs; Vincent d'Indy, composer of the symphonic variations *Istar,* who later became his master's biographer and artistic successor; the gifted but short-lived Ernest Chausson, composer of the well-known *Poème* for violin and orchestra, and a splendid symphony. The following were not pupils of Franck but came within the orbit of his artistic influence: Gabriel Pierné, Emmanuel Chabrier, and Paul Dukas.

Franck's tolerance apparently extended to his criticism of his own works; for of the great quantity of music which he turned out with such methodical earnestness, only a comparatively small amount merits performance today. His fame as a creative artist rests on the following compositions, all late works: the Prelude, Chorale and Fugue, and the Prelude, Aria and Finale for piano solo; the Symphonic Variations for piano and orchestra; the Sonata for Violin and Piano in A major; the String Quartet in D major; the Piano Quintet in F minor; the Symphony in D minor (Franck composed only one work in each of these categories); several pieces for organ of which the *Piece héroïque* is the best known; and an oratorio, *Les Béatitudes.*

Franck's Style

Franck as a composer invites comparison with Brahms, for his outlook was thoroughly classical, and as examination of the list of his great works shows, he was a master of the larger forms. But here the analogy ends. Brahms was indifferent to most of what was going on around him. Franck, while still employing the classical forms, introduced into them all of those additions to the vocabulary of music for which Liszt and Wagner were largely responsible.

The first of these features is the principle of thematic transformation employed by Liszt in his symphonic poems. Franck applies this to absolute music by recurrently introducing one theme, suitably modified, in each of the several movements comprising a work, thereby creating a community of interest in the movements which serves to integrate them into a unified whole. The procedure had, of course, been anticipated by Berlioz with the *idée fixe* of the *Symphonie fantastique,* and it had already been observed in the works of Liszt and Tchaikovsky. An instrumental work so constructed is called a *cyclical* form. An excellent example is Franck's Piano Quintet in F minor. Here the theme which pervades the three movements of the work makes its appearance in the first movement in this form:

Ex. 1

In the course of the slow middle movement it recurs as:

Ex. 2

Its final appearance is as a pianissimo reminiscence in the middle of the coda of the last movement:

Ex. 3

Franck's harmonic language stems directly from the chromaticism of Wagner and carries it on to new levels. His harmonic idiom is characterized by continual modulation, often so subtle as to obscure tonality, by elusive cadences and by semitonal progressions. The Franck melodies, unlike those of his German contemporary Brahms, are uniformly short-breathed, and have a curious tendency to cluster about a focal note. The theme from the Piano Quintet quoted above is typical.

But the music of Franck, like that of all the great masters, eludes characterization in terms of a particular brand of musical syntax. The underlying spirit of his works is one of deep sincerity and earnestness which while reserved in its utterance is of a highly personal nature.

PRELUDE, CHORALE AND FUGUE

The Prelude, Chorale and Fugue for piano, which had its first performance at a concert of the Société Nationale in 1885, is one of the results of Franck's close contact with the music of Bach. But in typical fashion he has utilized the old forms in the spirit of the late nineteenth century. Between the units of the customary prelude and fugue combination he has inserted a movement which, although written for an instrument, is appropriately entitled *Chorale*. The three movements, which are joined one to the other, comprise a cyclical form whose motto-theme may be represented as:

Ex. 4

The Prelude, in the improvisational mood associated with the form, commences with a series of arpeggio figures out of which the motto theme emerges as:

Ex. 5

The Chorale is based on two themes, the first of which is a transformation of the motto-theme:

Ex. 6

etc.

The second theme is a somewhat monastic melody, which recalls the Knights of the Holy Grail of Wagner's *Parsifal*:

Ex. 7

etc.

The subject of the four-voiced Fugue is another transformation of the motto-theme:

Ex. 8

etc.

The development contains a fine example of inversion,[1] the fugue subject appearing as:

Ex. 9

etc.

[1] See pages 70–71.

The development reaches a climax and is followed by a section which Franck entitles *come una cadenza* (like a cadenza). This commences with reminiscences of the opening arpeggios of the Prelude into which the melody of Example 7 is eventually introduced with great delicacy. A long crescendo finally culminates in a dramatic contrapuntal combination of the chorale melody and the fugue subject. The entire work is brought to a close with a series of fanfares derived from Example 7.

SYMPHONY IN D MINOR

The celebrated Symphony in D minor, completed in 1888, is Franck's best-known work and occupies an important place in the symphonic repertoire as a universally accepted classic. The work is ostensibly in only three movements but, as will be shown later, the second movement combines the functions of a slow movement and a scherzo.

The first movement is in sonata form, but the slow introduction and the entire first group are literally repeated in a different key. The introduction opens with a solemn questioning motive which had already found employment in Beethoven's String Quartet in F major (Opus 135), in Liszt's *Les Préludes,* and in Wagner's *Die Walküre*:

Ex. 10

The introduction also contains a fervent theme harmonized in Franck's characteristically chromatic manner:

Ex. 11

The introduction is now followed by the conventional Allegro commencing with an energetic diminution of Example 10:

Ex. 12

The introductory and allegro sections are now repeated in F minor. After a brief transition the key shifts to F major, the key of the second group. Two important themes are heard in the new tonality. Both exhibit Franck's predilection for melodies which pivot on one note, in this instance:

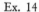

The first, a quiet limpid theme, is given out by the strings with effective imitation in the outer parts:

Ex. 13

After some characteristically elusive modulations the music attains the level of a fortissimo and the second theme of this group appears in jubilant syncopation:

Ex. 14

Franck takes leave of this motive rather reluctantly, and it is only after much pensive manipulation of it that the development finally gets under way. This section, although of considerable length, is filled with dramatic interest through ingenious treatment of the subject matter. It culminates in a grandiose canonic statement of Example 10 in a slow tempo and in its original key of D minor. After some remote modulations the recapitulation settles down into the conventional restatement of the exposition. The coda consists of an extended crescendo over a modulating ground-bass derived from Example 14:

Ex. 15

The movement is brought to a triumphant conclusion with another canonic statement of Example 10.

As has already been mentioned, the second movement is in reality two movements telescoped into one. Its first section corresponds to the usual slow movement. The introduction, for strings pizzicato and harp, also serves as accompaniment for the principal theme, a plaintive melody in B-flat minor sung by the English horn:

Ex. 16

A wholly unexpected modulation turns the course of this theme into B-flat major, in which key another melody appears as a contrasting middle section:

Ex. 17

Example 16 now returns for what is ostensibly a *Da capo*. But the procedure is abandoned, and the muted strings commence a delicate passage in the mood of a Mendelssohn scherzo:

Ex. 18

The scherzo part of the movement also has its contrasting middle section, a graceful tune given out by the clarinet:

Ex. 19

The scherzo returns, and after two preliminary trials in different keys appears in combination with Example 16 in the tonic key of B-flat minor:

Ex. 20

The beautiful coda is based on variants of Examples 17 and 19 and concludes with a pianissimo chord of B-flat major adorned by a quiet harp arpeggio.

The last movement starts out as though it planned to follow the normal sonata form pattern. The suave first subject is given out by the bassoons and 'cellos:

Ex. 21

The second group in B major introduces a solemn theme scored for brass alone—an excellent example of the influence of Wagner:

Ex. 22

Instead of proceeding to develop these themes Franck returns to the material of the second movement, and the English-horn melody (Example 16) is heard again. After this interruption the development of Examples 21 and 22 commences and reaches a climax in the presentation by the full orchestra of Example 16. This is followed by the introduction of two themes from the first movement, Example 10 and Example 14. The coda, like the corresponding section in the first movement, is worked out over a modulating ground-bass; and the movement terminates with a canonic treatment of its first theme, Example 21.

Suggested Readings

The inception of the Société Nationale is described by Romain Rolland in the chapter "The Awakening," included in his *Musicians of Today* (Holt). The work of Franck and his pupils is copiously treated in *Modern French Music* by Edward Burlingame Hill (Houghton Mifflin). The only life of Franck is the *César Franck* of his pupil Vincent d'Indy (Lane). It should be borne in mind that this is the work of a disciple and is, therefore, occasionally overlavish with its praise. A concise statement of the part which the music of Wagner played in the development of the French school is to be found in d'Indy's *Richard Wagner et son influence sur l'art musical français* (Delagrave).

Chapter XXVII

POST-WAGNERIAN MUSIC
IN GERMANY AND AUSTRIA

O F THE numerous Teutonic composers who ventured to follow
in the footsteps of Wagner, only a handful escaped being mere
imitators. The composers achieving the greatest success were those
who effected a transference of the Wagnerian technique to non-
operatic spheres by utilizing the Wagner orchestra and Wagner's
methods of thematic development for symphonic music, and his manner of associating the spoken word with instrumental music for the
art-song. The only significant dramatic work which adhered faith-
fully to Wagnerian precepts and yet showed an individual style was
the fairy opera *Hänsel und Gretel* of Engelbert Humperdinck (1854–
1921), produced at Weimar in 1893.

Richard Strauss

The most outstanding German composer since Wagner is Richard
Strauss, born in Munich June 11, 1864. Strauss' father was a famous
horn player of ultraconservative temperament, who saw to it that his
precocious son received a thorough musical training at the hands of
various Munich pedagogues. Most of Strauss' earlier works were
written in a classical idiom, and for a time his musical development
seemed to be progressing in the direction of Brahms. An early symphony of Strauss written in the best classical tradition was given its
première under Theodore Thomas in New York in 1884. Strauss'
conversion to the aesthetic principles embodied in the works of Liszt
and Wagner is attributed by the composer himself to his contacts with
a contemporary musician, Alexander Ritter, who was not only close
to the Weimar circle but also had married a niece of Wagner. Strauss

RICHARD STRAUSS

described Ritter's influence upon him as follows: "He urged me on to develop the expressive, the poetic in music after the example set by Berlioz, Liszt and Wagner." [1]

Strauss' Tone-Poems

The result of Ritter's exhortations was to divert Strauss' creative gifts into the channels of program music. During the interval 1887–1898 a notable series of symphonic poems, or as the composer called them, "tone-poems" (*Tondichtungen*), came from his facile pen. Of these the following have become firmly established in the modern orchestral repertoire: *Don Juan* (1888), *Tod und Verklärung* (Death and Transfiguration) (1889), *Till Eulenspiegels lustige Streiche* (Till Eulenspiegel's Merry Pranks) (1895), *Also sprach Zarathustra* (Thus Spake Zarathustra) (1896), *Don Quixote* (1897), *Ein Heldenleben* (A Hero's Life) (1898). The high artistic level of the tone-poems has not been attained by Strauss in his later program symphonies, the *Symphonia domestica* (1903) and the *Alpensymphonie* (Alpine Symphony) (1915). Although the tone-poems are directly descended from the symphonic poems of Liszt, Strauss, thanks to the wide scope of his imagination and to his complete mastery of all of the many factors which enter into the art of orchestral composition, has invested the symphonic poem with an entirely new musical significance. This technical mastery is particularly evident in his sense of form, in his polyphonic skill, and in his orchestration.

Don Juan is the only work of Strauss which is closely modeled after a poem, in this instance the *Don Juan* of the Hungarian poet Nicolaus Lenau. Although a poem by the composer's friend Alexander Ritter prefaces the score of *Tod und Verklärung,* the poem was written after the work was completed and hence may be regarded as an *ex post facto* literary interpretation bearing the composer's approval. None of the other tone-poems possesses a detailed literary program. *Till Eulenspiegel, Don Quixote,* and *Also sprach Zarathustra* are rather freely conceived musical elaborations of the basic ideas involved in three works of literature. *Ein Heldenleben* is frankly autobiographical.

Although all the Strauss tone-poems are pure program music, their

[1] Max Steinitzer—*Richard Strauss,* page 56.

formal designs are of almost classical perfection. Strauss has maintained that he recognizes no difference between absolute music and descriptive music, and that a program is merely an incentive to the creation of a new musical form. The formal plan of each of the tone-poems represents a notable advance over Liszt's system of "transformation of themes," although that device has been freely employed, and *Don Juan* and *Tod und Verklärung* show the strong influence of Liszt. In *Till Eulenspiegel* Strauss reverts to the classical rondo. In *Don Quixote* the adventures of the knight are described in a series of variations. *Ein Heldenleben* is a huge orchestral movement whose formal outlines bear a very close resemblance to those of the classical sonata form.

The texture of the tone-poems is extraordinarily rich and full, due to Strauss' command of orchestration and to his natural inclination towards a polyphonic manner of expression. Some of the finest examples of Strauss' contrapuntal fluency are to be found in *Ein Heldenleben*. But this fluency also leads Strauss to indulge in polyphonic complexities which in their wealth of melodic freight occasionally defeat their own purpose.

Strauss possesses unusual melodic gifts. His melodies, most of which are conceived along large lines, are characterized by impetuosity and vigor, and a certain boldness. The opening theme of *Ein Heldenleben* (quoted on page 33) and the horn theme of *Till Eulenspiegel* (quoted on page 354) are typical examples of the great range of many of Strauss' melodies. A curious feature of his melodic idiom, however, is the frequency with which it falls into a straightforward diatonic gait which, while far from commonplace, is somewhat difficult to reconcile with the complex melodic formations abounding in his works. Although almost every composition of Strauss exhibits this peculiarity, it may best be observed in his opera *Der Rosenkavalier* (The Rose Cavalier).

Strauss' Orchestration

The works of Strauss have established new standards of orchestration as well as of orchestral performance. Strauss has taken Wagner's orchestra, but has discovered new usages for its constituent instruments and has added to their number. Strauss writes almost habitually for large orchestras. A performance of *Ein Heldenleben,* for example, requires an orchestra of one hundred and five players. This insistence on large orchestras originates in Strauss' apparent need for great volume of tone, a need which is met not only by using a large number of instruments, but also by making frequent use of their intense upper registers; he occasionally goes so far as to write passages beyond the normal ranges of the orchestral instruments. As a result of Strauss' originality in this sphere his works have played an important part in the development of the art of orchestration. But it should be noted that all of the many devices for which he is responsible were the outcome of a need for a more accurate means of musical communication, and not mere attempts at musical perversity. The demands which Strauss has made on the orchestral instruments, by breaking down traditional concepts regarding their range and their possibilities of execution, have done much to raise standards of orchestral proficiency. This has been particularly apparent in the case of the brass instruments, from the players of which great virtuosity is demanded. The Strauss tone-poems remain among the most difficult of orchestral works.

Strauss' uncanny skill at using the orchestra as a delineative agency has won for him the appellation of "realist." In *Don Quixote,* for example, he has produced an amazingly effective imitation of the bleating of a herd of sheep by having muted brass instruments play querulous dissonances in a rapidly tongued tremolo, called "flutter-tonguing." The same work also calls for a wind machine. In *Ein Heldenleben* Strauss revenges himself on those critics who have belittled his works by depicting them in a series of haggling, carping passages given out by wood-wind instruments. To stress the realistic aspect of Strauss' orchestral wizardry, however, is to do him an injustice. Few composers have achieved the rich glow which emanates from certain contemplative sections of *Don Juan, Don Quixote, Ein Heldenleben,* and the *Symphonia domestica.*

"TILL EULENSPIEGELS LUSTIGE STREICHE"

To *Till Eulenspiegel* has been accorded the place of honor among Strauss' tone-poems. Of all his works it is the most concise in form, the most human in its sympathies, the most universal in its outlook.

Above all it bears the stamp of sincerity, a quality which, unfortunately, is not to be found in all of Strauss' music. The full title of the work is *Till Eulenspiegels lustige Streiche, nach alter Schelmenweise —in Rondeauform,* the translation of which is, "Till Eulenspiegel's Merry Pranks, after the old roguish manner—in rondo form."

Till Eulenspiegel is supposed to have lived during the fourteenth century. He was a clever knave who used his wits to perpetrate all manner of practical jokes on the simple-minded members of the bourgeoisie. According to the medieval *Volksbuch* of a Dr. Thomas Murner, in which Till's life and exploits have been chronicled, he even succeeded in evading a sentence of death which had been passed upon him, and his end was a peaceful one. In Strauss' musical account of Till Eulenspiegel's career, however, the rogue's life terminates on the gallows.

When Strauss composed *Till Eulenspiegel* he merely gave the above title, hoping that "after the old roguish manner" would indicate the mischievous nature of his piece. The accounts of Till's exploits were household tales in Germany, and Strauss naturally assumed that his work would need no further elucidation. In reply to a request for an explanatory program, Strauss declared that it was impossible to give a detailed description of the contents of his work. But his refusal included the following succinct statement: "Let us therefore leave it to the hearers themselves to crack the nuts the rogue hands to them. By way of helping them to a better understanding, it seems sufficient to point out the two Eulenspiegel motives which in the most manifold disguises, moods, and situations pervade the whole up to the catastrophe, when, after he has been condemned to death, Till is strung up to the gibbet. For the rest let them guess at the musical jokes which a rogue has offered them." [1]

Strauss has stated that his work is in rondo form, but his conception of the rondo form is a late nineteenth-century one. The rondo element in Till consists in the frequent reappearance of the two motives associated with the hero; but as opposed to classical practice, these motives undergo many transformations. The recurring feature of the work is, therefore, the personality of the knave as seen in his various exploits.

[1] Henry T. Finck—*Richard Strauss, The Man and His Works,* page 174.

The first of the two motives upon which the composition is based is given out in genial fashion by the violins in a short prologue:

Ex. 1

The second basic motive, of characteristic breadth and of much rhythmic originality, is entrusted to a solo horn:

Ex. 2

Of these two motives, the first is subjected to the greater number of transformations. One of the most typical variants is a saucy figure given out on its first appearance by the E-flat clarinet:

Ex. 3

In a subsequent episode the same theme is broken up into fragments:

Ex. 4

The following transformation of the second theme evidently depicts one of Till's wooings. The composer has marked it *liebeglühend* (ardently loving) and has directed that the violins add a humorous touch by playing a *glissando* at the end of the phrase:

Ex. 5

Strauss, in characteristic fashion, cannot resist the temptation to effect a combination of motives derived from the two basic themes:

Ex. 6

Till is finally apprehended and after a short trial, whose atmosphere is created by low-pitched repeated chords and side-drum rolls, is condemned to death. Strauss himself has stated that the following figure given out by bassoons, horns, trombones, and tuba represents the meting out of the death sentence:

Ex. 7

The E-flat clarinet, later joined by the oboes and English horn, describes Till's end on the scaffold. A flutter in a flute adds the typically Straussian touch of realism:

Ex. 8

The work ends with a blithe epilogue which seems to indicate that Till's demise is not to be taken too seriously.

Till Eulenspiegel is a fine example of humor in music though, to be sure, a different type of humor from that of Beethoven. Touches of the humor and geniality which characterize so much of *Till Eulenspiegel* also manifest themselves in Strauss' other works.

Songs

Although Strauss' primary importance is in other types of composition, he has made a few significant contributions to the repertory of song. His song production taken as a whole, however, has been uneven, and in many instances surprisingly unoriginal. The only successful works in this genre are the predominantly lyrical songs, many of which have won wide popularity.

Operas

Strauss had written operas as early as 1892, but his great triumphs in operatic composition did not occur until after the advent of the twentieth century. Of Strauss' numerous operas, three are conceded to be great masterworks. These are *Salomé* (1905), *Elektra* (1909), and *Der Rosenkavalier* (1911). The vocal writing, particularly in *Salomé* and *Elektra,* is often cruel and inhuman, although there are occasional moments in which the voices are allowed to shake off the tremendous orchestral weight mercilessly loaded upon them. The operas are further testimonials of Strauss' ability to manipulate a huge orchestra with telling effectiveness. Wagnerian influences are evident in the use of leading motives, but Strauss' motives often lack distinction, a defect which their elaborate orchestral development cannot conceal. The emphasis which Strauss places upon the orchestra often relegates the voice to a secondary position, with consequent impairment of the intelligibility of the words.

Der Rosenkavalier, one of the world's great comic operas, contains some notable departures from Strauss' normal operatic methods. The work includes vocal ensembles of ravishing beauty and numerous Viennese waltzes, the charm of which more than atones for the historical error which Strauss perpetrated in introducing them into an opera whose action takes place about the middle of the eighteenth century, many years before the waltz had achieved popularity in Vienna.

Strauss has lived to see his tone-poems, which once created such a stir, become classics. But while his craftsmanship has increased with the years, his imagination and his faculty for self-criticism have waned considerably. No truly great work has come from his pen since *Der Rosenkavalier.*

Anton Bruckner

Among Wagner's most reverent disciples was the intensely religious Austrian composer Anton Bruckner (1824–1896). Bruckner, initially

a country schoolmaster, was for some time organist at the cathedral at
Linz and later held the position of professor of theory and organ at
the Vienna Conservatory. His works include eight symphonies and
three movements of an uncompleted ninth, in addition to a considerable amount of sacred choral music. All of Bruckner's symphonies
are large-scale compositions in which the influence of Wagner's harmonic procedures and methods of orchestration is particularly evident.
Bruckner was an intensely earnest soul for whom composition was an
act of devotion. His symphonies, however, are prolix and diffuse—
fervent passages of great inspiration alternating with sections which
are merely pious attenuations of commonplace materials. The works
of Bruckner have achieved great popularity in Germany and Austria.
American audiences, however, have on the whole failed to be impressed by them.

Gustav Mahler

Gustav Mahler (1860–1911) is usually grouped with Bruckner, for
he is also a composer of colossal symphonies, nine in number. Many
of the symphonies bear explanatory titles, often with autobiographical
connotations. Mahler had spent many years at the conductor's desk
and had thus acquired an intimate knowledge of the inner workings
of the orchestra. The orchestration of his works, planned with great
attention to detail, is rich and colorful. Four of the symphonies contain important vocal parts. The loftiness of Mahler's conceptions and
the overwhelming intensity which characterized his life as well as his
music fail to make themselves apparent to most listeners because of
the composer's tendency to indulge in overstatement and overelabora-
tion. The inordinate length of many of Mahler's works has been another hindrance to their ready acceptance in America, but no orchestral conductor who has possessed implicit faith in Mahler and his
music has ever failed to stir an audience with a rendition of the symphonies. The position of Mahler in musical art is still a disputed
one; but appearances of his works on orchestral programs are continually increasing in number.

Hugo Wolf

Wagner's methods of combining poetry and music were transferred
to the song by the Austrian composer, Hugo Wolf (1860–1903).

Wolf, however, was no mere imitator of Wagner. Proceeding from Wagner's assumption that the purpose of a musical setting was to heighten the effectiveness of poetry, Wolf developed new standards of declamation, new harmonic methods, new ways of employing the piano in association with the voice.

Wolf's period of productivity, extending from 1888 to 1897, was amazingly brief; the majority of his songs were written before 1891. It was Wolf's custom to make a thorough study of one particular poet and, after having thoroughly absorbed his literary style, to commence to set his poems to music. Once composition was begun, Wolf turned out one master song after another at a furious rate. His fifty-one settings of Goethe's poems, for example, were written within the space of three months. The greater part of Wolf's creativity is included in the following six groups of songs: fifty-three Mörike songs, twenty Eichendorff songs, fifty-one Goethe songs, forty-four songs from the *Spanisches Liederbuch* (Spanish Song Book) of Heyse and Geibel, forty-six songs from the *Italienisches Liederbuch* (Italian Song Book) of Heyse, three sonnets by Michelangelo.

Wolf's vocal writing is predominantly declamatory. His declamation, however, is not to be confused with that of Wagner. Wagner's methods were designed to meet the needs of the operatic stage and involved settings of dramatic poetry of heroic proportions. Wolf, on the other hand, dealt largely with short lyrical poems, every nuance of which stands revealed through the subtleties of his declamation. Wolf's emphasis on a declamatory style, while resulting in a certain melodic impoverishment of the vocal part, adds immeasurably to the meaning of the poem. It also demands that the listener have some knowledge of the poem prior to hearing it sung. It is worthy of note that whenever Wolf performed his songs before his friends it was always his custom to preface his renditions by careful and expressive readings of the texts he had set.

An important feature of Wolf's style is the utter objectivity of his approach to poetry. In a letter to a fellow composer, Engelbert Humperdinck, he spoke of himself somewhat humorously as "an objective lyricist who can pipe in all keys." [1] This objectivity, combined with an acute literary sensitivity, was responsible for the success with

---

[1] Ernst Decsey—*Hugo Wolf*, Vol. II, page 77.

which Wolf met the diverse needs of his poems. Wolf's attitude towards his poets is shown by the titles he gave his collections, for example, *Gedichte von Goethe für eine Singstimme und Klavier von Hugo Wolf* (Poems by Goethe set for voice and piano by Hugo Wolf).

The above title also indicates Wolf's concept of the function of the piano in his songs. He lists it as an associate of the voice; the word "accompaniment" is significantly absent. Wolf assigns to the piano a role which in its relation to the poem is somewhat analogous to that of the Wagnerian orchestra. Like Wagner's orchestra, the piano in Wolf's hands is an instrument capable of expressing subtle shades of emotion, of accurately delineating character, and of creating atmosphere. Unlike Wagner, however, Wolf is capable of expressing a great deal in an amazingly short space. Many of his songs are masterpieces of condensation; Wolf may well be called one of the greatest of musical miniaturists. The piano parts, which are always intimately associated with the voice, while thoroughly pianistic, are often difficult and demand pianists of virtuoso attainments for their correct performance. Like Schubert, Wolf realized the dramatic possibilities of carefully planned modulation. He had, in addition, thoroughly digested Wagner's harmonic methods, notably his chromaticism. Wolf's songs abound in harmonic procedures of great originality and telling psychological effectiveness.

Suggested Readings

The authoritative biography of Strauss, Max Steinitzer's *Richard Strauss* (Schuster and Loeffler) is in German. The two major treatises in the English language—Ernest Newman's *Richard Strauss* (John Lane) and Henry T. Finck's *Richard Strauss: The Man and His Works* (Little, Brown) are somewhat out of date. The latter work, however, includes some interesting anecdotal material. A provocative article on Strauss is included in Cecil Gray's *A Survey of Contemporary Music* (Oxford). The following are useful guides: Thomas Armstrong—*Strauss: The Tone Poems* (Musical Pilgrim Series, Oxford); Lawrence Gilman—*Salomé, A Guide to the Opera* (John Lane); Eric Blom—*Strauss: The Rose Cavalier* (Musical Pilgrim Series, Oxford). *Philip Hale's Boston Symphony Programme Notes,* edited by John F. Burk, includes discussions of Strauss' principal symphonic works.

The best treatises in their respective fields are Gabriel Engel's *The Life of Anton Bruckner* and *Gustav Mahler, Song-Symphonist,* both published by the Bruckner Society of America. There are many important works in German on these composers.

The standard work on Wolf is the four-volume treatise of Dr. Ernst Decsey,

Hugo Wolf (Schuster und Loeffler). Dr. Georg Bieri's *Die Lieder von Hugo Wolf* (Paul Haupt) is a detailed study of the technical aspects of Wolf's art. An early work is Ernest Newman's *Hugo Wolf* (Methuen). The second volume of *The Heritage of Music* (Oxford) contains an article on Wolf by Walter Ford. The amount of material on Wolf in the English language is surprisingly small, especially when his importance as a song-writer is taken into account.

Chapter XXVIII

JEAN SIBELIUS

IT IS difficult to assign a position in the development of music to the great Finnish symphonist Jean Sibelius. He may conceivably be grouped, on a geographical basis, with such nationalistic composers as Grieg or Borodin, but he is of far greater artistic stature than most of the nineteenth-century nationalists. While most of his great works have been composed during the twentieth century, Sibelius is no modernist in the accepted sense of the term. The style of his writing, the forms which he has chosen, and his indifference to contemporary trends recall the situation of Brahms in the previous century. His larger works, like those of Brahms, were slow in winning public recognition; but today his preëminence as the foremost modern master of the symphony is unquestioned.

Sibelius was born on December 8, 1865, at Tavastehus, Finland. His family were cultured members of the middle class. As a boy he played the violin and made some amateurish attempts at composition but, like Wagner, he showed no signs of any unusual musical aptitude during his youth. Like many other composers before him, Sibelius was for a short time a student of law before he decided to devote himself exclusively to music. After a period of study in Helsingfors he left Finland in 1889 for further instruction in Berlin and Vienna. He returned to his native land in 1892. A few years later the Finnish government conferred an annual allowance upon him, with the highly beneficial result that he has been freed from all financial care, and has been able to devote himself to composition without interruption. With the exception of occasional appearances as conductor of his own works, his life has been uneventful. Sibelius came to America in 1914 to conduct his compositions at a festival held at Norfolk, Connecticut.

Yale University conferred the degree of Doctor of Music upon him at this time, and three of his compositions were played at the commencement ceremonies. He is today Finland's foremost citizen.

Of the many works of Sibelius, the following may be said to have won a firm place on American programs: Two symphonic poems, *En Saga* and *Finlandia*; a "Legend" for orchestra, *The Swan of Tuonela;* the *Valse triste,* from the incidental music to a play; the string quartet, *Voces Intimae*; and five of his seven symphonies, Nos. 1, 2, 4, 5, 7. The excessive technical difficulties of his fine violin concerto have apparently militated against its acceptance among the few great compositions in this category.

Sibelius was the first composer of his nationality to win international recognition. Inasmuch as his music had a peculiar flavor, it was but logical that its divergences from prevailing idioms should be attributed to the influence of Finnish folk music. Sibelius, however, is no self-conscious nationalist. At no time has he employed actual Finnish folk tunes in his music. Attempts have also been made to explain Sibelius in terms of the peculiar topography and climate of Finland; but the roots of Sibelius' style probably rest on much less tangible concepts, such as his own personality, as well as on the racial characteristics of the Finnish people. One of Sibelius' strongest traits of character is his love of nature. He has expressed himself in this regard as follows: "It pleases me greatly to be called an artist of nature, for nature has been truly the book of books for me. The voices of nature are the voices of God, and if an artist can give mere echo of them in his works, he is fully rewarded for all his efforts." [1] It is in this sense that Sibelius' style may be viewed as the outcome of the unique character of the Finnish scene.

Sibelius' specifically national works are the numerous programmatic pieces on subjects from Finnish folk-lore, including the works inspired by the great Finnish epic *Kalevala,* of which *The Swan of Tuonela* is the best known. According to Sibelius' biographer Cecil Gray, the popular *Finlandia* was written to serve as incidental music for a series of historical tableaux. It is regrettable that this work and the

---

[1] Quoted by Philip Hale in a Boston Symphony Orchestra program book, from an article in *Musical America* for January 14, 1934.

JEAN SIBELIUS

Valse triste are Sibelius' best known compositions, for neither is typical, and the emphasis placed upon them has served to delay recognition of Sibelius' more substantial creations.

Sibelius' best works are his seven symphonies, none of which bears a descriptive title or a program. These symphonies, like those of Beethoven and Brahms, are highly individual in character, and generalizations concerning them are both difficult and hazardous. With the exception of the Seventh Symphony, which is in one movement, the formal outlines of the symphonies do not represent radical departures from conventional procedures. The various movements retain a degree of independence unusual for an age in which the constructional principles fostered by Liszt had become standard usage in symphonic composition.

The feature of Sibelius' style which makes him a worthy associate of the world's greatest symphonists is the degree of concentration to be found in his works. His thematic material is brief and concise, its development a natural process of organic evolution which remains under firm control and is not the product of either caprice and fancy on the one hand, or pedantry and mere craftsmanship on the other. The rhythmic, melodic, and harmonic aspects of his writing, like those of Brahms, are thoroughly original without constituting a radical departure from accepted methods. Sibelius is responsible for no new theories, no innovations.

In an era in which orchestral color as an end in itself seems to have become an indispensable factor in orchestral composition, Sibelius, in a manner which again recalls Brahms, has resisted the temptation to exploit the coloristic potentialities of the modern symphony orchestra. His orchestration, while lacking in sensuous appeal, is at all times thoroughly colorful, but the color of any given passage in his works is an integral part of the music itself and not an added condiment. Sibelius has also found an orchestra of more modest size to be adequate for his purposes. The instrumentation which he specifies for his Third, Fourth, and Seventh Symphonies, for example, is practically identical with that of the Fifth Symphony of Beethoven. It may be observed at this point that Sibelius' orchestration has remained immune to Wagnerian influences.

SYMPHONY NO. 2, IN D MAJOR

At the risk of placing misleading emphasis upon a single composition, Sibelius' Symphony No. 2, Opus 43, composed in 1901–1902 has
been chosen for examination here. All that can be accomplished,
however, is to indicate briefly the structure of each of the four movements and identify their thematic elements.

The first movement of the Second Symphony may be divided into
three sections which are somewhat analogous to the various parts of a
movement in sonata form. The first section is given over entirely to
the presentation of several terse melodic fragments. The first of these
is a rising figure in the strings:

Ex. 1

This is followed by a blithe tune for the oboes and clarinets:

Ex. 2

An episode in the bassoons leads to this melody played by the violins
alone:

Ex. 3

A series of sequences for the strings, pizzicato, leads up to this vehement subject given out by the wood-winds over a string figure based on Example 1:

Ex. 4

The second section of this movement is akin to the familiar development, but instead of breaking the themes up into smaller units, Sibelius joins them into larger wholes. The third section might be described as a greatly abridged recapitulation.

The second movement begins with a kettledrum roll. This is followed by a long pizzicato passage in the lower strings over which the bassoons enter with this forlorn tune:

Ex. 5

With the entrance of the violins the pace of the movement is accelerated, giving rise to a dramatic episode which culminates in this intense phrase:

Ex. 6

After a particularly forceful presentation of this theme in the full brass, two lyrical themes of singular expressiveness are heard. The first is given to the strings:

Ex. 7

The second of these themes is sung by the oboes and clarinets:

Ex. 8

The rest of the movement consists of a series of dramatically contrasted episodes based on each of these subjects in turn. Special importance is assigned to the lyrical Example 7.

Although specific indications are lacking, the two contrasting sections of the third movement may be regarded as the familiar combination of Scherzo and Trio. The predominant note of the Scherzo is established by an epigrammatic motive:

Ex. 9

While the strings maintain the rapid pace of Example 9, flutes and bassoons intone:

Ex. 10

The brief Trio contains an oboe tune which is as beautiful as it is simple:

Ex. 11

Both Scherzo and Trio are repeated, but with change of orchestration, after which a tense passage effects a dramatic transition to the concluding movement.

The last movement lacks the complexity of its predecessors; it is in the conventional sonata form and is based on two well-contrasted subjects. The first of these, an impressive martial theme, is given out by the upper strings over an insistent accompaniment in the trombones, timpani, and double basses:

Ex. 12

The second group begins with a folk-like tune for the wood-winds accompanied by an *ostinato* figure in the strings:

Ex. 13

The development is based largely on Example 12. In the recapitulation, the second group is materially lengthened and its underlying *ostinato* is intensified by a dramatic accumulation of instrumental weight. The coda consists of a triumphant presentation of Example 12 by the full orchestra, with trumpets and trombones blaring forth this version of the theme over a thunderous kettledrum pedal:

Ex. 14

SUGGESTED READINGS

The best work on Sibelius is the brief but informative treatise *Sibelius* by Cecil Gray (Oxford University Press). The most recent biography is the *Jean Sibelius* of Karl Ekman (Wilmer). Alfred H. Meyer's article, *Sibelius: Symphonist,* in *The Musical Quarterly* for January 1936, discusses the elements of Sibelius' style. The symphonies have been analyzed by Cecil Gray in *Sibelius: The Symphonies* (Musical Pilgrim Series, Oxford University Press). *Philip Hale's Boston Symphony Programme Notes,* edited by John N. Burk (Doubleday, Doran) includes commentaries on the more frequently performed orchestral works.

Chapter XXIX

CLAUDE DEBUSSY

THE EFFORTS of the Société Nationale in behalf of French music had, to be sure, created a French musical literature worthy of a place beside the great masterpieces of Germany; but hard as Franck and his contemporaries may have striven, they did not free themselves entirely from the German yoke. The final break was not made until the very end of the nineteenth century, and it was brought about by the advent of a new musical style in the works of one composer, Claude Debussy. The new style is known today as Impressionism. Unlike Romanticism or Nationalism, Impressionism, insofar as music was concerned, was not a movement in which many artists participated. It was the highly personal idiom of one man, which, like other individual styles, has attracted many imitators, few of whom, however, have been able to transcend its limitations.

Claude Debussy was born on August 22, 1862, at St. Germain-en-Laye, a small town about thirteen miles from Paris. His parents, humble shopkeepers, moved to Paris shortly after his birth, and almost all of Debussy's life was spent in that city. He studied the piano for a time under a pupil of Chopin, and when he was eleven years old entered the Paris Conservatory. In 1879 he was engaged as household pianist by the selfsame Madame von Meck who had assisted Tchaikovsky.[1] Debussy went with Madame von Meck to Switzerland and Italy and finally to Moscow, where he became acquainted with a few of the compositions of Rimsky-Korsakoff and Borodin, those of the latter exercising a strong influence upon him. The works of Moussorgsky were little known at the time, and Debussy's wide knowledge of them dates from a later period in his life. Debussy spent eleven

[1] See pages 330–332.

CLAUDE DEBUSSY

years in all at the Paris Conservatory, not without creating a reputation for himself as a wilful breaker of academic rules of harmony. In 1884 he won the coveted *Prix de Rome* which entitled him to three years at the Villa Medici, but he did not stay in Rome the required length of time, and 1887 found him back in Paris.

Upon Debussy's return several forces helped to mold his artistic outlook and musical style. The first of these was his keen interest in Wagner; Debussy visited Bayreuth in 1888 and 1889. Not a few aspects of Debussy's harmonic style are traceable to Wagner's methods, particularly as displayed in *Tristan und Isolde*. Another molding force was his presence at two concerts of Russian music which Rimsky-Korsakoff conducted at the great International Exposition held in Paris in 1889. At these concerts Debussy had his first real contact with Russian symphonic music. A much more important part of the exposition so far as Debussy was concerned, however, was the performance of native musicians from Java and French Indo-China. The highly original flavor and particularly the unique scales of this Oriental music stirred his imagination.

A fourth formative influence at this time was his association with a group of artists and writers who were the prime movers in the symbolist and impressionist movements, notably Stéphane Mallarmé and Paul Verlaine. Debussy met many kindred spirits among the artists who frequented Mallarmé's salon and found himself in sympathy with their attempts to suggest fleeting moods or emotions in a manner which placed especial emphasis on fidelity of representation of sensory impression to the obscuration of detail. A fifth influence was his discovery of the music of Moussorgsky. The directness of Moussorgsky's style, unhampered by any academic considerations, met with Debussy's enthusiastic approval. It seemed to him to be the ideal escape from the tyranny of conventional standards as well as from the complexities of Wagner. Moussorgsky's influence on Debussy was, however, purely catalytic; Debussy regarded him as a precedent, but not as a model. It is important to notice that with the exception of the music of Wagner, all these influences were such as to affirm Debussy's deep-seated iconoclasm.

Debussy's life in Paris was rather uneventful. His public appearances were comparatively rare. Although a fine pianist, he seldom played in public; he lacked ability as a conductor, and he appeared in some of the larger European capitals as director of his own works largely because of financial exigencies. His compositions, particularly the opera *Pelléas et Mélisande,* aroused much controversy so that Debussy, even if not universally appreciated, was at least well known. Debussy, like Schumann before him, was an astute critic and contributed numerous articles to the Parisian journals. Despite their ironic tone and the caustic manner in which Debussy aired his anti-Wagnerian prejudices in them, these articles contain much sound criticism of the music, the musicians, and the musical instruction of his day. During his last years Debussy's productivity as a composer fell off considerably due in large measure to a wasting sickness. He died on March 25, 1918.

Included among Debussy's more important works are many beautiful songs, notably those with poems by Beaudelaire, Verlaine, and Mallarmé; many fine piano pieces; a string quartet (1893); *L'Après-midi d'un faune* (The Afternoon of a Faun) (1894), *Nocturnes* (1899), *La Mer* (The Sea) (1905), and *Iberia* (1908) for orchestra; and the opera *Pelléas et Mélisande* (1902).

Impressionism

Debussy's music, like that of his romantic predecessors, was only one manifestation of a well-defined movement in the arts. This movement reached its zenith during the latter part of the nineteenth century in the compositions of Debussy, in the poetry of Mallarmé and Verlaine, and in the paintings of Monet, Pissaro, Sisley, and Renoir; the designation *Impressionism* given to it had its origin in a picture of a sunrise at sea which Monet entitled *Une Impression.* The Symbolist poets stressed imagery and fantasy in writing; their aim was to suggest rather than actually to describe sensory impressions. The result of this restriction to indirect suggestion was a certain vagueness. It is important to observe, however, that the Symbolists let no accepted convention retard what they considered to be their presentation of artistic truth. Mallarmé, for example, invented a new punctuation and a new grammatical construction for his verse. The Impressionist painters aimed to reproduce on canvas the first impression which an object made on the painter's eye. The impressionistic style, again in opposition to traditional procedures, excluded detail and precision, and concentrated on the reproduction of an object precisely as the artist saw it. The Impressionist painters thus strove for a higher degree of realism than that permitted by adherence to orthodox standards. The music of Debussy echoes the work of these poets and painters in its departure from conventional standards of melodic construction, its total avoidance, with the exception of the string quartet, of orthodox formulas, its suppression of detail and its emphasis on atmosphere. Debussy has described his music as follows: "I desired for music that freedom of which it is capable perhaps to a greater degree than any other art, as it is not confined to an exact reproduction of nature, but only to the mysterious affinity between Nature and the Imagination." [1]

The impressionism of Debussy also constituted a revolt against orthodox standards, in this case standards of harmonic procedure, of dissonance, and of the function and progression of chords. The first of the Debussy innovations involved a new concept of dissonance. Dissonance was now regarded as an end in itself and not an episode on the route to a consonance. Each of the chords in this excerpt from a piano piece *La Cathédrale engloutie* (The Engulfed Cathedral), for example, is dissonant; none is resolved according to older canons of harmonic propriety:

Ex. 1

Debussy was especially fond of concatenations of chords of the type shown by this excerpt from *Pelléas et Mélisande,* Act I, Scene 3:

Ex. 2

---

[1] Leon Vallas—*Claude Debussy: His Life and Works,* page 85.

It will be observed that both examples contain successions of consecutive fifths, a procedure which recalls the *organum* [1] of a thousand years previous.

The second important feature of the impressionistic idiom is the frequent use of modal scales.[2] An example of Debussy's use of one of the modes has been cited on page 36. Debussy has also used the pentatonic scale, a five-tone scale, one of whose forms can be created by striking only the black keys of the piano. The pentatonic scale, while extensively used for much Western folk music, has certain Oriental connotations and consequently is aptly introduced in Debussy's piano piece *Pagodes*. A less restricted use of this scale is found in *Nuages* (Clouds) in a beautiful episode for flute and harp:

Ex. 3

The most unusual scale employed by Debussy is the whole-tone scale.[3] Although the absence of half-steps limits the melodic potentialities of this particular scale pattern, its harmonic implications are both numerous and valuable and have been a fructifying influence in the development of modern harmony. Debussy's use of this scale is best exemplified by a piano piece *Voiles* (Sails), from which this typical whole-tone passage is quoted:

Ex. 4

The various innovations of Debussy listed above were important

[1] See page 39.
[2] See pages 35–36.
[3] See page 38.

factors in the development of modern music. The use of parallel progressions of chords as shown in Example 2 ran counter to the traditional concept of chordal functions. Debussy treated chords as independent units which could be arranged in successions apparently at variance with conventional standards, and yet of undeniable beauty. But with this new usage of chords, their older tonality-fixing function was either weakened or wholly obliterated. In addition, many of the scales employed by Debussy, particularly the whole-tone scale, lack the pronounced tonal centers of the conventional major and minor scales. But Debussy's artistic use of them has resulted in the creation of entirely new standards of melodic and harmonic values.

Debussy's break with tradition, despite its radical nature, was motivated purely by a desire to achieve new beauties and to create an idiom more sensitively attuned to what he wished to portray. It is interesting to note that Debussy harbored a deep admiration for another colorist, Carl Maria von Weber. It is difficult to divorce Debussy's style from the subjects which he portrayed in his works, almost all of which bear descriptive titles. Typical designations, which might have served with equal facility for impressionistic paintings, are *Jardins sous la pluie* (Gardens in the Rain), *L'Isle joyeuse* (The Isle of Joy), *Reflets dans l'eau* (Reflections on the Water), *Poissons d'or* (Goldfish) *Des Pas sur la neige* (Footprints in the Snow), *Feuilles mortes* (Dead Leaves). Like the Impressionists of other arts, Debussy suggests rather than actually portrays. His music has an elusiveness, a reticence, a delicacy of touch, which, while giving his works a definitely personal cast, have at the same time robbed them of emotional depth, persuasiveness, and vitality. The scope of his art is narrow, but within its limits Debussy has created works of consummate beauty.

Piano Works

The literature of piano music has been considerably enriched by Debussy, and his many works for the instrument have become standard concert fare. Debussy ranks with Liszt and Chopin as a significant contributor to the development of pianism. His works abound in colorful passages based on new concepts of sonority involving subtle adjustment of dynamic values, skilful use of the pedal, and imaginative employment of the lower register with its wealth of faint yet effectively dissonant overtones.

Pelléas et Mélisande

Pelléas et Mélisande, Debussy's only opera, is a setting of the play by the Belgian symbolist Maurice Maeterlinck. The work was of almost revolutionary significance, for it represented the first really new contribution to the technique of dramatic composition since the music-drama of Wagner. The most important feature of the opera is the manner in which the orchestra has been treated. The orchestral music of Pelléas et Mélisande is not a symphonic commentary which is vitally bound up with the stage action, but a sensitively conceived background which remains comparatively unobtrusive. The vocal parts are written in a chant-like recitative from which melodic elements are almost entirely absent. Despite all of Debussy's vindictiveness toward Wagner, he has utilized the Wagnerian leading-motive, although in a much less complex fashion. Throughout the work Debussy has achieved a remarkably successful fusion of spoken word, music, and stage action. But the highly rarefied atmosphere of the opera has prevented it from achieving any great measure of popularity.

Orchestral Music

Debussy's orchestral works, of which the more important have been mentioned, exhibit a style of orchestral writing which was at marked variance with the accepted standards of his time, particularly those whose origins were traceable to Wagner's influence. Debussy placed his emphasis not on volume or brilliancy of tone, but rather on delicacy and subtle contrast. Here again his contribution has been an important one. The exquisite refinement of his writing and the delicacy of texture of his works, all brought about with the greatest economy of means, were based on technical devices which have now become a definite part of the vocabulary of modern orchestration. It is in his masterful use of orchestral color as an expressive medium that Debussy shows his closest affinity with the painters of the Impressionist School.

PRÉLUDE À L'APRÈS-MIDI D'UN FAUNE

The *Prélude à l'après-midi d'un faune* is Debussy's most celebrated orchestral work. This composition, which had its première in 1894 at a concert of the Société Nationale, is based on a pastoral poem by Mallarmé. The poem, called by the English critic Edmund Gosse "a famous miracle of unintelligibility," describes the musings of a faun, a Roman god of the woods and fields, of human shape but with a tail, short horns, and goat's feet. The faun, drowsy and surfeited with wine, attempts to recall his pursuits of nymphs and naiads. But the effort is too much for him, and he falls asleep in the warm rays of the sun. Debussy's title *Prélude* is difficult to interpret, but it seems to suggest that the music was conceived as a sort of introduction to Mallarmé's poem. According to the composer the music evokes "the successive scenes of the faun's desires and dreams on that hot afternoon." [1] The work is scored for a small orchestra from which trumpets, trombones, tuba, and kettledrums are absent.

The principal theme is given out by a solo flute:

Ex. 5

Beautifully scored repetitions, in which the flutes play an important role, are followed by the introduction of a new theme by the oboe:

Ex. 6

Motives derived from this theme are developed, and after a brief forte episode another theme is announced in the wood-winds:

[1] Leon Vallas—*Claude Debussy: His Life and Works,* page 102.

Ex. 7

This is also brought to a climax, after which Example 5 returns in an augmented form, played first by the flute and then by the oboe, interrupted, however, by fleeting episodes in which harp glissandi and querulous wood-wind passages play an important role. At the conclusion of the work Debussy introduces antique cymbals, tiny plates which give out a bell-like tone of definite pitch when struck together. Just before the final chords muted horns and violins give out an exquisitely harmonized version of the principal theme in a hushed pianissimo:

Ex. 8

SUGGESTED READINGS

The authentic life of Debussy is Leon Vallas' *Claude Debussy: His Life and Works* (Oxford). The same author has assembled a series of abstracts from Debussy's writings under the title *The Theories of Claude Debussy* (Oxford). Excerpts from Debussy's journalistic writings have been published in book form with the title *Monsieur Croche, The Dilettante Hater* (Viking). *Philip Hale's Boston Symphony Programme Notes,* edited by John N. Burk (Doubleday, Doran), includes commentaries on the important orchestral works. Lawrence Gilman has written *Debussy's Pelléas et Mélisande: A Guide to the Opera with Musical Examples from the Score* (Schirmer). *French Piano Music* by Alfred Cortot (Oxford) includes commentaries on Debussy's works. A little booklet by F. H. Shera entitled *Debussy and Ravel* (Musical Pilgrim Series, Oxford) includes a concise statement of the impressionistic method and short discussions of a few important works.

Chapter XXX

SOME RECENT TRENDS

FROM the vantage point of a great distance, the stars can be grouped as constellations, but within these constellations not all stars are of the same magnitude. Up to this point we have been examining the more luminous stars of the more sharply defined constellations of composers. That we can make distinctions such as "The Viennese School," "Romantic Composers," and "Nationalistic Composers," with a reasonable degree of accuracy, we owe to our removal in time, for art periods have always overlapped.

Continually bearing in mind the highly approximate nature of our measurements, it may be stated that the end of the nineteenth century marked the close of an epoch in the history of music, an epoch which commenced in about 1600 with the advent of the opera. Two great epochs had preceded it. The first of these was the epoch of single-voiced music, reaching its high point in about 900 in the chant of the Roman Catholic Church.

The second epoch, the great polyphonic period, extended from about 850 to 1600. It was during this long interval that a complex musical language based on the combination of melodies evolved. The polyphonic idiom reached its high point at the hands of such masters as Palestrina, Lassus, Victoria, and the Elizabethan madrigalists in the sixteenth century, a period which has been rightly called the "Golden Age" of music.

The third epoch, which may be called the era of harmonic-tonal music, extended from 1600 to approximately 1900. It was ushered in by the first experiments in opera and was brought to a close in the works of Debussy. During this period the elaborate modal system of the earlier centuries was abandoned in favor of two scales, our conventional major and minor; but the close of the nineteenth century also witnessed a revival of the older modes. The emerging opera, placing its emphasis on melody, was in large measure responsible for the development of a homophonic idiom. A harmonic language based on the recognition of the function of the chord as an entity developed, and with it those concepts of tonality and key relationship upon which the formal design of the larger instrumental forms rests. Instrumental music experienced a remarkable growth, thanks again to the initial acceleration imparted to it by the opera.

It is important to notice that the activity which characterizes the beginning of any new art epoch is of a highly experimental nature, and that its first products are usually inferior as art works to those of the period which is drawing to a close. The first crude experiments of the early Florentine opera writers, for example, took place as Palestrina's life was nearing its end; the forerunners of the Haydn symphony were contemporaneous with the cantatas of Bach.

The changes which have occurred in the language of music during the twentieth century have been so numerous and so drastic that it is obvious to infer that a new epoch has begun. Whatever these changes have been, they constitute sincere efforts to open up new avenues of expression, arrived at not through an empty desire for novelty, but rather through inner necessity. Many of these innovations have already become part and parcel of musical language. Others are still in an evolutionary stage. The language of many modern composers, furthermore, is deeply rooted in the conventions of the nineteenth century, and while these composers have not disdained to use the contributions of their more intrepid colleagues, their works may follow those of Wagner or Strauss on a program without producing too violent a contrast.

The great changes in the language of music which have taken place during the twentieth century are best discussed in terms of new concepts of such elements of musical language as harmony, rhythm, and instrumentation.

Atonality

In one of the early chapters of this volume melody was defined as "a meaningful succession of single tones." It was also pointed out that the materials of melodies were represented by scales and that certain tones of the scale, the dominant, the leading-tone, and the tonic, were of supreme importance in melody formation. The modern composer has questioned the apparent inexorability of the function of these tones as well as the conventional concepts of tonality. Melodies in whose construction the conventional concept of tonality plays no part are said to be atonal, and the result is called *atonality*. The individual who has done most to establish atonality as a legitimate musical idiom is the Viennese composer, Arnold Schoenberg, now living in America. The atonal melodies of Schoenberg are based on a system of relationships existing between all of the twelve notes of the chromatic scale. These relationships, however, are independent of all prior concepts usually associated with tonality, and the twelve tones may therefore be regarded as twelve pitches lacking functional significance. In some of his later works Schoenberg has arranged the twelve tones in a particular order, an arbitrarily erected scale called a "row." This row represents one of the first attempts to systematize the twelve-tone technique. Schoenberg himself calls his system "composition with twelve tones." The following excerpt from the first of his Three Pieces for Piano, Opus 11, is a typical example of the atonal process:

Ex. 1

Polytonality

Polytonality is the simultaneous employment of different tonalities. The origin of this practice can be traced as far back as the music of

Bach; but it has remained for twentieth-century composers to investigate the artistic possibilities of combinations of tonalities in precisely
the same way as their forerunners investigated combinations of melodies. The following example is from *L'Histoire du soldat* (The Soldier's Tale) by Igor Stravinsky, a composer in whose works polytonality has found frequent employment. The passage quoted is
written for violin and clarinet; the violin plays in B-flat minor, the
clarinet in A major:

Ex. 2

The excellent delineative purposes to which polytonality may be
put is shown by the following excerpt from *Mars*, the first of a set of
pieces by Gustav Holst entitled *The Planets*. Tenor-tuba and trumpets play in highly dissonant canon:

Ex. 3

Rhythm

Almost all of the new rhythmic devices used by modern composers attempt to avoid the regularity of rhythmic systems which proceed in orderly groups of two or three pulses, or multiples thereof. To the now commonly accepted quintuple rhythm have been added rhythms based on pulse groups of seven, eleven, and thirteen. But the most novel and at the same time most effective of the twentieth-century rhythmic devices consists of the frequent change of rhythms. This again is not a discovery of modern composers. Changes in rhythmic patterns are to be found in many of Beethoven's works, notably in the Third Symphony. But the composer of today does not hesitate to write music whose rhythmic scheme changes with almost every measure. For him rhythm is capable of endless variety and need not be governed by any system of regularly recurring stresses. In the *Danse sacrale* of Stravinsky's ballet *Le Sacre du printemps* (The Rites of Spring), an extreme instance of modern rhythmic procedures, the rhythm changes with almost every measure. The following sequence of time signatures is typical:

$$\frac{3}{16} \quad \frac{5}{16} \quad \frac{3}{16} \quad \frac{4}{16} \quad \frac{5}{16} \quad \frac{3}{16} \quad \frac{4}{16} \quad \frac{3}{16}$$

Instrumentation

Modern composers have on occasion demanded larger orchestras than their predecessors, but they have not been responsible for any radical change in the essential constitution of the orchestra. What new instruments have been introduced are to be found in the percussion group. A phonograph has been employed to create extra-orchestral sounds associated with the programs of two works, *The Pines of Rome* of Ottorino Resphigi and *Station WGZBX* of Philip James.

One of the most important instrumental developments of the present day has been the "chamber orchestra," but here again we find that what is apparently an innovation had already been anticipated by earlier composers. The chamber orchestra is merely a return to the use of a small body of performers on orchestral instruments, usually with not more than one player to a part—the same type of instrumental aggregation for which Bach wrote the orchestral parts of his cantatas. The roots of the modern chamber orchestra style are to be found, however, in Wagner's *Siegfried Idyll,* originally written for a group of sixteen performers.

The motivating factor in the development of the chamber orchestra seems to have been expediency, for a work scored for a small number of instruments enjoys a far better chance of being performed than one written for a full orchestra. The leader in the development of ensembles composed of only a few instruments has been Igor Stravinsky. His *L'Histoire du soldat,* for example, is written for only seven performers—clarinet, bassoon, cornet, trombone, violin, double bass, and a percussion group of eight instruments under the care of one player. The sharply contrasted colors of the chamber orchestra make it an ideal medium for the presentation of modern polyphony and there is hardly a composer in the modern idiom who has not written for it.

Suggested Readings

Among the many treatises on contemporary music, the following are readable and instructive:

Marion Bauer—*Twentieth Century Music* (Putnam).
George Dyson—*The New Music* (Oxford University Press).
Cecil Gray—*A Survey of Contemporary Music* (Oxford University Press).
John Tasker Howard—*Our American Music* (Crowell).
Guido Pannain—*Modern Composers* (Dutton).
Lazare Saminsky—*Music of Our Day* (Crowell).

INDEX OF MUSICAL EXAMPLES

Anonymous
  Adeste fideles, 30
  Dies Irae, 247
  Drink To Me Only With Thine Eyes, 55
  Le Pont d'Avignon, 29

Bach, Johann Sebastian
  Cantata—*Alles nur nach Gottes Willen,* 45
  Chorale—*Ich ruf' zu dir, Herr Jesu Christ,* 79
  Chorale-Prelude—*Ich ruf' zu dir, Herr Jesu Christ,* 79
  Chromatic Fantasia and Fugue, 73
  Concerto for Two Violins in D minor, 32
  Concerto for Violin in E major, 85
  Fantasia and Fugue in G minor, 75
  French Suite No. VI, in E major, 62
  Mass in B minor, *Crucifixus,* 95
  Passacaglia and Fugue in C minor, 76
  Passion According to St. Matthew
      Aria—*Aus Liebe will mein Heiland sterben,* 92
      Chorale—*O Haupt voll Blut und Wunden,* 92
  Sonata in D minor for Violin Solo, *Chaconne,* 86
  Suite in D major, Overture, 82
  Toccata in F major, 75
  Two-Part Invention in F major, 42
  Well-Tempered Clavichord, The
      Part I—Prelude in C major, 46
          Fugue in C major, 69
          Fugue in C minor, 47
          Fugue in D minor, 70
          Prelude in E-flat minor, 52
          Fugue in E-flat minor, 71
      Part II—Fugue in E major, 71

Beethoven, Ludwig van
  Concerto for Violin in D major, 177
  Egmont, Overture to, 178
  Leonore No. 3 overture, 31

Sonata in C minor, Opus 13 (*Pathétique*), 56
Sonata in F minor, Opus 57 (*Appassionata*), 165
String Quartet in E minor, Opus 59, No. 2, 182
Symphony No. 5, in C minor, 11, 49, 171
Symphony No. 7, in A major, 29
Symphony No. 8, in F major, 17
Symphony No. 9, in D minor, 21, 30, 32, 49, 50

Berlioz, Hector
  Symphonie fantastique, 244

Borodin, Alexander
  Symphony No. 2, in B minor, 326

Brahms, Johannes
  Concerto for Violin in D major, Opus 77, 312
  Piano Quintet in F minor, Opus 34, 307
  String Quartet in A minor, Opus 5, No. 2, 306
  Symphony No. 2, in D major, 31
  Symphony No. 3, in F major, 308
  Symphony No. 4, in E minor, 303
  Wiegenlied, 54

Chopin, Frédéric
  Ballade No. I, in G minor, Opus 23, 235
  Ballade No. IV, in F minor, Opus 52, 232
  Mazurka in C-sharp minor, Opus 34, No. 4, 236
  Polonaise in A-flat major, Opus 53, 237

Debussy, Claude
  Jumbo's Lullaby, 36
  La Cathédrale engloutie, 374
  L'Apres-midi d'un faune, 378
  Nuages, 375
  Pelléas et Mélisande, 374
  Voiles, 375

Dukas, Paul
  L'Apprenti sorcier, 14

Foster, Stephen
  The Old Folks at Home, 50

Franck, César
  Piano Quintet in F minor, 340
  Prelude, Chorale and Fugue, 341
  Symphony in D minor, 31, 50, 343

Giardini, Felice de
  Come, Thou Almighty King, 29

Gluck, Christoph Willibald
  Iphigénie en Aulide, Overture to, 113
  Orfeo ed Euridice
      Aria—*Che faro senza Euridice,* 112

Grieg, Edvard
  Sonata for Piano and Violin in C minor, Opus 45, 318

Handel, George Frideric
  The Messiah
      Aria—*He Shall Feed His Flock,* 106
      Aria—*The People That Walked in Darkness,* 105
      Chorus—*And With His Stripes,* 106
      Chorus—*Surely He Hath Borne Our Griefs,* 106
      Overture, 105

Haydn, Joseph
  String Quartet in C major, Opus 33, No. 3 (*Bird Quartet*), 128
  String Quartet in D minor, Opus 76, No. 2, 43
  String Quartet in G minor, Opus 74, No. 3 (*Horseman's Quartet*), 129
  Symphony in G major, B. & H. No. 94 (*The Surprise*), 124

Holst, Gustav
  The Planets, 383

Liszt, Franz
  Concerto for Piano in E-flat major, 257
  Les Préludes, 258
  Sonata in B minor, 254

Mendelssohn, Felix
  Music for Shakespeare's *A Midsummer Night's Dream*
      Nocturne, 218
      Overture, 215
      Scherzo, 218

Moussorgsky, Modeste
  Boris Godounoff, 328, 329
  Pictures at an Exhibition, 330

Mozart, Wolfgang Amadeus
  Concerto for Piano in D minor (K.V. 466), 149
  Fantasia in C minor (K.V. 475), 141
  Le Nozze di Figaro
      Aria—*Non so più cosa son,* 140
      Overture, 141
  Requiem Mass
      Kyrie eleison, 154
  Sonata in A major (K.V. 331), 141
  String Quartet in C major (K.V. 465), 138
  String Quartet in D minor (K.V. 421), 143

String Quartet in E-flat major (K.V. 428), 138
Symphony in G minor (K.V. 550), 17, 145

Palestrina, Pierluigi da
Exaltabo Te, Domine, 41
Stabat Mater, 44

Rimsky-Korsakoff, Nicholas
Overture—*The Russian Easter,* 322

Schoenberg, Arnold
Three Pieces for Piano, Opus 11, 382

Schubert, Franz
Der Erlkönig, 199
Der Leiermann, 196
Die Forelle, 196
Die Post, 196
Gretchen am Spinnrade, 197
Heidenröslein, 195
Ständchen, 196

Schumann, Robert
Carnaval, 224
Concerto for Piano in A minor, 226
The Merry Farmer, 34

Sibelius, Jean
Symphony No. 2, in D major, Opus 43, 365

Smetana, Bedřich,
The Moldau, 317

Smith, John Stafford
The Star-Spangled Banner, 50

Strauss, Johann
The Beautiful Blue Danube, 45

Strauss, Richard
Burleska, 21
Ein Heldenleben, 33
Till Eulenspiegels lustige Streiche, 352

Stravinsky, Igor
L'Histoire du soldat, 383

Tchaikovsky, Peter Ilitch
Symphony No. 4, in F minor, 330
Symphony No. 6, in B minor, 30

Wagner, Richard
Das Rheingold, 47, 283

Der fliegende Holländer
    Overture, 48
Die Meistersinger von Nürnberg
    Prelude, 286
Die Walküre, 49, 283
Götterdämmerung, 283, 284
Lohengrin
    Prelude, 51
Parsifal
    Prelude, 34
Siegfried, 50, 283
Tristan und Isolde
    Prelude, 138
    Prelude to Act III, 285
    Shepherd's Tune, Act III, 11

Weber, Carl Maria von
    Der Freischütz, Overture to, 208

Williams, R. Vaughan
    Pastoral Symphony, 36

Albéniz, Isaac, 261
Allegri, Gregorio, 136
Allemande, the, 63
Arpeggio, the, 22
Atonality, 381–382
Augmentation, 70–71

Bach, Johann Sebastian, 45, 46, 47, 55, 57–95, 96, 116, 137, 154, 272, 297, 338, 339, 381, 385
Bach, Karl Philipp Emanuel, 81, 118
Bach, Wilhelm Friedemann, 81
Balakireff, Mily, 261, *320–321,* 322, 327
Ballade, the, 234, 236
Bardi, Count Giovanni, 100
Bass clarinet, the, 13
Bass drum, the, 22
Bassoon, the, 13–14
Basso ostinato, 76
Beethoven, Ludwig van, 18, 21, 30, 43, 72, 116, 128, 130, 137, 140, 142, 149, *155–184,* 186, 189, 197, 207–208, 248, 263, 272, 275, 297, 302, 329, 333, 364, 384
Bellini, Vincenzo, 268–269
Bells, the, 22
Berlioz, Hector, 112, 186, 204, 231, *239–247,* 257, 321, 322, 337, 340
Bizet, Georges, 66
Borodin, Alexander, 261, 320, *325–327,* 370
Bourrée, the, 64
Brahms, Johannes, 54, 177, 215, 220, 222, 261, *297–313,* 314, 315, 340, 361
Brass instruments, the, 14–20
Briffault, Robert, 315
Bruckner, Anton, 356–357

Bülow, Hans von, 75, 275, 308, 330
Busoni, Ferruccio, 75

Cadence, the, 50–53
Cadenza, the, 148
Calzabigi, Ranieri, 111
Canon, the, 42–43
Cantata, the, 87–89 (Bach)
Carissimi, Giacomo, 98
Carpenter, John Alden, 66
Cavalli, Francesco, 101
Celesta, the, 23
'Cello, the, 6–7
Cembalo, the, 60
Chabrier, Emanuel, 339
Chaconne, the, 76, 86–87
Chausson, Ernest, 339
Chopin, Frédéric, 186, *231–238,* 268
Chorale, the, 78, 87, 92, 341
Chorale-prelude, the, 78–80
Chords, 45–47
Chromaticism, 138 (Mozart), 284–285 (Wagner), 343 (Franck)
Chromatic scale, the, 38
Clarinet, the, 12–13
Clavecin, the, 60
Clavichord, the, 60
Clavier, the, 61
Coda, the, 72, 123, 162
Concertino, the, 82
Concerto, the, 82–86 (Bach), 114, 147–153 (Mozart), 176–177 (Beethoven), 226–229 (Schumann), 257 (Liszt), 312–313 (Brahms)
Concerto, grosso, the, 82–83, 86, 107
Concert-overture, the, 214–215, 322–325

Conductor, the orchestral, 25–26, 188
Consonance, 40–42
Continuo, the, 81
Corelli, Arcangelo, 83, 98, 107
Counterpoint, 39–40
Courante, the, 63
Cui, César, 320, *321*
Cyclical form, 340
Cymbals, the, 22
Czerny, Carl, 248

Da capo, the, 65–66, 102
Dargomijsky, Alexander, *320,* 327
Debussy, Claude Achille, 22, 36, 261, *370–379,* 380
Decibel, the, 2
Diminution, 70–71
Dissonance, 40–42
Donizetti, Gaetano, 268
Double bass, the, 7
Double fugue, the, 78
Drone, the, 47
Dukas, Paul, 14, 339
Duparc, Henri, 339
Duration, 1
Dvořák, Antonin, 316, *317*

Elgar, Sir Edward, 75
English horn, the, 11–12
Erard, Sébastien, 22
Étude, the, 67, 235 (Chopin)

Fantasia, the, 74–75
Figured bass, 81
Flower, Newman, 107
Flügel, the, 60
Flute, the, 8–10, 33
Form in music, 49–56
Franck, César, 43, 261, 338, *339–347*
Frequency, 2
Fugato, the, 72
Fugue, the, *68–73,* 74, 75, 76

Gavotte, the, 63–64
Gigue, the, 64–65
Glazounoff, Alexander, 322, 325
Glinka, Michael, 320

Glissando, the, 22
Glockenspiel, the, 22
Gluck, Christoph Willibald, *109–113,* 140, 278
Gong, the, 22
Grand opéra, the, 267–268
Gray, Cecil, 362
Grieg, Edvard, 66, 261, *317–318*
Ground bass, 76–77
Guitar, the, 23

Handel, George Frideric, *96–108,* 109, 114, 116, 132, 154
Harmonic series, the, 3–4
Harmony, 43–48
Harp, the, 22–23
Harpsichord, the, 60–61
Haydn, Joseph, 116, 117, *118–133,* 134, 137, 142, 143, 144, 156, 169, 311, 314, 381
Holst, Gustav, 383
Homophony, 44–45
Horn, the, 17–18
Humperdinck, Engelbert, 348, 358

Idée fixe, the, 245
Impressionism, 370, 372, *373–376,* 377
Impromptu, the, 235
d'Indy, Vincent, 339
Instruments, musical, 5–27, 58–61
Intensity, 2
Intervals, 37
Invention, the, 66–67
Inversion, 70–71, 342
Inverted pedal, the, 48

James, Philip, 72 (note), 384
Joachim, Joseph, 298, 300, 312

Kettledrums, the, 20–21
Key, 38
Köchel Verzeichnis, the, 139

Lassus, Orlandus, 40, 380
Leading-motive, the, 282–284
Leoncavallo, Ruggiero, 295
Lessons, 62

Liadoff, Anatol, 322
Liszt, Franz, 75, 186, 192, 226, 231, 247, *248–261,* 273, 275, 276, 284, 298, 300, 302, 316, 321, 338, 339, 340, 350, 351, 364
Lully, Jean Baptiste, 268 (note)

Mahler, Gustav, 357
Mandolin, the, 23
Mascagni, Pietro, 294–295
Mass, the, 87, 93–95 (Bach), 153–154 (Mozart), 183–184 (Beethoven)
Mazurka, the, 234, 236
Meck, Nadejda von, 330–332, 333, 370
Melody, 32–38, 381–382
Mendelssohn, Felix, 8, 58, 186, *211–218,* 220, 338
Meyerbeer, Jakob, 268, 337
Minuet, the, 64 (Bach), 126 (Haydn)
Modes, 35–36
Modulation, 38
Monteverdi, Claudio, 101, 284
Motive, the, 49–50
Moussorgsky, Modeste, 320, 325, *327–330,* 370, 372
Mozart, Wolfgang Amadeus, 116, 119, 123, 128, *134–154,* 201, 314, 320
Musical tone, characteristics of a, 1–4
Music-drama, the, 270, 277–289

Nationalism in music, 261, 292, *314–315,* 315–317 (Bohemian), 317–318 (Norwegian), 319–336 (Russian), 337–347 (French)
Nocturne, the, 215, 218 (Mendelssohn), 235 (Chopin)

Oboe, the, 10–12
Octave, the, 2, 37
Opera, the, 44, 100–102, 102–103 (Handel), 110–113 (Gluck), 116, 139–141 (Mozart), 177–178 (Beethoven), 202–209 (von Weber), 263–269 (Italian Opera of the Early Nineteenth Century), 267–268 (*Grand opéra*), 270–290 (Wagner),

291–296 (Italian Opera of the Late Nineteenth Century), 316 (Smetana), 385 (Glinka), 328–329 (Moussorgsky), 356 (Strauss), 377 (Debussy), 380
Opera buffa, the, 266–267
Opera seria, 266
Oratorio, the, 99–100, *103–107,* 340
Orchestra, the, *5–26,* 81, 104–105, 112, 121, 169–170, 187–188, 207, 214, 243, 280–284, 322, 332–333, 351–352, 364, 377, 384–385
Orchestration, 25
Ordre, the, 62
Organ, the, 23–24
Organ-point, the, 47
Organum, 39
Overtones, 3–4
Overture, the, 81–82 (Bach), 102 (Scarlatti), 105 (Handel), 112–113 (Gluck), 140–141 (Mozart), 178–181 (Beethoven), 208–209 (von Weber), 214–217 (Mendelssohn), 267 (Rossini), 285–289 (Wagner), 322–325 (Rimsky-Korsakoff)

Paganini, Niccolo, 192, 250, 303
Palestrina, Giovanni Pierluigi, 40, 41, 44, 380
Partita, the, 62
Passacaglia, the, 76–78, 303
Passepied, the, 65
Passion, the, 87, 90–93
Pedal, the, 47
Pepusch, John, 99
Percussion instruments, the, 20–22
Pergolesi, Giovanni, 267
Peri, Jacopo, 101
Phrase, the musical, 49–50
Piano, the, *23,* 33, 116, 187, 232–234 (Chopin), 253–254 (Liszt), 376–377 (Debussy)
Piccinni, Niccola, 110
Piccolo, the, 8–10
Pierné, Gabriel, 339
Pitch, 1–2
Polka, the, 316–317

Polonaise, the, 64 (Bach), 237–238 (Chopin)

Polyphony, 39–43, 44, 380

Polytonality, 381–383

Prelude, the, 68 (Bach), 235 (Chopin), 285–289 (Wagner), 341–342 (Franck)

Prokofieff, Serge, 322

Program music, 170–171, 187, 242–243, 244–247, 254, 258, 350

Puccini, Giacomo, 295

Purcell, Henry, 99

Raison, André, 77

Rasoumovsky, Count Andreas, 181, 320

Ravel, Maurice, 23, 25, 330

Recitative, 90–91

Reményi, Eduard, 298, 305

Resolution, 41–42

Respighi, Ottorino, 75, 322, 384

Rhythm, 28–31, 384

Riesemann, Oskar von, 327

Rimsky-Korsakoff, Nicholas, 20, 66, 215, 261, 320, 321–325, 329, 370, 372

Ripieno, the, 82

Ritornello, the, 84

Ritter, Alexander, 348, 350

Rolland, Romain, 161

Romantic composers, the, 186–187

Romanticism in music, 185–188

Romantic Opera, the, 201, 205–209, 277

Romanza, the, 151, 228, 318

Rondo, the, 65, 129, 151

Rossini Gioacchino, 192, 263, 264–268, 269, 291

Round, the, 43

Russian Five, the, 320–330, 332

Saint-Saëns, Camille, 247, 261, 338

Sarabande, the, 63

Scale degrees, nomenclature of the, 36–37

Scales, 33–38

Scarlatti, Alessandro, 98, 102

Scarlatti, Domenico, 98

Schelling, Ernest, 247

Schering, Arnold, 132

Scherzo, the, 163 (Beethoven), 214, 217 (Mendelssohn), 235–236 (Chopin)

Schoenberg, Arnold, 76, 382

Schubert, Franz, 186, *189–200,* 314, 317

Schumann, Clara Wieck, 220, 222, 301

Schumann, Robert, 186, 188, *219–230,* 298, 313

Schweitzer, Albert, 88

Sentence, the musical, 50

Sibelius, Jean, 361–369

Singspiel, the, 193, 201

Smetana, Bedřich, 72, 261, *316–317*

Snare drum, the, 22

Societé nationale de musique, 337–338, 339, 341, 370, 378

Sonata, the, 86, 87, 114, 121–123, 162–164, 254–256

Sonata form, 121–123

Song, the, 193–200 (Schubert), 226 (Schumann), 305–306 (Brahms), 355–356 (Strauss), 357–359 (Wolf), 373 (Debussy)

Stokowski, Leopold, 76

Strauss, Johann, 44, 305

Strauss, Richard, 13, 21, 242, 243, 261, *348–356*

Stravinsky, Igor, 20, 31, 322, 383, 384, 385

Stretto, 71

String instruments, the, 5–7

String quartet, the, 114, 121, 127–131 (Haydn), 142–144 (Mozart), 181–183 (Beethoven), 306–307 (Brahms)

Suite, the, 61–66, 81–82

Sullivan, J. W. N., 162

Süssmayer, Franz X., 153

Symphonic poem, the, 257–261 (Liszt), 316–317(Smetana), 350–355(Strauss)

Symphony, the, 114, 121, 124–127 (Haydn), 144–147 (Mozart), 169–176 (Beethoven), 307–311 (Brahms), 326–327 (Borodin), 332–336 (Tchai-

kovsky), 343–347 (Franck), 356–357
(Bruckner), 357 (Mahler), 364–369
(Sibelius)
Syncopation, 31

Tausig, Carl, 75
Taylor, Deems, 72
Tchaikovsky, Peter Ilitch, 30, 66, 215,
   330–336
Tempo, 31–32
Three-part form, 55–56
Timbre, 2
Timpani, the, 20–21
Toccata, the, 75
Tonality, 38
Tone-quality, 2–3
Transcription, the, 253–254
Triad, the, 45
Triangle, the, 22
Trio, the, 66
Trombone, the, 19–20
Trumpet, the, 18–19
Tuba, the, 20
Tuning, the tempered system of, 67
Two-part form, 54–55

Van Vechten, Carl, 325
Variations, 76, 125–126, 164, 224, 255,

282–284, 302–303
Verdi, Giuseppe, *291–294*
Verismo, 294–295
Victoria, Tomás Luis de, 40, 380
Viennese School, the, 114–184
Viola, the, 6
Violin, the, 5–6
Violoncello, the, 6–7
Vivaldi, Antonio, 83
Vogler, Abbé Georg, 202

Wagner, Richard, 11, 19, 20, 22, 47,
   48, 72, 88, 113, 137, 138, 161, 186,
   188, 205, 207, 214, 219 (note), 242,
   244, 250, 251, 254, 268–269, *270–290,*
   294, 295, 297, 301–302, 315, 328, 338,
   341, 342, 346, 348, 350, 356, 357, 358,
   359, 364, 372, 377, 385
Waltz, the, 43–44, 236, 305
Weber, Carl Maria von, 140, 186, *201–
   210,* 263, 270, 314, 316, 376
Wesendonk, Mathilde, 274, 282
Williams, Ralph Vaughan, 36
Wolf, Hugo, 357–359
Wood, Sir Henry, 76
Wood-wind instruments, the, 8–14

Xylophone, the, 22